Transforming Public Services by Design

T0362347

For policy makers and policy implementers, design challenges abound. Every design challenge presents an opportunity for change and transformation. To get from policy intent to policy outcome, however, is not a straightforward journey. It involves people and services as much as it involves policies and organizations. Of all organizations, perhaps government agencies are perceived to be the least likely to change. They are embedded in enormous bureaucratic structures that have grown over decades, if not centuries. In effect, many people have given up hope that such an institution can ever change its ways of doing business. And yet, from a human-centered design perspective, they present a fabulous challenge. Designed by people for people, they have a mandate to be citizen-centered, but they often fall short of this goal. If human-centered design can make a difference in this organizational context, it is likely to have an equal or greater impact on an organization that shows more flexibility; for example, one that is smaller in size and less entangled in legal or political frameworks.

Transforming Public Services by Design offers a human-centered design perspective on policies, organizations and services. Three design projects by large-scale government agencies illustrate the implications for organizations and the people involved in designing public services: the Tax Forms Simplification Project by the Internal Revenue Service (1978–1983), the Domestic Mail Manual Transformation Project by the United States Postal Service (2001–2005) and the Integrated Tax Design Project by the Australian Tax Office. These case studies offer a unique demonstration of the role of human-centered design in the policy context.

This book aims to support designers and managers of all backgrounds who want to know more about reorienting policies, organizations and services around people.

Sabine Junginger, PhD heads the Competency Center for Research into Design and Management at the Lucerne University of Applied Sciences and Arts. She is a Fellow of the Hertie School of Governance. She is Visiting Professor at Jiangnan University, China and Macromedia University of Applied Sciences and Arts, Germany.

Transforming Public Services by Design

Re-orienting policies, organizations and services around people

Sabine Junginger

Routledge
Taylor & Francis Group

LONDON AND NEW YORK

First published in paperback 2024

First published 2017
by Routledge
4 Park Square, Milton Park, Abingdon, Oxon OX14 4RN

and by Routledge
605 Third Avenue, New York, NY 10158

Routledge is an imprint of the Taylor & Francis Group, an informa business

Publisher's Note
The publisher has gone to great lengths to ensure the quality of this reprint but
points out that some imperfections in the original copies may be apparent.

British Library Cataloguing in Publication Data
A catalogue record for this book is available from the British Library

Library of Congress Cataloging in Publication Data
A catalog record for this book has been requested

ISBN: 978-1-409-43625-6 (hbk)
ISBN: 978-1-03-283691-1 (pbk)
ISBN: 978-1-315-55018-3 (ebk)

DOI: 10.4324/9781315550183

Typeset in Bembo
by Apex CoVantage, LLC

To Mark and Sebastian

Contents

Figures

Preface

The origin of this book can be traced to my doctoral studies at Carnegie Mellon. It was then that my interest and research into design in places where few people think designing has a role began in earnest. I was encouraged by Richard Buchanan, the head of the School of Design at Carnegie Mellon, to look into the Integrated Design Project by the Australian Tax Office. He also enabled me to pursue my research further as a participant observer for the redesign of the Domestic Mail Manual with the United States Postal Service. The potential of design in the organizational context was just unfolding in these projects and made me curious about earlier design projects in government. When I found out about the IRS Tax Simplification Project, the differences in design understanding, design concepts and the perceived role of design along with their implications and consequences were striking. More so than ever, governments today are engaging with design, designers and designing. The lessons from these earlier efforts should therefore not go unheeded. A theoretical scaffold will be useful to structure, organize and make sense of the variety of approaches and methods that are now being experimented with. Incidentally, I wrote about my aim to develop a scaffold for design in my application for my PhD. Practice, it seemed to me, generates a lot of insights and knowledge. But just like a sculpture or building can grow higher and taller on its own for some time, there comes a point when structural support is needed to strengthen the construction and to allow it to continue to grow. The inquiry into the relevance of design in public services, administrative innovation and new approaches for policy work has just begun. I hope to contribute to a solid foundation on which we can all continue to build. We cannot help but design, but we can all design better.

Sabine Junginger

Acknowledgements

I share with most scholars that I am standing on the shoulders of giants: People who nurtured and fed my interest in design; people who encouraged my curiosity about policy; people who engaged with me in practice and in research on issues of design, management and organization; people who provided me with opportunities to engage hands-on. Richard Buchanan was already mentioned in the preface. Denise Rousseau, Craig Vogel, Bruce Hanington and Steve Stadelmeier remain influential. Michael Howlett and Ramesh deserve special mentioning because it was their depiction of the policy cycle that drew me deeper into policy studies. On the practitioners' side, I am particularly grateful to the great team at Mindlab in Denmark where I could gain additional insights during my time on its advisory board. Credit goes to the innovation team at Nesta, led by Geoff Mulgan and Brenton Caffin, who have never shied from a critical conversation to foster new educational approaches. Christian Bason, the current head of the Danish Design Center and former director of Mindlab has been an outstanding supporter. Dr. Sidney Heimbrock Smith from the US Office of Personnel Management in Washington, D.C.; Jocelyne Bourgogne, Director of the Public Innovation Group in Canada; Stephane Vincent from La 27e Région in France and Marco Steinberg, the former head of Helsinki Design have all helped me gain new insights on the pitfalls and challenges design in government presents. Jeanne Treadwell, who led the Australian initiative DesignGov, contributed not only plenty of anecdotal material but also enabled me to identify relevant themes. My gratitude extends to everyone who was involved in any of the projects I had the opportunity to work on, study or otherwise engage with. This includes staff at the United States Postal Service, the Australian Tax Office and those working on the Document Design Project and the Tax Simplification Project for the Internal Revenue Service. It includes members of the design teams in each of these projects, as well as the School of Design at Carnegie Mellon. Thank you all and know that any omission is unintentional.

Jonathan Norman from Gower has accompanied my journey and allowed me to change the direction of the book as it evolved and as I experienced personal changes that made it difficult at time to focus. Throughout this process, I also had the unwavering support from friends and my family. Danke!

Abbreviations

I am hopeless with acronyms, nonetheless, every now and then, I, too must resort to a short version of a long term:

ATO   Australian Tax Office (Tax Office of the Australian Government)
DMM   Domestic Mail Manual
HCD   Human–Centered Design
IRS   Internal Revenue Service of the United States Government
ITD   Integrated Tax Design
PTAX   Personal Tax
TACSI   Australian Center for Social Innovation
UCD   User–Centered Design
UCD   User–Centered Design
USPS   United States Postal Service

Section I

Re-orienting policies, organizations and public services around people

1 Design and transformation as a problem for the public sector

The only way in which social is honorific is when it enhances human living.

—John Dewey

Transformation by design might be read as a promise or a hope. A new design always promises change, and for this reason design inherently offers hope to make life better for people. However, we cannot take this promise or hope for granted. Many people design with good intentions, yet many design outcomes neither fulfill the hopes we put in them nor the promises they make. This is particularly obvious in the public realm where people are busy designing new laws, new policies, new programs and new services with the intent to make a positive contribution to peoples' lives. The public sector is an area that constantly engages in design. Services are developed and delivered, policies created and implemented. Yet we seem to know very little about designing in this key area that shapes and impacts the lives of millions of people. This book explains how design activities, design methods, design practices and design principles apply to the public sector.

Public sector design concerns citizens, civil servants, public managers and policy makers alike: Though they engage with a specific design at different points in time for different reasons, a successful product enables the civil servant to do her job, the policy maker to fulfill policy intent and the individual to fulfill his obligation as citizen. Yet we lack a clear understanding or awareness of how the design of services relates to policy implementation or policy making. This book connects these threads and weaves them together.

Above all, this book proposes a design perspective on organizations, services and policies. It is a perspective that differs in key aspects from traditional ways of studying the public sector. For one, it recognizes human experience and human interaction as central to all three. It shows how human experience and human interaction can inform the design of public policies, public organizations and public services and re-orient them around people. A design perspective offers an integrated view that connects issues we have traditionally looked at and dealt with in isolation: policy making and policy-implementation; service design and organizational change; policy goals and public services.

Transformation by design demands a systematic approach that inquires into people, situations and systems to understand the kinds of products and services that are needed to invite, engage and enable people in matters of public concern. It is a rather serious undertaking and – as the cases presented in the second part of the book show – is marked by headaches and pushbacks. The effort is worthwhile, though, not only for the obvious economic gains in productivity and efficiency. When we design with the human experience and human interaction in mind, we can generate gains for everyone: we can arrive at more meaningful policies, achieve faster implementation and create the kinds of services that support people and provide positive experiences.

With a design perspective, we open up to new kinds of problems. As Rittel and Webber (1973) explain, there are certain kinds of problems people struggle with more than others.[1] They point to 'wicked problems' in planning and in design thinking. Problems of a wicked nature go beyond the complexities of systems and their interacting parts that can be found, for example, in infrastructural projects. The building of the seemingly never-to-be-finished Berlin airport involves a gamut of challenges experts need to tend to. But Rittel and Webber maintain that even such a project mostly poses 'tame' problems. They would argue that although the building of a new airport in a capital European city involves many new and unforeseen problems, they are tame because we already know what we want to build: an airport. We also know what makes a 'good' airport. Accordingly, our design activities are focused and targeted around the clear objective from the inception of the project. Basic parameters and basic specifications exist, the problem is stated and action can be taken accordingly.

In contrast, it is much more difficult to address and engage with situations where we do not yet know what problems we might be dealing with. How do we inquire into such a situation? Where do we start? What to include? What principles can we apply for guidance? Such situations encapsulate 'wicked problems in design thinking' (Buchanan 1992).[2] Wicked problems present us with unique design challenges: their complexity is overwhelming and can act as a deterrent for any action towards addressing them. Wicked problems in design concern our efforts to improve specific human situations in changing human contexts.

It comes as no surprise then that wicked problems abound in the public sector.[3] They are framed by questions like 'how do we eliminate child poverty in society?' 'How do we ensure social and legal justice?' or 'what kind of policies do we need to achieve the kind of society we want to be part of?' They are implicit in the search for 'how can we reduce bureaucracy for citizens?' and in efforts to 'make governance more effective'. None of these questions present a problem statement akin to 'how do we build an airport?' But all of them inherently concern the ways in which people experience society and government and can engage with both. Wicked problems in the public sector thus demand attention to human experience and human interaction. This book demonstrates how the principles of human-centered design can help us generate valuable and actionable insights. In a short amount of time, requiring comparatively few resources, they generate new ideas that can lead to novel and sustainable solutions. A design perspective acknowledges that there are different ways we can go about generating ideas and bringing them to life through actual products and services. I discuss different design approaches to clarify how distinct methods lead to specific outcomes and express different forms of thinking that are manifested in particular design practices. Organizational design practices are of particular interest because new approaches to design call for fundamental changes in how organizations approach design issues. Unfortunately, there is no app for that and while a three-day design thinking workshop will support these efforts, it will not suffice to foster new sustainable skills and new thinking among its staff. Transformation does not happen simply as a result of applying one or two methods, no matter how creative they are. Organizational systems are known for devouring and spitting out 'new methods' with predictable regularity. Therefore I do not discuss specific methods but rather seek to explain the design approaches organizations do and may pursue as they go about their business. My aim is to show how different design approaches work with different design methods to achieve strategic outcomes.

For those interested in discovering new ways to think about design in the public sector, particularly those who wonder what designing has in common with policy making or who want to explore the role of services in generating and instilling organizational changes, this book provides plenty of material for thought and new arguments to advance their own design understanding. It offers substance to those who have discovered design in brief workshops, be that on design thinking, service design or design-led innovation. At the same time, it challenges traditional design management thinkers and practitioners who have contributed amazingly little to help us grasp issues of managing design in the public sector.

Some will find this book theory heavy. Admittedly, it was never conceived as a coffee-table book on design in the public sector. Instead my aim is to introduce and explain basic theoretical concepts in an effort to engage the interested reader in an evolving conversation. I want to provide access to material that complements and makes sense of the many design-driven methods that currently keep our heads spinning. If successful, the book serves as a foundation for those who seek to develop sustainable design practices tailored to policy making and policy implementation. I am thinking of ministerial staff concerned with new citizen participation initiatives; I am thinking of lawmakers who make an effort to reduce the bureaucratic burden on citizens and businesses. I am thinking of behavioral economists, sociologists and other experts who currently collaborate closely with their government and citizens to find out new ways to provide accessible and meaningful information. I would be happy if anyone working in a civil society organization found this work useful and an incentive to initiate internal changes. Too often, these places are full of goodwill and energy and yet obstructed by their own hierarchical, anachronistic management regimes.

The book, in short, is for all those who have not resigned to cynicism when it comes to government but who are actively looking for new ways forward. The diversity of people who form this group means that some parts of this book may be more interesting to a public manager than to a design professional while other parts may speak more to the issues of a policy- or lawmaker. For each of them, this book seeks to provide access to design thinking in the public realm as it relates to government and governance.

Design in government: Current developments

Many efforts are currently underway to transform the public sector. The design outcomes of each will be of utmost consequence for at least some, if not for many people. This book is a reminder that people across all stages of policy making and policy implementation engage in a wide range of design activities. They apply design methods and establish design principles. They develop and deliver policies and public services with the intent – and mandate – to enhance human living. While the strategies of the state as an organization have changed over time to fulfill this mandate, the mandate itself has not changed. No matter if a government seeks to impose law and order, strives to ensure liberty and welfare or aims to do more with less, the measurement of success will be its ability to make a positive impact on the lives of people it answers to. This is something to keep in mind when some experts seek to convince us that the purpose of government is to create a leaner, more efficient state. Creating a lean state cannot replace the purpose of a government nor fulfill its overall mandate but it can be a useful or necessary strategy to get there.[4]

We are at a moment in time where many governments are desperately looking for new approaches to policy making and policy implementation. Traditional models and problem-solving processes are under attack by frustrated, impatient and vocal citizens.[5] They receive support from scholars who are pushing for a new understanding of policy work (cf: Torfing et al. 2013). Some, like Matt Andrews use explicit design language to argue for more integrative policy development that includes rapid and iterative prototyping (Andrews et al. 2012). Others, including Guy Peters (2015) call on policy planners to design policies 'like we design cars'.[6] At the same time, few civil servants receive adequate support as they go about these new design challenges. They are asked to develop citizen-centric policies and services but have little if any access to learn about different design methods that can help them to get there. Understandably, many resign to their default mode of action: tactical moves that postpone and delay urgently needed solutions.

Nonetheless, design has moved into the focus of some practitioners and public organizations. Special organizational units created on a local, regional or national level have begun to explore how new design methods and new approaches can help them address concrete problems. We find such design initiatives across the spectrum of the policy cycle. They are collectively known as 'Public Innovation Labs', though they differ – often very strongly – in form, purpose, legitimacy and authority. What most of these initiatives share, however, is that they explicitly employ designers and seek to introduce ideas and concepts of design thinking and design practices into government work. *Image 1* shows an excerpt of a map of public innovation labs generated by attendees of a June 2015 workshop in Paris. The event, 'Immersion in Public Design' was co-organized by the French Ministry of Decentralization and Public Services; La27eRegion, Mindlab and the OECD in Paris. Those mapped in this image present but a small sample of the various Public Innovation Labs that have been set up to explore new approaches to policy making and policy implementation. Just a few months later that same year, the annual LabWorks conference organized by the UK National Endowment for the Sciences and Arts (NESTA) counted representatives from more than 200 government related 'innovation labs'. The London event offered them opportunities to participate in skilling workshops and to network with like-minded civil servants, consultants and designers.[7]

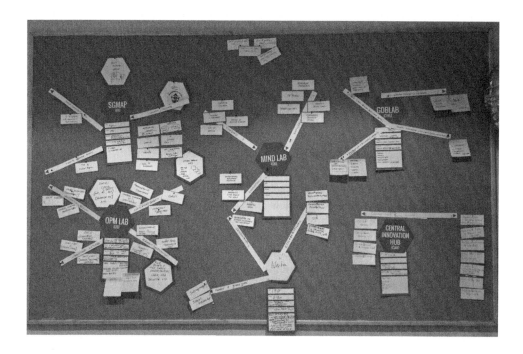

Design is moving to center stage in the public realm. And it is doing so on the tactical, operational and also on the strategic level. This is evident in the locations of some of the public innovation labs and the goals they are stating. Chile's Laboratorio Gobierno, for example, is directly reporting to the Chilean President and does not perceive of itself as 'the fire department for the government.' Instead, members of this Lab are interested in 'changing the way government works.'[8] In contrast, the US Office of Personnel Management focuses on developing its internal design capabilities and on changing the mindset among its employees to instill new human resource practices across federal organizations.[9] 'Agentes de Innovaçion' is yet another example and presents an effort by the Mexican Prime Minister's office to engage public servants in the development of human-centered digital services across different ministries.[10]

So what is it about design that gets the attention of people across the policy cycle? What captures the imagination of policy makers, public managers and others? How does a design perspective contribute to our urgent challenges? In its essence, designing is about conceiving, planning, developing and delivering 'products', whatever form they may take (Buchanan 1995).[11] But design can also be viewed as an art of change. Designers, observed Noble Laureate Herbert A. Simon, include all people who 'device courses of actions to improve existing situations into preferred ones.'[12] For Simon, policy makers and public managers are rightfully designers, too. They 'are not passive instruments, but are themselves designers who are seeking to use the system to further their own goals' (Simon 1996 [1969], p. 153). Moreover, they are also 'members of an organization or a society for whom plans are made.'[13]

Many Public Innovation Labs function as a reminder to public servants in their various roles that they are both designers and citizens. The point is to recognize and become aware of these opportunities and responsibilities because many set out 'to improve an existing situation into a preferred one' but end up contributing to a design outcome that is worse for people than it was before their design attempt. Many a policy begins with the best intentions and yet, by the time it is being implemented through specific products and services, after running through the full course of a policy cycle, fails to fulfill its intent and misses its objectives. Design theory refers to such outcomes as 'unintended consequences.' When products fail people in the market, we have an incentive to find out why. Better products result in increased profits, higher customer satisfaction and greater market shares. When government policies and government services fail people, we have a responsibility to find out because better products not only lead to greater economies but also foster much needed trust in government by instilling a sense of social justice.

A new research area has emerged around 'design for policy' (Bason 2014).[14] Already, we know that transformations in government and in governance require new forms of collaboration (Eppel et al. 2011; Sørensen and Boch 2014; Torfing and Ansell 2014);[15] new opportunities for citizen involvement (Arnstein 1969) and a renewed focus on creative problem-solving (Peters 2015).[16] Leading these innovative changes poses new challenges for public leaders (Bason 2010), who like many professional designers, find themselves taking a fresh look at design.[17]

Some people still cling on to the idea that design solely applies to lifestyle choices and consumer goods. Others see everything as a design outcome and everyone as a designer. The first view denies design a role within organizations and overlooks that people not trained in the design professions often conceive, plan, execute and deliver products and services for or with other people. The second view raises the question of the value and relevance of design because if everyone does it anyways, then what is so special about it and what is it that design researchers and experienced designers can possibly contribute?

If we seek to innovate the public sector, if we are to transform our public organizations and our approaches to policy making, we need to change the ways we think about design in these important areas, but also introduce new design principles, practices and methods. This means that transformation by design has consequences for the discipline of design, for design scholars, design researchers and design practitioners on the whole. For them, transformation by design presents what Richard Buchanan (2016) has described as 'the turn to action, services, and management' in design.[18] It is a shift that invites us to broaden our own design understanding in an area where action, service and management play an important role: in the public sector or, more precisely, in government.

Matters of design in government

Broadly stated, matters of design in government concern the design of policies and their implementation. The latter includes aspects of administration and compliance monitoring.[19] As the internal *Design Guide* by the Australian Tax Office observed already in 2002, policy makers, public managers and other civil servants often find themselves filling the role of a designer, though for many the idea of being a designer remains novel and a bit uncomfortable, if not outright worthy of rejection. They think of themselves as 'product builders', or as 'exercising a delivery or compliance function' without realizing that this puts them in a design role or that this engages them in design work.[20] They are members of a larger group that have been identified as 'silent designers' in a seminal paper on design in the organization by Peter Gorb and Angela Dumas (1987).[21] Silent designers, according to Gorb and Dumas, are people within organizations and within institutions who are actively involved in creating artifacts, systems, procedures or other kinds of products, yet who do not recognize how their thinking and doing give shape to and produce outcomes other people have to live with or make use of. As a consequence, silent designers rarely consider how their design work affects the ability of other people to accomplish a task or to make an informed decision. Though invisible to the eye (Burckhardt 1985), it is not uncommon for citizens to experience the benefits and flaws of policies, organizations and services on a daily basis. Design methods and design principles employed in silence are difficult to challenge or question. Things and situations we are not aware of and cannot articulate are even more difficult to improve on or change. This is why we need a greater awareness of design in government if we are serious about public sector innovation. For this we need a more nuanced design discourse concerning matters of design in government.

Such a discourse makes sense of historical developments. Programs like the *Federal Design Improvement Program*, which was initiated by US President Nixon in 1971, remind us that design has a history in government. But this particular initiative, like so many others, stopped at shaping federal buildings and the look and feel of public spaces. Design *in* government became synonymous with the design of office buildings and office spaces and served governments to develop their 'brands'. The intent of the *Federal Design Improvement Program* was not to help us understand the design work and the actual design activities civil servants, elected lawmakers and frontline workers continuously engage in and often struggle with.[22] In this early example, design was celebrated as a cultural art form and used by government to give expression and form to its advanced cultural and technical status. As Beatriz Colomina (2001) writes in 'Enclosed by Images: The Eames' Multimedia Architecture', for Nixon design was a way to demonstrate American superiority in these two areas. He assigned the American design team Charles and Ray Eames with the task to create the 1959 American Exhibition in Moscow. This exhibit formed the official part of a bilateral exchange on science, technology and culture. In 1959, the American contribution celebrated the ideal of the American suburban home, complete with modern appliances and distinct gender roles.[23] The *Federal Design Improvement Program* echoed earlier moves by other national governments to parade technological and cultural achievements to other nations. Design was not understood as a tool to improve, innovate or change government and governance to achieve better social outcomes. Instead, governments took pride in enabling their national designers to produce advanced and modern goods. Design served to demonstrate and affirm existing values of a governance system and government but had no role in actual government work.[24]

Such a discourse inquires into the specific contexts of policy making and policy implementation where design has been consistently treated as an element of the policy response toolbox. In the 1980s, the *Paperwork Reduction Act* posed an enormous challenge for most government agencies. This new law required all US government agencies to reduce their burden on citizens in significant and quantifiable ways. Among the biggest government agencies, the US Internal Revenue Service (IRS) now had to provide easier and faster ways for taxpayers to report their annual incomes, and do so quickly. To resolve this problem, the IRS called on a design team to simplify its tax forms. The *Tax Forms Simplification Project* – a project this book will continuously revisit and reflect on – centered on the redesign of the personal income tax form.

It was not until the late 1990s that the IRS realized that to improve its services to citizens, well-designed paper forms were *essential* but not *sufficient*. By that time, the IRS acknowledged that forms were only *one element* in their service. To innovate and to improve services, a special *IRS Customer Service Task Force* reported in 1997 required changes not only to forms and service provisions but also to the organization itself. In *Reinventing Service at the IRS*, then Vice President Al Gore together with members of the Treasury Department, the National Performance Review and roughly 30 front-line IRS employees explain how services and organization are related and what changes are necessary to improve the citizen experience.[25]

The story of the IRS and its organizational struggle to satisfy the demands of the *Paperwork Reduction Act* while developing better and more citizen-friendly services highlights the centrality of services to governments. It remains one of the earlier government testaments of how services mediate the relationships between people external to an organization and people within an organization. It points to the importance of services in establishing and enabling relationships of individuals with institutions and presents them as an opportunity for public managers and policy makers to engage people. This implies that any attempt at innovating and transforming the public sector around people must allow for and embrace changes to organizational design practices, too. Improving our design capabilities can lead to new efficiencies and cost savings while reducing frustrations, confusions and skepticism for both government and citizens. It is this 'turn to action' (Buchanan 2016) that prevents us from being stifled by complexities and doubts and encourages us to cultivate new practices that are better suited to the challenges ahead. Design does not hold all the answers and it is not the answer to everything. But, as *The Economist* exclaimed, in the new world that presents itself to governments and their citizens, 'doing something is surely better than nothing.'[26]

The book chapter by chapter

This book contributes to the theoretical foundation of a new public sector design discourse supported by insights and lessons from actual design projects in government. It offers a nuanced design understanding and shares new design practices in policy making and policy implementation. Following this brief introductory chapter, chapter 2 sets the stage by introducing and explaining relevant concepts, keywords and characteristics that inform the subsequent chapters. It describes the activities of designing, changing, organizing and managing as interconnected and as core to every organization. It also explains how human-centered design is related to, but not synonymous with, user-centered design.

Chapters 3 to 5 develop the argument for why a focus on people, on human experience and human interaction presents a path to re-orient services, organizations and policies around people. Chapter 3 inquires into what this means for design in policy; chapter 4 elaborates on the implications for services and chapter 5 shows how we can rethink organizational design practices. Each of these chapters presents a shift in perspective. Chapter 3 engages with existing views of design in policy and shows off some of their limitations. It contrasts these with an explicit design perspective on policy that allows us to think of policies as outcomes of applied design thinking and as results of concrete design doing. Chapter 4 situates the problem of services in the public sector. It establishes that services are central to policy intent, to policy making and to policy implementation. It also calls for the inclusion of services in policy research and practice because it is services people experience, not policies. It concludes that human experience and human interaction are currently blind spots in policy literature and policy practice. Chapter 5 presents an organizational perspective, and discusses common organizational design practices. It argues that organizational design practices are a manifestation of organizational doing. Transformation by design requires a change in the way we think and act. Becoming aware of organizational design practices allows us to reflect on them and encourages us to engage in other ways of doing. Chapter 5 concludes the Section I of this book.

Section II of the book presents three different examples of design in government organizations: The US Postal Service's Domestic Mail Manual Transformation Project, The United States Internal Revenue Service's Tax Simplification Project and the Australian Tax Office's Integrated Tax Design Project. Together chapters 6 through 11 share rare and valuable insights from real design projects in government organizations that have, in one way or another, approached transformation as a design problem.

Chapters 6 through 9 tell the story of the United States Postal Service and its multi-year project to redesign the *Domestic Mail Manual,* a core operational 'document.' This multi-year project covers a lot of ground and is organized into background and introduction to the project (chapter 6); phase I (chapter 7); phase II; (chapter 8) and phase III (chapter 9).

Chapter 10 presents a remarkable historic example of transformation by design by the Internal Revenue Service of the United States. This example illustrates how easy it is to miss opportunities despite best intentions. It provides valuable lessons for today's organizations and designers who find that designing services cannot be done successfully without organizational engagement and without understanding and addressing organizational design practices. Chapter 11 reports on the Australian Tax Office and its efforts to integrate all aspects of tax design around human experience and human interaction. The Australian example illustrates why governments that aim to become more citizen-oriented have to rethink the relationship between policy makers, public organizations and services. Moreover, it demonstrates once again that this must remain an ongoing effort because designing goes on every day and it is easy to fall back into default design practices and default design thinking. Section II closes with chapter 12, where I draw on the insights and theories of the book to discuss some of the issues I encounter in my present design work in government.

Each chapter, though connected with each other throughout the book, also stands on its own. This is true for the theoretical discourse in Section I and for the organizational examples in Section II. Taken together, though, they develop the design discourse in policy work and policy studies around the conception, planning, development and delivery of meaningful public services – services that are in line with the intent of the policies they implement and realize. If John Dewey (1948) is right and 'the only way in which social is honorific is when it enhances human living', we have to improve our abilities and capabilities to design.

Notes

1 See Rittel, H. and Webber, M. (1973). 'Dilemmas in a General Theory of Planning', *Policy Sciences*, Vol. 4: 155–169.

2 For an elaboration of wicked problems in design see Buchanan, R. (Spring, 1992). 'Wicked Problems in Design Thinking', *Design Issues*, Vol. 8 (2): 5–21.

3 See Head, B.W. and Alford, J. (2013). 'Wicked Problems – Implications for Public Policy and Management', *Administration and Society*, Vol. 47 (6): 711–739; Head, B.W. (2008). 'Wicked Problems in Public Policy', *Public Policy* [Online], Vol. 3 (2): 101–118.

4 See Micklethwait, John and Woolridge, Adrian (2015). *The Fourth Revolution–The Global Race to Reinvent the State*, Penguin Random Books, UK.

5 See OECD Report, Public Governance and Territorial Development Directorate Public Governance Committee, February 2013.

6 Peters, G. (2015). *Advanced Introduction to Public Policy*, Edward Elgar, Northampton, MA, USA.

7 See Labworks, NESTA: http://www.nesta.org.uk/event/labworks-2015 [accessed November 2015].

8 Both statements made by a key member of the Chilean Government Lab during private conversations but also in the context of a class lecture at the Hertie School of Governance in Spring 2015.

9 Statements made by representatives of the US OPM LAB, during a presentation at the 2013 Symposium *Human-Centered Design in Government and Social Innovation*, Hertie School of Governance, April 23, 2015.

10 See http://www.presidencia.gob.mx/agentesdeinnovacion/#proyectos.

11 Buchanan, R. (1995). 'Rhetoric, Humanism and Design', in Buchanan R. and Margolin, V. (eds.), *Discovering Design: Explorations in Design Studies*, University of Chicago Press, Chicago, IL, pp. 23–66.

12 Simon, Herbert A. (1996 [1969]). *The Sciences of the Artificial*, MIT Press, Cambridge, MA, p. 111.

13 Ibid.

14 Bason, C. (2014). *Design for Policy*, Gower, Farnham, UK.

15 Torfing, J. and Ansell, C. (2014). 'Collaboration and Design: New Tools for Public Innovation', in Chris Ansell and Jacob Torfing (eds.), *Public Innovation through Collaboration and Design*, Routledge, Oxon, UK; Sørensen, E. and Boch Waldorff, S. (2014). 'Collaborative Policy Innovation: Problems and Potential', *Innovation Journal*, Vol. 19 (3): 1–17; Eppel, E., Turner, D. and Wolf, A. (2011). 'Future State 2–Working Paper 11/04', Institute of Policy Studies, School of Government Victoria University of Wellington, New Zealand, June 2011.

16 Arnstein, S.R. (1969). 'A Ladder of Citizen Participation', *Journal of the American Institute of Planners*, Vol. 35 (4): 216–234; Peters, *Advanced Introduction to Public Policy*.

17 Bason, C. (2010). *Leading Public Sector Innovation*, Policy Press University of Bristol, Great Britain.

18 Buchanan, R. (2016): 'Design on New Ground: The Turn to Action, Services, and Management', in S. Junginger and J. Faust (eds.), *Designing Business*, Bloomsbury, London, UK, pp. 17–26.

19 Both terms are used broadly here, with implementation also including administration and monitoring of compliance, for example.

20 *The Guide*, Version 2, April 2002, Australian Tax Office.

21 Gorb, P. and Dumas, A. (1987). 'Silent Design', Design Studies, Vol. 8 (3), pp. 150–156.

22 Source: Federal Design Improvement Program, website: For a summary and critical review see Kleinman, Neil (July/August, 1973). 'Design and the Federal Government', *Print*, Vol. 27 (4), pp. 54–59, 83.

23 See Colomina, Beatriz (2001). 'Enclosed by Images: The Eames' Multimedia Architecture', *Grey Room*, Vol. 2: 6–29, Grey Room and Massachusetts Institute of Technology.

24 Jonathan Woodham alludes to this in Woodham, J. (2010). Formulating National Design Policies in the United States: Recycling the "Emperor's New Clothes"? *Design Issues*, Vol. 26 (2), pp. 27–46.

25 See *Reinventing Service at the IRS* by Vice President Al Gore and Treasury Secretary Robert E. Rubin with Front-line Employees of the IRS. Published by the Department of Treasury Internal Revenue Service: Publication 2197 (3–98) Catalog Number 25006E, Government Printing Office 1998.

26 *The Economist*, 'Test-Tube Government–Governments Are Borrowing Ideas about Innovation from the Private Sector', Schumpeter, December 6th Print Edition.

2 Design foundations for transforming policies, organizations and public services

Design thinking makes things hang together. It makes strings of products hang together into families. It makes intent hang together with user expectations. It makes economic goals hang together with administrative requirements, and with IT capabilities. It fights to keep things connected, and its enemy is often the silos of specialisation which optimise one part of the system to the exclusion of others.[1]

Principles, practices and methods of design are intrinsic to every form of government and to every governance approach. Constitutions, policies, laws and the structure of cities and states are matters of design because they are a consequence of human thinking and doing. Since their intent is to accomplish something for people – both for the individual and society as a whole – we can argue that public sector design in principle is human-centered.

This chapter explains the relationships between designing, organizing and changing in the government context. It reveals organizations as products of human making and establishes design as essential to organizational life. It presents designing as one of four core organizational activities, that is, as an activity inseparable from changing, organizing and managing. This forms the foundation for organizational change as a problem of design. The current interest in design by policy makers, public managers and civil servants rests not only on the ability of design to generate and implement creative changes. Design appeals because design research involves techniques and methods suitable for developing useful, usable and desirable products people can access easily. Many have already heard about human-centered design and user-centered design. These two concepts are of particular relevance to public sector innovation around people and a theme throughout the book. Because human-centered design is not synonymous with user-centered design though both play a role in public sector innovation, I explain each concept and describe their principal differences.

Organizations as products: By people for people

Organizations are made up of distinct elements that one way or another have to be brought together into a functioning whole. Despite the many varieties and forms organizations assume around the globe, there are four elements they have in common: people, resources, structures and purpose. It is design thinking that makes these elements 'hang together'. Design thinking here is not a method but describes the organizational principle around which the different elements of the organization are being connected to each other. We may also say that design thinking informs the logic of an organization. This comes often as a surprise to people who have learned about design thinking as a set of methods. What they find is that design thinking calls for a different design understanding and a greater awareness of design in general. They find that design relates to all aspects of organizational life. The following section explains how so:

Every form of governmental organization requires people. Government presents a system created by and for humans.[2] Without people, government cannot exist because there is no one to govern. Without people, any organization loses its reason for existence. While we focus on developing more citizen-centric policies and services, it easy to overlook that those people working within often dreary federal office buildings are humans, too. Many of those I work with chose a public sector career because they were hoping to make a difference and a contribution to society. In different organizations, 'people' may include staff, managers, stakeholders or customers – or all of the above. Though it is possible that the advances of self-driving cars and robotic humanoids may change the role of people in organizations over the long term, for the foreseeable future, people will remain essential to organizations.[3] They cannot do without them.

All organizations must own and make use of some kind of resource, be that money, skills, creativity, information, knowledge, time or something other. Resources have to be identified and employed. The fact that an organization requires resources says little about its ability to recognize, transform or employ them. Yet, much of an organization's success depends on how it identifies, generates and allocates resources. This is true for a private business, an NGO or a government organization. An organization without resources is not able to act. What an organization considers a resource is not fixed. Even within the same organization, today's resource may become tomorrow's liability. This is the case when expertise and competencies that initially afford organizational routines turn into core rigidities that make the organization less efficient.[4] Vice versa, what seems worthless in the current context may become valuable in another.

Structures have to be developed and put in place. This is common to all organizations. Structures can be rigid and archaic but they can also be fluid and follow self-organizing principles. Social media provides interesting examples of new approaches to organizing outside established and formalized organizations.[5] Structures clarify tasks, hierarchies, processes, procedures and responsibilities. They enable people within an organization to work together, to act together. An organization without any kind of structural agreement, be that formal or informal, is merely a temporary assembly of people and stuff. Structure is essential to organizational life.

While a structure is essential to an organization, it is bound to be random in isolation from an organizational vision or purpose. In the public sector, the organizational purpose is sometimes treated as synonymous with or reduced to a legal mandate. In other instances, the purpose or vision of an organization may be linked to a situation that is perceived to be problematic by a group of people.[6] In either case, it is the vision and/or purpose of an organization that galvanizes people to come together and to commit to coordinated action.

This clarifies that an organization comes into being when one or more people share a purpose and organize around it. It does not matter so much if this is a legal mandate or a voluntary passionate pursuit of an ideal. An organization begins to exist when a group of people, no matter their number, utilizes available resources in an agreed manner to pursue a common or shared purpose. Moreover, purpose clarifies that an organization is not a result of natural forces or an accidental occurrence. Instead, it reminds us that organizations are the result of a mindful human undertaking. When people lose interest for what an organization stands for or no longer understand what its purpose is, the organization is in trouble.

The above definition underlines that the core elements of any human organization are people, resources, structure and vision or purpose. It applies to private businesses, NGOs and government agencies just as it applies to organizational forms emerging by means of social media. It embraces society as a whole but also people in government who are organizing around special interests.

We can therefore establish organizations as products of design, made by people for people, and declare the integration of the four elements as an organizational design challenge that directly links designing to organizational change: The moment people in an organizational context engage in design activities, they are pushing and pulling on the four elements of the organization. Each push and each pull can shift the meaning, weight and direction, that is, the relationship among the four elements. Each 'combination' or 'arrangement' gives form and shape to a specific kind of organization that expresses a certain kind of design thinking.

Designing as an organizational core activity[7]

The recognition that designing is a necessity for organizations assigns designing the role of a core organizational activity. A core organizational activity is an activity that is essential to the existence of an organization. But designing is an activity that cannot be undertaken in isolation. It is inseparable from the activities of changing, organizing and managing. How so? And what does this mean?

Designing, understood as the conceiving, planning, developing and delivering of plans, strategies, services or policies, always requires us to initiate or make changes to some 'thing'. The redesign of the appearance of an object cannot be done without making some change. The change can be as simple and superficial as in changing colors, using new materials or developing a new shape. But such a redesign can also change the function of some 'thing', which require changes in ideas and perceptions of what that 'thing' might be. Another change generated through design may involve a change in meaning.[8] There are times when designing aims for changes in behavior. Behavioral economists are currently exploiting this potential of design.[9]

The moment we undertake some form of change, we find it cannot be done without engaging in an exercise of re-organization. We find it necessary to re-organize materials, processes and tasks, and even our own thoughts to allow for the changes we seek, to make the changes possible, to realize the design. Organizing is crucial to the activity of preparing the path for a specific action. Organization facilitates action because, in the process of organizing, unrelated pieces and bits are put into purposeful relationships. Meaningful roles and functions emerge that clarify responsibilities, the kinds of tasks needed and their sequences.

This links organizing to managing; how we go about managing in an organization can shape the opportunities and starting points for our design work. For example, when management is understood to function as an activity of containing, controlling and monitoring, we are bound to employ design approaches and design processes that prevent any surprising, i.e. innovative, outcomes. Predictability will dominate over uncertainty, specification over ambiguity. When managing considers itself in the business of designing, it is more likely to support emergent and experimental design approaches. The design activities are encouraged to exploit uncertainties and complexities, ambiguities and tensions to arrive at innovative outcomes.

Designing, changing, organizing and managing are interdependent activities that constantly interact in organizational life (Figure 2.1). Together, these activities enable the organization to conceive, plan, develop and deliver plans, strategies, services and policies suitable for achieving organizational goals and intent. This means that all four

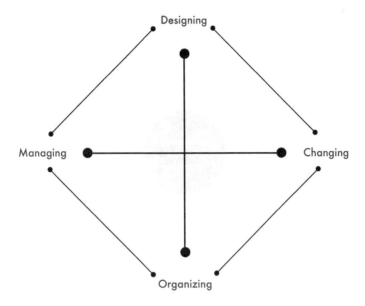

**Designing, changing, organizing and managing are organizational
activities that depend on each other.**

Figure 2.1 Designing constitutes one of the four core organizational activities

activities must be linked to the purpose of an organization and directed by the same
design principle. Looking at the problem of organizing from the perspective of the
individual human experience allows us to redefine the meaning of *being organized*: being
organized means to have prepared the path for a specific action. Because the mandate
of the public sector is human-centered, its design principle must be human-centered,
too (Figure 2.2). This is easier said than done. The task is complicated by the reality
that governments have to 'be organized' for many different needs and radically different
groups of users.

Human-centered design suggests that the purpose of an organization is to provide useful,
meaningful and usable services to people that help the organization fulfill its mandate or
vision.[10] Nowhere is the necessity to integrate the organization as pronounced and obvious
as when we engage in the development of services. Any service, as we will learn in chapter 4,
weaves through an organization's system and depends on the integration of relevant
resources, structures and people for its success. It follows that when we change a service, we
inevitably make some changes to one or more elements of the organization. This is problematic when we develop or change services without consideration for the organizational
system. The result is bound to cause some system breakdowns that affect the new service
negatively. However, if we are aware and conscious about how services relate to the core
elements of an organization, we can develop innovative services to transform and re-orient
organizations around people. In other words, the development of services around people
can serve to introduce and implement changes into the organizational system. This is
what designers like Tim Brown from IDEO (2009) have alluded to for some time with

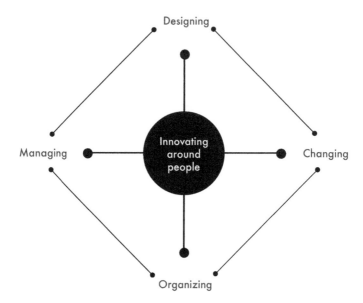

Innovation around people gives direction and purpose to the activities of designing, changing, organizing and managing.

Figure 2.2 Innovating around people gives purpose to organizational activities

claims that design thinking can transform organizations and inspire innovation.[11] Their short-comings were to treat design thinking solely as an innovation method but not as an organizing principle. Before we explore the implications this has for policy makers and public managers in chapter 3, we have to address why human experience and human interaction have a role in public sector innovation and clarify what we mean by human-centered design.

Designing as exploring and exploiting organizational abilities

The concept of exploiting existing organizational capabilities versus exploring new organizational capabilities was introduced by James G. March in 1991.[12] He was very much concerned with organizational learning. In the context of innovation, we can think of exploitation as following the paths that already exist and that are laid out in front of us. March described 'the relation between the exploration of new possibilities and the exploitation of old certainties' as 'a central concern of studies of adaptive processes'. He explained exploration as an activity that involves 'search, variation, risk taking, experimentation, play, flexibility, discovery, innovation.' In contrast, he considered exploitation activities to be concerned with 'refinement, choice, production, efficiency, selection, implementation, and execution'. The words March uses to describe exploration are remarkable for their ability to *investigate* new criteria for decision-making (search, variation, risk-taking, experimentation, play, flexibility and discovery), while the terms that describe exploitation relate mainly to the logistics of administering and decision-making where a frame of reference already exists: selection, choice, implementation and execution.

When the aim is to re-orient services, organizations and policies around people, both exploration and exploitation have a role and a place. To take advantage of their respective powers, we need to briefly reflect on the terms March associates with each activity. Taking a closer look at how he characterizes exploration reveals some interesting contradictions and potential problems for transformative changes. We might begin with the meaning of 'search'. There are many different ways to interpret the meaning of a search. However, they all have in common that when we search, we have something in mind we are looking for. This means that on the onset of the search, we already have a concept, an idea of that we are trying to find, however vague. We are searching for a solution, which implies that we have a problem in mind. As a method, a search can be part of an inquiry, but a search in itself does not constitute an inquiry. To give an example, we do not inquire when we use our web browsers to find something. We conduct a search. We provide names and terms we are familiar with and associate with what we are looking for and type these into the browser. Based on our input, the search engine conveniently pulls a list of associated terms, events, people and things. A search can be inspiring and lead to new discoveries and new knowledge. Nonetheless, our search still takes place within the framework of thought we are already familiar with. Our search does not question this framework unless we are very conscientious about its existence. We will find indeed what we are looking for.

'Variation' is another characteristic of exploration according to March. Variations, as their name implies, depend on something that can be varied upon. This implies that variations, too, are a theme of something that already exists. Although March lists variations as part of explorations, variations are really a form of exploitation of an existing concept. We can extent this argument to other terms March reserves for exploration, namely 'flexibility' and 'discovery'.

This suggests that March rooted exploration in exploitation. It is indicative that March does not mention design in his original paper and makes no mention of innovation. Gupta et al. (2006) have pounded out the links to innovation and design inherent in March's concepts in an article for the Academy of Management Journal.[13] However, they do not address the constraints March's understanding of exploration imposes on both innovation and design.

For organizations that seek transformative changes, at least some of the exploration activities need to be freed from the limitations of exploitation. More often than not, they need to open new spaces that allow new practices, new thinking and new doing to overcome the current limitations. To achieve this, they need to inquire and invent beyond varying existing approaches and playing within their current operational and strategic framework. Designers, if we can believe Polanyi (1963), have a great advantage over many of the businesses they work with: They are not bogged down or discouraged by 'knowing too much' about the organization they work with. This, according to Polyani is a key for opening new lines of research and practice:

> I would never have conceived my theory, let alone have made a great effort to verify it, if I had been more familiar with major developments in physics that were taking place. Moreover, my initial ignorance of the powerful, false objections that were raised against my ideas protected those ideas from being nipped in the bud.
>
> (Polanyi 1963, p. 1013)

March has aptly described two different approaches to innovation, which for him was manifested in organizational learning. Organizational learning remains key to the current efforts at public sector innovation. In the end of the day, it is about learning more about one's own organization, about new ways of seeing and about new ways of developing and delivering solutions that produce desired outcomes. We must remain attentive, though, to the fact that it is easy to embed exploration within exploitation. Keeping this in mind means to remain aware that exploration depends on how we frame it. Inquiries into organizations can exploit the abilities and resources of an organization to explore new unknown territories, some of which may benefit from invention.

About human-centered design

As more practitioners and scholars consider the role of design, we should revisit and clarify what human-centered design might imply in specific practices. In contemporary design research and practice, human-centered design often appears in the context of interaction design, user-centered design and experience design. We might therefore ask: Do all of these design activities represent different forms of human-centered design? Or does each of these design activities constitute a specific element of a human-centered design approach? An argument can be made that the moment one begins to design around people, be it by considering how people interact with products, ensuring easy access and usability or by paying attention to their overall experience, one enters into the realm of human-centered design. But there remains a tension between designing for the individual and designing for the common good.

Being human-centered means different things to different people. In order to make this concept meaningful, we need to draw some boundaries. Winograd and Koch (1997) explored human centered design for its relevance and implications to the field of human computer interaction.[14] They found a gamut of interpretations of this concept, from 'wide' to 'strong'. A 'wide' interpretation puts 'human-centered design' on equal footing with 'user-centered design' and 'user experience.' User-centered design has its roots in human factor studies, which today forms the field of ergonomics. Henry Dreyfuss, an influential American industrial designer was among its early advocates in the 1960s. He thought it important that design products like chairs, tables or bicycles could be used by average sized people with average mobility. At the time, no such information was available to industrial designers. So he begun to measure and size up American men (and only much later women). 'Designing for people' for him meant to understand the weights a person can lift or the lengths of the radius that the arm and hand draw around a desk when a person writes a letter. Knowing this, he could design items that work for people.[15] In contrast, user experience centers on the idea of 'pleasurable products'. According to Patrick Jordan, whose book with of same title introduced the term in 2002, products are pleasurable when they consider a person's psychological, ergonomic, emotional and social implications.[16] Since both user-centered and experience design pay attention to the human being, a wide interpretation of human-centered design would include them.

A 'strong' interpretation of human-centered design, in contrast, refers to first principles of human rights and human dignity and also to issues of sustainability and the social. A core distinguisher between the wide and strong interpretation of human-centered design is thus the understanding of people. In the wide interpretation, human beings are categorized, classified, and labeled, for example, as a user, operator, patient or consumer. Being so classified, people are assigned a role in a *transactional* exchange-based relationship: we offer, you use; you use, we offer or provide. Our ability to arrive at the kinds of human environments and human experiences we are striving for hinges on our ability to distinguish between transactional exchange models and design approaches that consider and respect a person as a full human being.

A strong interpretation of human-centered design positions us to evaluate our design efforts along human dimensions: Are we achieving the kinds of human experiences and human environments we want to create? Do our services help us fulfill our strategic and organizational purposes, which ultimately have to 'serve' people in ways that contribute to sustainable, just and dignified human living? And if not, how could they? This strong interpretation insists that our actions, our constructions, our inventions, our organizational systems operate at their highest level of efficiency and their maximum capability when they work for, support and enable people.

Strong and wide interpretations of human-centered design relate to Rittel and Webber's (1973) distinction between tame and wicked problems, from which we can draw parallels to the 'wide' and 'strong' interpretation of human-centered design.[17] We find that 'tame' problems typically apply user-centered design principles and methods that focus on user experiences. The strong interpretation, in contrast, is much more likely to engage with wicked problems. If we believe Rittel & Webber, our ability and success in mastering tame problems has led us to the gates of wicked problems. Neither policy making nor policy implementation, neither service design nor organizational design alone are prepared to address these wicked problems on their own when they concern open societal problems:

> The difficulties attached to rationality are tenacious, and we have so far been unable to get untangled from their web. This is partly because the classical paradigm of science and engineering – the paradigm that has underlain modern professionalism – is not applicable to the problems of open societal systems.
>
> [. . .]The kinds of problems that planners deal with – societal problems – are inherently different from the problems that scientists and perhaps some classes of engineers deal with. Planning problems are inherently wicked.

A human-centered design approach can therefore not ignore the social, political, ecological and economical contexts in which individual interactions take place. Furthermore, human-centered design concerns itself with the ways in which *any* product or service enables, encourages or discourages, even disables, a person to engage with other people, objects, services and environments. The focus of human-centered design rests on the human relationships people and groups of people have or may have. Products and services (in the broadest sense) are understood to mediate these relationships.[18] Because of their mediating role, human-centered design pays attention to what, why and how we communicate, build or interact and what, why and how we organize these communications, things and interfaces into systems that work well for people. The lingering question is are we achieving the kinds of human environments and human experiences we are striving for? Products and services here can become stepping-stones, learning opportunities and evidence for possible alternative futures – not seldom all at once.

Human-centered design in this interpretation, too, begins with the individual experience of people and involves user-centered design approaches. But this focus on the experience of an individual person differs in significant ways from having a wonderful experience with a product that, for example, due to its material uses becomes a liability to society and a detriment to the environment. Because both society and the environment are essential to human wellbeing, sustainability is a major concern in any kind of human-centered design.

It is important to notice the differences of a human-centered design approach and a user-centered design approach. A human-centered approach, as is evident from the above areas of inquiry, begins with the experiences of individuals as they engage with a particular system. But while a user-centered approach remains focused on the interactions of one person with a specific product, service or system, a human-centered approach concerns itself with the implications on a wider social scale, situating the human experience in the context of communities and environments, concerning itself with issues of justice and human dignity. The theoretical foundations for human-centered design are influenced by the pragmatic philosophy of John Dewey and the writings of Richard Buchanan (2001).[19] A slightly different take that also embraces a 'strong' interpretation is offered by Klaus Krippendorff (2006).[20]

Arriving at meaningful, accessible and effective public services, organizations and policies

It is easy to demand that products and services have to be meaningful and relevant to people; that laws and policies should be citizen-centric. But how does an organization or lawmaker find out what a person needs to be able to access relevant and appropriate information in a format useful and usable to him or her at the right time and in the right place? How can we know what is appropriate and relevant information in a specific context? What forms (i.e., printed book, mobile app, etc.) are desirable, useful and usable by those very people who need this information? What locations are meaningful for them? And what do people try to achieve when they get in touch with a specific public organization?

Answers to these questions follow from inquiry. A design inquiry identifies how people interact with and how they can access current products and services. This includes when, where and why people struggle, and when, where and why they succeed. The methods range from ethnographic observations to diary studies and system analysis. A design inquiry is contextualized and participatory, requiring the involvement of people inside and outside of the organization. A design inquiry reveals hitherto unknown patterns, bottlenecks and contradictions in procedures as well as in information; developing new ideas and concepts through strategic conversations and participatory design practices–these are the characteristics of a comprehensive, human-centered design approach.

This is a good time to address a common misperception about users and user-centered design: the solid focus on the everyday experience of people should not lead us to forget that members, i.e., staff and employees within an organization, are 'users', too. They often share the struggles and frustrations of those external to the organization, yet for different reasons and with different 'everyday-realities'. If the re-orientation is to be successful, any co-designing effort will involve members of the organization from all levels: those at the frontline and those at the top of the public management hierarchy and policy making.

The question we have to answer today is *how* do we – those who are in positions to shape the lives of others – go about designing policies, products and services? How do we establish criteria for our designs? In light of our economic and environmental challenges and technical opportunities, how do our design activities help or hinder people? How do our designs contribute to the social and human environments we seek to foster and to maintain? It is a question more and more government organizations are posing in their search for new and innovative approaches to fulfill their organizational goals. They want to develop products and services that reach people at the right time in the right places and in a form that speaks to their life experiences and life circumstances. They want to ensure that the intent of a policy remains intact throughout the implementation process by changing from relay style design processes to integrated, participatory and iterative design approaches that include important stakeholders across all policy levels from the start. They want to know that the policy they put in place addresses the right problem and achieves the desired outcome because it works for the people involved. Among other things, they want to shift from being reactive and responsive to proactive steering (Bason 2014).[21]

This inability to recognize ongoing design work and design issues has several implications. One is that products and services 'get made' without benefitting from the lessons, insights and knowledge generated by generations of designers. Another implication is that we miss many opportunities for change and transformation. Yet another is that we are stuck with methods that produce the same old over and over again.

One of the tasks ahead is to develop greater design awareness and a more nuanced design understanding. Transformation by design in the public sector calls for the integration of policy making, public management and service design around human experience and human interaction. Over the next three chapters we learn what this means for design in policy, the design of services and for organizational design practices.

A design approach suggests that we remain focused on what we want to achieve for people, what we want people to be able to do. A design approach accepts that when everyday people engage with government on different levels, they worry little about who is responsible for what. They seek assurance that they have access to the information they understand and tools they need to do what they are asked to do at the time they have to make a decision or take action. Many civil servants struggle precisely with these demands. It is not what they are trained or prepared for. It is not what they currently get rewarded for within their own high-pressure work environments. But it is something that is of increasing importance to deliver on the demands for more citizen-centric policies. They may find consolation in the following statement by Gui Bonsiepe, an internationally renowned design scholar: 'To design means to deal with paradoxes and contradictions; in a society plagued by contradiction; design, too, is affected by them'.[22] This will become even more obvious as we explore design in policy and services over the next two chapters.

Notes

1 From *The Guide*, Version April, 2002, Australian Tax Office (ATO), p. 74.
2 Churchman, C.W. (1968). *The Systems Approach*, Dell Publishing, New York.
3 See Velonaki, Marie, Geminoid-F: http://www.techradar.com/news/world-of-tech/meet-the-geminoid-f-the-first-humanoid-robot-to-star-in-a-movie-1310108 [accessed January 2016].
4 See Leonard-Barton, D. (Summer, 1992). 'Core Capabilities and Core Rigidities: A Paradox in Managing New Product Development', *Strategic Management Journal*, Vol. 13 (S1): 111–125.
5 Clay Shirky's (Penguin Books, 2009) *Here Comes Everybody: Organizing without Organizations* remains a must read on this topic. Also recommended: Ori Brafman and Rod A. Beckstrom's book on new and evolving organizational forms The Starfish and the Spider: *The Unstoppable Power of the Leaderless Organization* (Portfolio Trade, 2008).
6 For the full argument see Dewey, John (1927 [1954]). *The Public and Its Problems*, Swallow Press, Ohio University Press, Athens, OH.
7 Also see Junginger, S. (2015). 'Design Legacies and Service Design', *The Design Journal*, Vol. 18 (2), *Special Issue on Emerging Issues in Service Design*: 209–226.
8 See Diller, S., Shedroff, N. and Rhea, D. (2005). *Making Meaning–How Successful Business Deliver Meaningful Customer Experiences*, New Rider Press, Berkeley, CA; Verganti, R. (2009). *Design Driven*

Innovation: Changing the Rules of Competition by Radically Innovating What Things Mean, Harvard Business School Publishing, Boston, MA.

9 See Halpern, D. (2015). *Inside the Nudge Unit, How Small Changes Can Make a Big Difference*, WH Allen, London, UK.

10 Elizabeth Sanders first called for 'usable, useful and desirable' products. See Sanders, B.N. (1992). 'Product Development Research for the 1990s', *Design Management Journal*, Vol. 3 (4): 49–54.

11 Brown, T. (2008). *Change by Design: How Design Thinking Transforms Organizations and Inspires Innovation*, Harper Collins, New York, NY.

12 March, J.G. (1991). 'Exploration and Exploitation in Organizational Learning', *Organization Science*, Vol. 2 (1), *Special Issue: Organizational Learning: Papers in Honor of (and by) James G. March (1991)*: 71–87.

13 Gupta, A.K., Smith, K.G. and Shalley, C.E. (2006). 'The Interplay between Exploration and Exploitation', *Academy of Management Journal*, Vol. 49 (4): 693–706.

14 Winograd, T. and Wood, D.D. (1997). *The Challenge of Human-Centered Design*, Report from Working Group 3, Version of April 9, 1997. Unpublished Working Paper, http://www.ifp.illinois.edu/nsfhcs/bog_reports/bog3.html.

15 See Tilley, Alvin R. and Henry Dreyfuss Associates (1993). The Measure of Man and Woman: Human Factors in Design, Whitney Library of Design, New York. Originally published: New York: Whitney Library of Design, under title: The measure of man, 1960.

16 Jordan, P. (2002). *Pleasurable Products*, Taylor & Francis, London, UK.

17 Rittel, H. and Webber, M. (1973). Dilemmas in a General Theory of Planning, *Policy Sciences* 4, Elsevier Science, 1969, pp. 155–173.

18 Buchanan, R. (1995). 'Rhetoric, Humanism and Design', in R. Buchanan and V. Margolin (eds.), *Discovering Design: Explorations in Design Studies*, University of Chicago Press, Chicago, IL, pp. 23–66.

19 Keyworks are Dewey, J. (1934). *Art as Experience*, Minton, Balch and Company, New York, London. and Buchanan, R. (Summer, 2001). 'Human Dignity and Human Rights: Thoughts on the Principles of Human-Centered Design', *Design Issues*, Vol. 17 (3): 35–39.

20 Krippendorff, K. (2006). 'The Semantic Turn–A New Foundation for Design', *Policy Sciences*, Vol. 4: 155–169.

21 Bason, C. (2014). 'Design Attitude as an Innovation Catalyst', in Chris Ansell and Jacob Torfing (eds.), *Public Innovation through Collaboration and Design*, Routledge, Oxford.

22 Bonsiepe, Guy (2010). *Civi City Cahier 2: Design & Democracy*, ed. Jesko Fezer and Matthias Görlich, Bedford Press, London, UK.

3 New approaches to policy design[1]

Chapter 2 explained important design concepts and characteristics that help us discuss and engage with matters of public sector transformation by design. We will now begin to address issues more specific to transforming public services, re-orienting services, organizations and policies around people design. This involves the integration of policy making with policy implementation. To pave the way, this chapter situates and traces design in policy. It provides yet another theoretical backbone to our developing design discourse by zooming in on design issues in policy making and policy implementation. The chapter begins with a discussion of how design has been viewed in policy over time. From there it moves on to new and emerging views that are beginning to influence and transform some policy work around the globe.

Transformative thinking begins when we revisit and re-evaluate how design has contributed to policy research and practice over time and what forms its future contributions may take. Another way to initiate some fundamental re-thinking is by examining the policy cycle and its constituent elements for their use and understanding of design. Both inquiries challenge the way we commonly think about policies. They encourage us to recognize policies as design products and to perceive of policy making and implementation as closely connected design activities. The aim of this chapter is to lay the foundation for the two chapters that follow, which will explain how services link with policies and how organizational design practices have an impact on both, policies and services.

Explorations and experiments

First explorations into the relevance of design to public policy have already produced useful insights. Derek B. Miller and Lisa Rudnick, for example, (2011) have 'tried on design for size' in a paper that reflects on design´s relevance to the work and efforts of the UN organization UNIDIR. They agree that design holds the potential to generate new approaches to core problems of public policy. But they also point to the challenges involved in embedding new design practices in environments and organizations where employees and staff rely on bureaucratic processes and mechanisms:

> In international public policy, design is the dark space between knowledge and action. It is where the murky terms, metaphors, and conventional wisdom lurk that are often antagonistic to design as a professional activity. Design, after all, requires a certain humility before a problem – a respect for the challenge and complexity being faced, and a willingness to engage that problem on its own terms before rushing to action. This patience and humility are not often the qualities found in international public

policy, where civil servants too often treat their work mechanically and fulfill policy with known treatments. These tendencies suppress the curiosity needed to imagine new possibilities – to innovate, to solve.[2]

The ability of design to 'engage that problem on its own terms before rushing to action' is one that is rarely used. Instead, policy makers turn to design when they have agreed on an idea or a solution and want to see this idea or solution translated into something tangible. Design continues to be valued only for its role in implementing existing and new policies. A new logo creates visibility for an initiative, a brochure or website communicates the aims of a policy. This state of affairs was affirmed during a recent conversation with a former EU-level policy maker. Once he found out that I was a designer, he was brimming with pride and eager to share that he and his colleagues had just tasked a professional design firm with the re-branding of their group. 'We realized we need a new logo to better communicate our work.' I kept prodding him about possible links between designing and policy making and started to ask questions about his actual work. Subsequently, I was able to explain his current activities as advisor to EU policy makers in Brussels in design terms. Rather surprised, he shared: 'I have never thought of design that way'.[3]

Though there are already a number of people who are 'trying on design for size' in various policy contexts and at various levels of government, there are still more for whom design remains a practice external and peripheral to their own work. They cannot access design. Given the connection we established between designing and changing in the previous chapter, this might explain the difficulties we have in instilling changes in the public sector. When we cannot see designing going on, we are likely to overlook opportunities for change.

Some governments have begun to invest resources to engage design methods and to employ design thinking in the development of public policies and public services. Many of these take the form of a Public Innovation Lab. Public Innovation Labs are places dedicated to detect, learn about and experiment with new practices and methods in order to build the capacity of public organizations to experiment and adapt their tactical, operational and strategic and co-evolve with their environment. Public Innovation Labs promise to create new opportunities for interaction between policy makers, public managers and citizens. Their shared emphasis on collaboration, co-creation and other forms of participatory product development connects the insights generated through service design with the insights generated at the policy level. Public Innovation Labs can align policy design with the design of services when they are situated within governments and work closely with local communities and citizens.

Despite differences in form, resources and location within their respective governments, existing public innovation labs have in common that they seek to develop new organizational design capabilities and new organizational design practices relevant to policy making and policy implementation.[4] We find public innovation labs in surprising places, initiated and set up by the very civil servants and bureaucrats who are described by innovation experts as 'risk averse' and 'working in the absence of competitive forces,' 'lacking incentives' to engage in change, 'deterred' by a proliferation of 'red tape' that stifles any hope of innovation.[5]

Examples of current public innovation labs include the Lab at the US Office of Personnel Management (US OPM) set up in 2012. The US OPM Lab is explicit about its use of human-centered design: 'We apply HCD to uncover insights into unique experiences, systemic challenges, and unmet individual needs. We integrate these insights into design application prototypes that are rapidly tested with users'.[6]

Mindlab in Denmark, a cross-ministerial innovation unit sponsored by the respective Ministries of Business and Growth, Education and Employment, may qualify as the longest running public innovation lab to date. As a former member of the advisory board, I had the wonderful opportunity to accompany parts of their journey. Mindlab was founded as a Creative Platform in 2002 and has changed its focus since several times, increasingly applying human-centered design principles to fulfil its respective role. Mindlab first moved from being a user oriented innovation unit to filling the role of a catalyst of an international movement in public sector innovation. Subsequently, it acted as a strategic change partner before it focused on the development of capacity. Most recently, Mindlab understood itself as an enabler of a new public sector culture.[7] With the arrival of Thomas Prehn as new director in 2015, another 'variation' of Mindlab will emerge. There are indications that this involves the idea of public sector start-ups.

Other examples of public innovation labs include the UK Policy Lab, which launched in 2014 with rather little commitment from the government in terms of budget and staff. It will be interesting to watch how it can fulfill its vision to create 'an experimental space for policy makers to trial new policy ideas using open policy making principles, exploring the most creative ideas through practical activities' while it continuously has to justify its existence and demonstrate that the Lab Model of working can improve policy making. The first Fellowship report on its work produced by Lucy Kimbell (2015) offered an optimistic outlook.[8] At the time of writing, the original 12-month funding has been extended by another year. The question is if this will be enough to satisfy the ambitious agenda, which includes:

- fully support up to five practical showcase projects working within and across government departments
- try out new and emergent tools and methods with departments on responsive or targeted basis – through shorter projects that offer more civil servants the opportunity to get involved
- develop the skills and capabilities of policymakers through practical projects and opportunities for shared learning
- build a robust and compelling evidence base to underpin the activities of the Lab
- the Lab will use a range of tools and techniques to gain new insights into policy issues. These include ethnographic research, service blueprinting, data science and digital tools.

Like the UK Policy Lab, many Public Innovation Labs work on shaky and wobbly grounds and lack the commitment necessary to achieve sustainable transformation. This is one of the motivations for this book. Working under the greatest level of scrutiny and with a minimum of budget, staff and commitment, the fact that the UK Policy Lab is clearly not in a position to say no to any project thrown at them is a cause to be concerned about its longevity and sustainability of this set-up.

Other public innovation labs have already come and gone. DesignGov by the Australian government, for example did not last beyond its initial 18-month funding.[9] As in the case of the UK Policy Lab, neither the budget nor the timeframe nor the personnel staffing were adequate for the demands put on it: set-up an innovation lab space and environment, identify and work on a project, analyze and report its findings to justify further investment. 'It took them six months to set up and skill the team', I was told by a fellow member of the DesignGov advisory board. We can compare the 18-month timeframe in Australia with the three-year plan afforded the US Office of Personnel Management Lab. The American team had the time, budget and staff to first create a work environment, then select and skill people for its initial team and then identify and work on project to generate learnings and insights on which it could build.[10]

Another case in point is the internationally influential team that made up the Helsinki Design Lab in Finland. It, too, was forced to close its doors because of lacking government support. In the Finnish case, however, it emerged that the local community engaged in public sector innovation felt excluded and disconnected. Despite its international successes (many based on Finnish case studies), the Helsinki Design Lab was not able to show the relevance of their work to their own funding unit SITRA.[11]

La27eRegion, the driving force behind French government public innovation lab Super-public (founded in 2014), has taken these lessons to heart.[12] From its inception it sought to 're-examine how public policies are designed and implemented – especially in the French regions.' In contrast with the Australian DesignGov, Superpublic benefits from the skills and knowledge of La27eRegion's team, which it has developed and honed since 2008. It has become the model for other regional innovation initiatives, which also can be classified as public innovation labs. One such example is the Social Innovation Lab for Kent in the UK.[13] It is perhaps one of the early achievements of successful public sector innovation labs to establish the link between social innovation and public sector innovation.

The latest countries to create new innovation spaces based on design-informed approaches to policy are located in Latin America. They include the Ministry of Planning, Development and Budget, The President's Offices in Mexico, and the Chilean Laboratorio Gobierno. Their common objective is to develop innovative social policies, which increasingly require the integration of the activities of policy making with the activities of policy implementation. Their quest to move beyond current methods, practise and concepts within the public sector also has led them to human-centered design.[14] It is an acknowledgment that policies are a result of human making.

Policy making as designing[15]

Policies do not just grow on trees. People create them. For this reason, it is possible to talk about policies as products of design. The Cambridge dictionary underlines that policies are a result of human doing when it defines a policy as

> A set of ideas or a plan of what to do in particular situations that has been greed to officially by a group of people, a business organization, a government, or a political party.[16]

This makes it necessary to inquire into the design concepts; the design practices; or the design principles and specific design methods policy makers employ to arrive at a policy product. Transformation by design encourages us to ask these questions and to understand policy making as a problem of design. A policy in design terms is a guideline or framework that delineates the kinds of services and products, the relationships and the manner of the interactions that are possible, encouraged or discouraged within and by a particular human system. Moreover, a policy perceived in design terms is the result of applied design practices that employ certain design concepts and specific design methods.

Thinking of policy making as designing enables us to see how these design activities connect with those design activities that are necessary to implement a policy: the design of products and services. A design approach builds the bridge that has been missing in policy work and that must be built if future policies are to be more citizen-centric. We will expand on the role of services in policy in the next chapter and will be satisfied for the moment with concluding that the design of services starts already at the policy making stage because policies effectively establish the criteria and the framework that make specific products and services possible.

Policies serve a dual role in overall policy design: On the one hand, a policy needs to be specific enough to provide guidance for future actions, products and services. At the same time, policies have to create the necessary space for people to take appropriate actions, to envision new products and services to implement them. This dual characteristic of policies is often a cause for conflict in practice. A policy can narrow the opportunities for future product development too much, leading to products and services that are unsuitable to fulfil the policy's intent. In this case, a policy is flawed because the idea and its intent cannot be realized through products and services people can use and find meaningful. Such a policy is flawed because it fails to create opportunities for action.

Design theories in policy

Andrews et al. (2012) complain that 'government and organizations pretend to reform by changing what policies or organizations *look like* rather than what the actually *do*.'[17] When a policy does not provide enough space and vision to embrace the kinds of products and services that are necessary to translate intent and ideas into action, little can be done in the implementation stage to remedy this situation. Blame for policy failures can be levelled against policy makers. It is their fault when policies tackle the wrong problem or address a problem only partially. A policy that is ill-perceived and ill-informed seldom provides a useful framework for implementation.

But what if a policy has been carefully crafted and is sound and comprehensive, yet, the people entrusted with policy implementation struggle? What if the organizations charged with developing products and services that bring that policy to life lack the means to do so? This, too is a problem and leads to policy failures. It is easy in such cases to blame managers and staff in public organizations for their inability to implement a policy appropriately. But both 'blame models', argue Andrews and his colleagues, overlook that many problems related to policy making and policy-implementation cannot be addressed by either policy makers or policy-implementers in a unilateral fashion (Andrews et al. 2012). Assuming we can fragment policies neatly into idea generation and practical translation overlooks the systemic nature of policy design and implementation.

Other scholars and practitioners concerned with policy-implementation have also called for re-connecting policy makers with frontline workers and for integrating policy making with policy-implementation.[18] Some have specifically demanded a new design perspective on policy making. Among those count Stephen Linder and Guy Peters, who co-wrote several papers on the topic.[19] Their exploration of 'dialogue versus decision' as 'traditions of institutional designing' (Linder and Peters 1995) followed their earlier call for a 'design perspective on policy implementation' (Linder and Peters 1987). In his most recent book, Peters embraces not only a design perspective but also calls for policy makers to embrace and apply design methods borrowed from product design.[20] He writes in his preface:

> One way to consider policy analysis from both the academic and practical perspectives is to use a concept of policy design. The fundamental argument behind this perspective is that making policy is a design science very much like architecture and

engineering. While the messiness of the political process involved in making policy makes such a perspective appear excessively optimistic, the analyst can still develop and attempt to implement more coherent designs of policy. Even if that designing fails, and few policies are adopted and implemented exactly as designed, beginning with a coherent conception of the policy is likely to produce a more coherent result.

Unfortunately, Peters does not engage more fully with the implications of a design approach, respectively how policy making as designing provides new avenues for reflection, critique and action. Indicative here is his fixation that designing is an activity that begins once a problem has been identified and stated. As so many others, Peters overlooks the 'fuzzy front end' of design, the initial stages were problems are being identified, agendas set and the stakes put in the ground for what kinds of products and services are possible and which not. Still, like Herbert Simon in 1969, Peters makes the case for design in policy.[21]

Peters' understanding of policy as design resonates with that of Richard Baxstrom, a trained anthropologist. Baxstrom argues that government plans are

> . . . originating as a virtual object, as an image of thought that exists as an object and that subsequently provides the grounds for a range of acts and outcomes that particularly in the present, we can make more precise determinations regarding the variety of possible effects and outcomes that particular plans have in specific contexts.
>
> (Baxstrom 2011, p. 65)

Peters and Baxstrom affirm Noble Prize Winner Herbert Simon's (1969) earlier observation that 'everyone designs who devices courses of action aimed at changing existing situations into preferred ones'.[22]

Research into rhetoric beyond power in policy studies further informs this emerging design discourse in policy making, as do explorations in narratives and storytelling.[23] Fischer and Forrester (1993) have summarized some of these approaches in their landmark book *The Argumentative Turn in Policy Analysis and Planning*.[24] But few scholars have made as strong an argument for a design perspective as Martin Rein and Donald Schön. In their individual as well as their collaborative work, they have sought to shift the focus on design issues and design-related problems in policy making – albeit without using the term design. In his 1983 book *From Policy to Practice*, Rein points to the nonlinearity of the policy design process that often fails to align social values, public intent and program design with actual practice.[25] Also in 1983, Schön provided new insights into professional practices.[26] Already in 1977, Rein and Schön co-wrote a paper on 'problem setting in policy research'. They expanded on this work in 1993 when they looked at methods of reframing and developed the concept of reframing further in 1994.[27] Because policies present frameworks, the ability to reframe policies remains vital to developing new and future-oriented policies. The design perspective assigns new relevance to these earlier works.

Articulating design in policy

The design discoveries made by policy researchers so far remain limited and have yet to enter the design discourse. Vice versa, the design discussions in the policy field still lack the depth and rigor of design research. One of the reasons for this situation is that historically, the public sector thought of design as an external expertise for which one can engage professional designers – graphic designers, product designers, communication designers, or more recently, service designers. In many fields, the public sector included, it is still common to think of design merely as a profession. As a profession, design remains distinct and removed from the activities involved in policy making and policy implementation. As a profession, design is assigned a role and place within the policy cycle that enters into the policy cycle long after key design decisions have been made and long after crucial design criteria have been established. As a profession, design offers expertise on the form and materials people get to touch and encounter. As a profession, design fulfills an important role in the public sector. What design for policy points at is a much more fundamental role, one that touches on the principles of human organization.

Another reason can be found in the traditional fragmentation between policy making and policy implementation. They are a direct consequence of the fragmentation current policy cycle models propose. This fragmentation has led to the perception that policy making is an abstract and theoretical task aloof of any practical implications. To this day, the tasks, skills and qualifications requested of policy makers emphasize analytic, legal and political abilities. These in turn promote decision-making and problem-solving approaches to policy making. As long as the need for a policy can be specified clearly, these methods work well. But many policy issues today defy problem solutions and are too fuzzy and complex to allow for decision-making. They involve many different people and stakeholders who need to be heard but also who can contribute to policy solutions. Policy making in these situations requires methods, skills and processes to engage people as much as it requires new strategies and processes for their overall development.

Too often, policies still emerge with little consideration for what their implementation involves and a lack of understanding of their impact on the everyday lives of people. There is agreement that poor policy practices are at the heart of many failed policies. And many scholars would agree with Brigid Freeman (2013) that policy failures are an indication of 'failure to understand the core objective of policy work: implementation.'[28] However, 'implementation' still remains a code word for institutional and procedural design flaws when the real flaws hinge on a lack of understanding what policies mean for people and how policies have to be designed to work for people. We are at a point where the traditional disregard for matters of policy implementation maintained by policy makers negatively interferes with policy outcomes.

Design problems and the policy cycle

A design perspective can help transform the ways policies are being developed and implemented. But in many cases, design is still slotted into the policy design process as an isolated, in-itself closed activity, a fragment or part of policy implementation. To illustrate this, we can take a closer look at the role and place typically assigned to design in the policy cycle. Any policy cycle describes but also often prescribes a specific design process. For this reason we can 'read' a policy cycle model like a design manual. I am continuously grateful for Michael Howlett and M. Ramesh to allow me to use their policy cycle to demonstrate different policy perspectives on design. Their policy cycle (Howlett and Ramesh 2003) begins with the identification of a policy need. This is followed by a clarification of the policy need and the formulation of a policy. It presents a classic approach where design is not thought to have a role until the implementation of the policy demands the development of specific services. In this perspective, design thinking and design methods do not apply to policy making or the policy process itself. They are

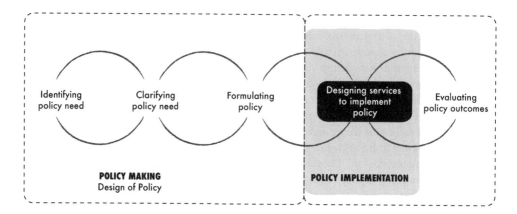

Design in the traditional policy cycle as decribed by Howlett & Ramesh 2003: Designing is not considered relevant for policy making. Design thinking, design methods and design practices are applied only in the context of policy implementation. Yet every depiction of the policy cycle articulates a specific design approach that promotes

Figure 3.1 Design in the traditional policy cycle

thought to be the domain of the service designer. Figure 3.1 depicts the complete policy design cycle described by Howlett and Ramesh.[29] I added the dotted lines to show how this perspective effectively breaks design into three different sections. This segmentation precludes the possibility that design has a role in the identification, framing or re-framing of a policy problem. It limits the usefulness and relevance of design concepts, methods and activities to matters of policy implementation – denying it a central role in the early stages of policy making.

I have labelled the largest outer box 'the realm of policy making as designing'. Within this realm, designing begins with policy identification and ends with policy evaluation. It therefore represents policy making as a comprehensive design problem and a synthesized design activity. Inside this all-encompassing dotted line, I have created two smaller rectangles. The left one encircles the areas and activities involved in policy creation. The smaller shaded one outlines the realm to which design is thought of as relevant in this model. Accordingly, innovation and transformation by design can only occur here. Furthermore, design in this perspective only concerns problem-solving. We can understand the implications better if we take a brief detour to discuss how problems frame design possibilities.

Design and its problems

Karl Ulrich (2007) has looked into various kinds of problems and how they relate to the development of products. He begins with the fair point that not all problems are problems of design. In Ulrich's view, problem-solving works this way: An agent operating in the world senses a gap between the current state and some desired state. The agent then defines a problem or problems, generates alternative solutions, selects an approach, and then takes action by implementing the solution. In most cases the problem solver then assesses whether the gap has indeed been closed and, if not, the problem solving process may be repeated iteratively (Ulrich 2007, p. 1). This sounds like a description of policy making as problem-solving.

Ulrich goes to great lengths to distinguish between a 'problem solving process' and a 'design process'. For him, the problem solving process is 'almost exactly' yet not the same as the design process. He argues that there are incongruences on the concept level where, in his understanding of design, designing focuses on 'plans' whereas problem-solving is concerned with 'outcomes' and actual practice. We can easily see how this line of argument drives a wedge between policy making and policy implementation. Ulrich denies the possibility of integrating policy making with policy implementation when he insists that the creation of a design does not necessarily mean its implementation or realization. He also releases designers from the responsibility of concerning themselves with the very issues that will ensure the realization of their plan.

What does this mean for a service designer who has developed a concept for a public service? Developing this concept constitutes a design process for Ulrich. But unlike this concept is translated into a real service, i.e., unless this designer can convince the public agency to give her a contract, the design remains an idea or plan, incapable of solving a problem.

If we translate this view into how policies are being designed and implemented, we are forced to separate the design of a policy ('the plan') from its implementation ('the outcome'). This is precisely what we can see in the Howlett and Ramesh policy cycle. It is almost ironic that policy makers according to Ulrich are 'designers' and 'planners' – not problem-solvers. That role and function is reserved for those who implement policies, thereby solving the problems planning has thrown at them. As in the policy cycle shown here, Ulrich also promotes the notion that design can only be part of a larger problem-solving effort. Design, in his view, can never address the whole.

Ulrich identifies one conceptual difference and several practical distinctions to underline his view that designing and problem-solving are distinct activities. The conceptual difference between design and problem solving, he argues, is evident in the difference between plans and outcomes. A design process, so Ulrich, results in a plan for action, but not necessarily in a realization of that plan. It is unclear why he overlooks that experienced designers are quite familiar with actual problem-solving.

Ulrich supports his view with a taxonomy of problems: Problems that need solving, he suggests, can be categorized into design problems, selection problems, system improvement problems, tuning problems, crises and wicked problems (Ulrich 2007, p. 5). Each kind of problem requires a specific problem-solving approach. A design problem is one that requires the creation of a new artefact in response to a gap. A selection problem is one in which it is possible to select from clearly articulated alternatives, i.e., by choosing from a given alternative. A system improvement problem is defined as the modification to existing artefacts or system(s). Ulrich defines a tuning problem as one where given variables are used to solve a riddle or puzzle to achieve the best or optimal outcome. An urgent or crises problem is one that needs to be resolved with a view to short-term impact. Finally, he allows for wicked problems, which he understands to be as 'problems where stakeholders' objectives are in fundamental conflict'.

Ulrich's classifications are worthwhile pondering as we seek to place design in policy, even though it may be a bit confusing to move from policy cycles to problem-solving to the nature of problems. Here is why: According to Ulrich, design is limited to areas of creating new artefacts and new systems where no artefact and no system existed before. He ignores that design never happens in a vacuum. The reason for this is rather simple: Reducing design problems to areas that concern only the invention of 'new' artefacts and 'new' systems ignores the reality that designing always takes place within systems: human, social, economic, political. There is no such thing as an empty or clean slate. New artefacts emerge from and within existing systems, new systems may develop parallel to existing systems but they are still part of the larger cultural system, though the relationship may be one of opposition rather than part of the mainstream.

In Ulrich's view, the integration of systems, a key challenge in policy making and policy implementation, ends up being reduced to a 'tuning problem' or to a 'system improvement problem'.

Like there are 'dominant, residual and emergent cultures' that continuously vie with each other, we can find dominant, residual and emergent systems that constantly negotiate their respective places.[30] Problem-solving as explained by Ulrich either denies or ignores this kind of dynamic as it has to assume an 'everything else being equal' (i.e., ceteris paribus) situation. Instead, a problem has to be treated in isolation to arrive at the desired outcome: selecting the right IT solution, reducing the defection rate, tuning elements of an organization.

In addition to this dilemma of design acting in and on the real world, not in a vacuum, there are other problems with approaching design solely as part of a problem-solving activity. To begin with, there is the real danger of getting lost in a round of classifying a problem before we have a chance to understand it. The urgency to assign a problem a category we are familiar with distracts us from looking into the nature of the problem at hand while we are busy seeking an appropriate category for a problem (which may or may not exist).

William Clancey's (1984) treatise on *Classified Problem-Solving* and his book *Heuristic Classifications* (Clancey 1985) explore these issues more fully.[31] It is easy to see how all this limits innovation. Innovation in a problem-solving mode can only happen within one of the categories we are ready to receive the problem into. A necessary condition for problem-solving is the existence of a problem. For a problem to be acknowledged as such, a problem has to be identified, perceived or stated. To do this, we need to have criteria in place. These criteria can include values, norms and beliefs. In other words, people have to wait (or do wait) until the data is in that affirms a problem exists. Pro-active inquiries and explorations, driven by curiosities and hunches that can generate new insights and change our perception of problems are rendered less valuable, if not a waste of time and effort.

We can detect another weakness in Ulrich's problem definition that concerns system integration. System integration involves many people with often conflicting views and territorial disputes, especially when the integration means a shift in responsibilities within an organization or within a government. Any redesign will involve shifting relationships, new forms of engagement and interaction. Not surprisingly we find that Ulrich's own problem taxonomy struggles with system integration, which is more akin to a wicked problem. In any case, the problem of connecting policy making with policy implementation does not fit neatly into any of these classifications and they should make us weary about the idea of problem-solving in policy making.

Weaknesses of policy making as problem-solving

The point of the above exercise is to illustrate that a problem-solving based approach to policymaking is based on a number of assumptions that limit our design options from the start. First, it builds on the notion that policymaking is a responsive, reactive activity. Policies then are not the forward-looking, future-oriented frameworks they could be. Instead, they are rooted in the past, responding to present and past facts, fears or other forces.

Policies in problem-solving are not so much tools to create future experiences but rather tools to regulate experiences of the past. We might say that 'the' problem shapes our policymaking and our lives because we only begin to shape policies that shape our lives in response to this problem. Second, the dependence on 'a' problem encourages policies to be developed in isolation from their larger contexts. Third, the problem-solving approach teaches policymakers to take action only when policymakers themselves are prepared to recognize a problem to be a problem. But it fails to consider and embrace people's everyday experiences and interactions.

It also pays little regard to the realities of employees in those organizations that have to implement and administer policies. What may seem to be a problem for policymakers may not be the problem experienced by people outside of policymaking. Furthermore, the problem-solving approach has a tendency to disconnect the different design activities that together constitute policy design by separating them into different design processes. The linear, top-down decision-making promoted in the policy cycle does little to remedy these fragmentations.

If we take all these aspects together, we can conclude that policy design driven by problem-solving does not lend itself to envisioning and inventing futures. It does not encourage or enable us to develop innovative policies towards achieving more desirable futures. It cannot, for example, achieve more humanizing outcomes as they prevent 'imaginative explorations through which new, more suitable and sustainable policies can be discovered'.[32]

Developing design thinking awareness in policy

Design thinking is intrinsic to policy and the public sector. Policy makers and public managers cannot help but apply some form of design thinking or another when they develop new policies, new procedures, new processes and new services. They have to design and redesign institutions for which they have to design procedures and structures. They have to be creative with using their resources in ways to fulfill their organizational mandates just as much as they have to care about achieving outcomes and fulfilling policy intent. The very existence of countless products and services are evidence of design thinking at work in the public sector.

But while design thinking *per se* may not be a new practice in the public realm, it has for long been taken for granted and treated as an implicit and tacit activity. The introduction of design thinking as a concept allows us to talk about and to reflect on existing design practices, design methods or design principles employed in the development of policies and public services. Moreover, it opens the door to new and different methods that are relevant and useful in our quest to arrive at effective policies and meaningful services. Design thinking as a concept enables us to hone new skills and new practices that advance our abilities to arrive at better and more effective outcomes, overcoming the weaknesses of our current, often un-reflected design practices and methods. Design thinking in this sense is about taking a stance, about developing a new attitude towards policy issues to generate new possibilities for public sector innovation.[33]

Many who attend design thinking workshops and seminars get introduced to a method or process.[34] All design thinking processes share that they are iterative and emerging. These characteristics distinguish design thinking from many design processes in place in the public sector that follow linear and deterministic approaches. The emergent characteristic means that the design problem is not understood or stated when the design process begins.

Rather, we are presented with a problematic situation. For John Dewey (1938) who I quoted above, a problematic situation is one where we find misfits in intent and outcome; where constituent elements do not line up to form a consistent and coherent unified whole. In contrast, a deterministic design process assumes that the problem is sufficiently identified and stated. Subsequently, the design process begins with the search for a solution for this problem.

Applying the concept of design thinking to policy means to think of policy making and policy implementation as design activities driven by design principles and applying design methods. Policy makers and public managers engage in designing the moment they conceive of a future product (i.e., a policy or service); when they plan and develop their idea (i.e., policy vision, purpose or intent) and finally give form to this idea through their thoughts and their actions. Design thinking thus extends the more traditional notion that views policy making as a decision-making and problem-solving activity. Moreover, design thinking can help us overcome the fragmented, linear, responsive and regressive tendencies implicit in current policy models.

It does so by embracing that at every stage of a design process, decisions and judgments are being made, criteria selected and weighted against each other, informed by dominant ethics and competing values. It does so by reminding us that policies are created and implemented by people with the intent to produce desirable, useful and usable outcomes for people in specific situations. In doing so, design thinking highlights that any policy is the result of applied design practices that employ certain design concepts and specific design methods. It is for this reason that we are able to discuss how representations of a policy cycle are an expression of design processes and what allows us to inquire into the kind of design principles and design methods that inform them.

Traditional and emerging professional design practices in policy

We can move away from the policy cycle and stop a moment to reflect on the traditional and emerging relationships for professional design in policy. The question is when and how do people associate design activities with policy. The answers reveal common places solidly anchored in various stages and at various levels of policy implementation and attached to specific design professions: Design for communication of existing policies (communication design); design for implementing existing policies (product and interaction design) and design for informing existing and new policies (service design):

Policy makers rely on design to communicate existing policies, for example, when they hire design professionals to create information brochures for citizens. Those designers have nothing to do with creating, shaping or influencing the policies since the policy is already in existence. The design practice can be limited to function as an instrument for announcement or extent to the role of a mediator. Communication and information are important to the success of a particular policy. As we have seen already, policy makers trust designers to support the implementation of existing policies through appropriate products and services. Traditionally, we would find product designers and, more recently, service designers active in this realm. Here the role of design is not only one of announcing but of implementing the policy, of making it happen. In this design practice, a designer acts a facilitator and enabler. More so than in the role of policy communicator, this can put professional design consultants in an ethical dilemma, for example, when a policy itself is disputed or flawed and not perceived beneficial by everyday citizens. It is possible to create a good experience for a potentially harmful policy.[35] Can professional designers mitigate the harshness of a policy? Should they? Independent of the answer to these questions, design gets more political the moment it engages in policy implementation.

The methods of information and interaction design, which are also evident in many service design practices, have recently opened new roles for professional designers in the policy context. Especially user research and participatory design methods are suited to inform new and existing policies with insights gained during the development of products and services. In this emerging design practice, professional design practices have a role in shaping the outcome of a policy itself. Existing policies can become amended and adjusted, new policies can build on insights from the design work. A good example for this new relationship is *Design for America*, (DFA) founded by Liz Gerber at Northwestern University in Chicago.[36]

In the design practices described above, the design of an object, an interaction or a service is the problem. This changes with the design practices that are currently emerging. Here policy making itself turns into a problem of design. In one relationship, design serves to envision human-centered policies. In the other, design serves to integrate the public system around people. More and more, though, the latter two design practices are coming together.

Designers are beginning to participate in envisioning future policies and changing organizational design practices based on human-centered design principles. This relationship of design and policy is notable for the way it views policy making as intrinsically linked with policy-implementation. As a result, methods of visualization, user research, co-creation, collaboration, co-production and co-design enter into the early stages of policy making and accompany the design process through all stages of product development needed for implementation.

From abstract problems to inquiries into human experiences

The moment we link policy implementation and policy making with the products and services that people actually experience, the human experience moves into the foreground. Human experiences can guide our questions and inquiries into ill-defined and problematic situations that we encounter in policy design. We might turn to human experience to guide

> . . . the controlled or directed transformation of an indeterminate situation into one that is so determinate in its constituent distinctions and relations as to convert the elements of the original situation into a unified whole.[37]

This definition of inquiry by John Dewey provides a rationale and a roadmap for policy making as designing, for connecting policy making with policy implementation. Policy making as designing adds two important elements to the current problem-solving mode: 1) the ability to inquire pro-actively into problematic *situations* and 2) to explore what makes them problematic for people. In other words, policy making as designing begins with an inquiry, not with a problem. The aim is to arrive at policies that are meaningful, useful and usable to people and society. The current problem-solving approach to policy design has proven to be incapable of supporting this kind of inquiry.[38]

In this context public services surface as starting points for such inquiries. They provide a missing link in any transformation by design in the public sector and they are therefore the topic of the next chapter.

Notes

1 This chapter brings together and develops ideas first presented in a paper for the 2012 RUCON Sunrise Conference *Innovating and Transforming Governments,* at Roskilde University in Roskilde, Denmark, and in a paper presented at the 11th European Academy of Design in Gothenburg in 2012, which has since been published by the online journal *Annual Review of Policy Design.*
2 Miller, Derek and Rudnick, Lisa (Spring, 2011). 'Trying It on for Size: Design and International Public Policy', *Design Issues,* Vol. 27 (2), p. 7.
3 Based on a personal conversation.
4 See Carmody, M. (2002). 'Listening to the Community: Easier, Cheaper, More Personalized', Presentation to the *American Chamber of Commerce,* Sydney; and Bason, C. (2014). *Design for Policy,* Gower, Earnham, UK.
5 Sahni, N.R., Wessel, M. and Christensen, C.M. (Summer, 2013). 'Unleashing Breakthrough Innovations in Government', *Stanford Social Innovation Blog.* See http://ssir.org/articles/entry/unleashing_breakthrough_innovation_in_government.
6 See http://www.federalnewsradio.com/520/3004758/OPMs-innovation-lab-spurs-new-way-of-problem-solving [accessed January 2016]. I provide an account of the US OPM Lab in Junginger, S. (2012). 'Public Innovation Labs: A Byway to Public Sector Innovation?' in P. Christensen and S. Junginger (eds.), *Highways and Byways of Radical Innovation,* University of Southern Denmark and Kolding School of Design, Kolding, Denmark, pp. 137–156.
7 http://mind-lab.dk [accessed January 2013].
8 See Kimbell, Lucy (2015). *Applying Design Approaches to Policy making: Discovering Policy Lab,* The University of Brighton, Brighton, UK. Also see: http://theiteams.org/case-studies/policy-lab-uk [accessed November 2015].
9 See http://innovation.govspace.gov.au/2012/01/27/a-pilot-centre-for-excellence-in-public-sector-design/ [accessed January 2013].
10 See Junginger, 'Public Innovation Labs.'
11 http://www.sitra.fi [accessed January 2016].
12 See http://www.la27eregion.fr/en/ and http://superpublic.fr [accessed January 2016].
13 http://socialinnovation.typepad.com/silk/meet-the-silk-team.html [accessed January 2016].
14 See http://www.presidencia.gob.mx/agentesdeinnovacion/#proyectos; http://mind-lab.dk/en; http://www.bnamericas.com/news/technology/public-innovation-lab-among-key-digital-initiatives-for-chile-govt [all accessed January 2016].
15 Also see: Junginger, S. (2014). 'Policy making as Designing: Policy making Beyond Problem-Solving and Decision-Making', in C. Bason (ed.), *Design for Policy,* Gower, Farnham, UK, pp. 57–69.
16 Cambridge online dictionary: http://dictionary.cambridge.org/dictionary/english/policy
17 Andrews, M, Pritchett, L. and Woolcock, M. (2012). 'Escaping Capability Traps through Problem-Driven Iterative Adaptation (PDIA)', Center for Global Development, Working Paper 299, June 2012.
18 See Adebowale, O. and Starkey, K. (2009). *Engagement and Aspiration–Reconnecting Policy making with Frontline Professionals,* Sunningdale Institute Report for the UK Cabinet, March 2009; Eppel, E., Turner, D. and Wolf, A. (2011). 'Future State 2–Working Paper 11/04', Institute of Policy Studies, School of Government Victoria University of Wellington, New Zealand, June 2011.
19 See, for example: Linder, S.H. and Peters, B.G. (1987). 'A Design Perspective on Policy Implementation: The Fallacies of Misplaced Prescriptions', *Review of Policy Research,* Vol. 6 (3): 459–475 and Linder, S.H. and Peters, B.G. (1995). 'The Two Traditions of Institutional Designing: Dialogue Versus Decision', in D. Weimer (ed.), *Institutional Design,* Kluwer Academic Publishers, Dordrecht, pp. 133–160.
20 Peters, G. (2015). *Advanced Introduction to Public Policy,* Edward Elgar, Northampton, MA, USA.
21 Simon, Herbert A. (1996 [1969]). *The Sciences of the Artificial,* MIT Press, Cambridge, MA.
22 Ibid., 111.

23   Kaplan, Thomas J. (1993). 'Reading Policy Narratives: Beginnings, Middles, and Ends', in Frank Fischer and John Forrester (eds.), *The Argumentative Turn in Policy Analysis and Planning*, Duke University Press, Durham, NC, pp. 167–185.

24   Fischer, F. and Forrester, J. (eds.) (1993). *The Argumentative Turn in Policy Analysis and Planning*, Duke University Press, Durham, NC.

25   Rein, M. (1983) *From Policy to Practice,* M.E. Sharpe, Armonk, NY.

26   Schön, D. (1983) *The Reflective Practitioner: How Professionals Think in Action*, Temple Smith, London.

27   See Rein, M. and Schön, Donald (1977) 'Problem Setting in Policy Research', in C.H. Weiss (ed.), *Using Social Research in Public Policy Making*, Lexington Books, Lexington, MA, pp. 235–51; Rein, Martin and Schön, Donald (1993) 'Reframing Policy Discourse', in Frank Fischer and John Forrester (eds.), *The Argumentative Turn in Policy Analysis and Planning*, Duke University Press, pp. 145–166; also see Rein, Martin and Schön, Donald (1994) *Reframing: Controversy and Design in Policy Practice*, Basic Books, New York.

28   Freeman, B. (2013). 'Revisiting the Policy Cycle', ATEM Developing Policy in Tertiary Institutions, June 21, 2013, Northern Metropolitan Institute of T AFE, Melbourne.

29   Howlett, M. and Ramesh, M. (2003). *Studying Public Policy*, 2nd Edition, Oxford University Press, Oxford.

30   Williams, R. (1977). 'Residual, Emergent and Dominant Culture', in I. Szeman, (ed.), *Cultural Theory*, Oxford University Press, New York, p. 121.

31   Clancey, W.J. (1985). 'Heuristic Classification', *Artificial Intelligence*, Vol. 27 (3): 289–350; Clancey, W.J. (1984). 'Classified Problem Solving', *Proceedings Fourth National Conference on Artificial Intelligence*, Austin, TX (August 1984), 49–55.

32   Lynch, K. (1965). 'The City Sense and City Design', *Design Issues*, reprint 2000, reprinted from *Scientific American*, Vol. 213 (3): 209–214.

33   Michlewski, K. (2015). *Design Attitude*, Gower, Farnham, UK.

34   For an example of design thinking as method and process see http://dschool.stanford.edu/dgift [accessed January 2016].

35   Ron Rosenbaum demonstrates this vividly in his book *Explaining Hitler–The Search for the Origins of His Evil*, Harper, 1999. Although he does not directly refer to design, it is clear how symbols, things, actions and systems work together as enablers and facilitators.

36   www.designforamerica.com [accessed January 2013].

37   Dewey, J. (1938). *Logic: The Theory of Inquiry*, Henry Holt and Company, New York, Chapter VI, "The Pattern of Inquiry," 104.

38   See for example: Sanderson, I (2002). 'Evaluation, Policy Learning and Evidence-Based Policy Making', *Public Administration*, Vol. 80: 1–22; Shields, Patricia M. (1998). 'Pragmatism as Philosophy of Science: A Tool for Public Administration', *Research in Public Administration*, Vol. 4: 195–225.

4 Services as key to effective government

It is clear, however, that *even governmentality begins as an image*; a perceptible virtual object which then proliferates through institutions, through discourse, and in the case of many large scale institutionally driven plans directly and concretely into the lives of everyday people.[1]

Chapter 3 positioned policy making and policy implementation as connected design activities and defined policies as products that delineate and guide the development of any future public service. Policy making emerged as a design activity that establishes the criteria for the kinds of services that are possible and encouraged within a human system. It showed that policy and design have much in common but also that designing is not new to policy making or policy implementation. At the same time, we could see that neither design research nor policy studies have made the case for design in policy making and in policy implementation just yet. This chapter turns our attention to services. It explains what makes services central to policy intent, policy making and policy implementation.

People are where policies begin and end. Policies begin with people because policy intent seeks to address an issue, problem or situation that concerns people. Policies end with people because policy fulfilment relies on people's compliance. The role of policy making is one of developing meaningful and sensible policies that can be successfully implemented and made accessible to people via some kind of service. Figure 4.1 links people with policy intent, policy making and policy implementation. The diagram reminds us that policies are not just for people but that people have a role in every step of policy design. People work on policy intent, frame policies and are responsible for their enactment.

Any policy effort involves eventually hinges on the question of what services do people need and how can the public sector create the policy framework and the organizational setting for these services. And the design of services has a long tradition and history in the public sector.[2] Yet, services have barely been looked at in the policy context so far.

Scholars like Donald Kettl and James Fessler (2009) can agree that the 'translation of politics into the reality that citizens see every day' is the task of public administration.[3] But they let policy makers off the hook and have little to say about the development of meaningful and useful public services, although that is what citizens 'see'. This reality is not without consequences: well-designed and appropriate services enhance trust in government; poorly and ill-conceived services reduce confidence in the public sector. Each interaction with a public service expresses and communicates values of equality and fairness to the individual citizen. Public services therefore contribute to social coherence and the sense of social justice.

Well-designed services provide meaningful tools or information at a time that is useful to people, in a place that is accessible, and in a format that is easy to understand and use. Well-designed services are efficient and effective from a policy perspective, from a public

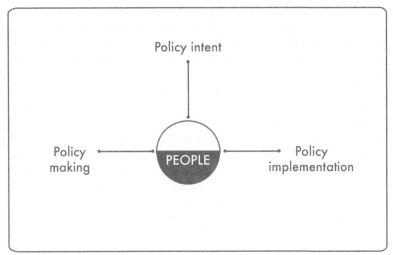

Human-centered design based on people's experiences and interactions can inform all aspects of policy development.

Figure 4.1 Policy intent, policy making and policy implementation depend on people

administration perspective and from a citizen perspective. They ensure that policy intent remains intact so that desired policy outcomes can be achieved. They reduce the burden on the public administration because people who have a clear understanding of what they are asked to do and are given the right tools to get the job done, require little additional support from the organization. Well-designed public services also help people make informed decisions or take deliberate actions.

In contrast, poorly designed services tend to be at the center of citizen complaints. Many complaints originate from problems citizens have in accessing them, using them or under-standing them. Sometimes, however, it is the nature of the service itself that fails to address real problems for real people. Such services might be accessible and usable. Nonetheless, people may not use them because they feel that they do not address the actual problems they are struggling with. Such services simply miss their target. They are a waste of time and resources on all levels of policy making and policy implementation. Once again it shows that public sector design cannot ignore human experience and human interaction without cost. It is yet another incentive to introduce human-centered design to policy makers and policy implementers. Further, it provides a rationale for applying the insights and methods of service design systemically, and systematically within public organizations.

To understand the complexities involved in designing public services, it helps to remind us of the characteristics of services in general and of the specific characteristics of public and private services. There exist some commonalities and some important distinctions.

Shared characteristics of public and private services

Public services share many characteristics with services private businesses provide. In pri-vate organizations, too, it is 'the service' people experience and associate with the organi-zation. Another shared characteristic of public and private services is that they are deeply embedded in the organizations that develop and deliver them.[4] This means that services continuously draw on an organization's resources and depend on the organization's staff. Services also interfere with processes and procedures and define specific tasks for employees. Any given service an organization offers simultaneously constitutes workload for some of their employees. That is true for both public and private services. Poorly designed services are therefore not only a problem for citizens; they are also a problem for the organization.

The general criteria service designers have set up to define services also apply to public services: they are intangible, heterogeneous, inseparable, and perishable. Most public services cannot be seen, smelled, tasted touched or felt in the same way goods, for example, as a mobile phone, can be sensed. Services are heterogeneous because the quality of their delivery depends on the time and place as well as on the people involved. Heterogeneity here means that there is no simple quality control. We cannot look for flaws in the material or in the production line. That services are inseparable is owed to the fact that services 'take place', that is, they come into being in the presence of people. Services do not exist without human interaction. This ephemeral characteristic of services is expressed in the criterion that services perish. Organizations cannot store an inventory of services like they can store a sufficient supply of coffee, for example. Instead, services 'depend on the ability to balance and synchronize demand with supply capacity.' Service Design literature refers to these criteria by its initials 'IHIP'.[5]

Characteristics unique to public or private services

There are important key characteristics that are unique to public services. The purposes, roles, forms and materials that constitute a public service are different from the kinds of services that originate in a commercial, manufacturing, or consumer-good-centered environment. The purpose of a public service is to make a positive contribution to a community or society.

Public services fulfill an important role in the policy cycle. They are first and foremost instruments for implementing public policy. They are the means through which policies get enacted and through which policies become real.[6] Thus services mediate not only the relationships between government organizations and citizens but also between organizations and policy or lawmakers. One of the consequences is that public organizations – unlike private companies – cannot choose to offer a particular service or not. Public organizations may not be excited about the services they are asked to develop and deliver. Still, they have to go ahead and get it done. Public organizations may not feel they have the capacity to develop and deliver a particular service. But here, too, the ability to say no is limited.

As if these constraints did not suffice, there are additional considerations private business does not have to worry about: Public organizations are required to provide the same services to all people regardless of their educational, earning, age, social, ethnic or religious background. As a principle, all citizens have the same rights to the same government services. Non-citizens, too, have a right to government services, regardless of demographics. Designing services under these circumstances is radically different from designing services for a private business that can choose to offer a service or not as well as to whom it wants to offer a specific service.

Public services are not an add-on or extension that adds value to a specific already exist-ing item. They have to constitute value in themselves and for themselves. The service system around a mobile phone is an example of a service that exists because of a product: without the network services, without mobile applications that offer additional specific services, the phone would be rather useless. Many services in the private sector are still attached to an object. Automobile services center on cars. Services in the public sector tend to exist independent of any tangible product.

The right to the same service also manifests an obligation for the citizen. Just like government agencies cannot pick and choose whom they want to engage with, people often have no choice but to make use of a public service. For example, they have to pay taxes and they have to register their cars. As private consumers, we can decide with which business we want to enter into a relationship; which company we want to give our business. This choice is not available when it comes to public organizations and public services.

To complicate matters further, some government services defy the common notion of 'a service' – at least in the sense that people expect to receive something. Prison services are one example. Tax services are another. In both cases, the 'service' serves to collect something from citizens: in one case freedom, in another money. Their service is to society first and to the individual second. Yet, these are public services necessary to fulfill our citi-zen obligations and to make society function as a whole. Thus, even these services provide 'a service' but in a much more complex fashion than many other services we are familiar with, say, the service we expect and receive in a restaurant.

Services and public organizations

The characteristics identified above are important for anyone involved in designing pub-lic services. They also help us position services in the policy context. Transformation by design here means to acknowledge services as mediators among policies organizations and human experience. Services provide opportunities for human interaction as much as they give shape to them. Because public policies are administered and monitored by public organizations and government agencies, and because services are central to these organizations and the key means through which they can fulfill their organizational mandates, policy makers would do well to pay attention to future services in the earliest stages of policy making. In addition, services touch an all four elements of an organi-zation described in chapter 1. Any change to a service provision is therefore likely to involve changes to the organizational system. Because services draw on monetary, mate-rial and technical resources as well as on the skills and knowledge of staff, any change in a service means to mess with procedures, possible assigning and defining new tasks. Vice versa, any change to a policy is likely to involve changes in an existing service.

This characteristic is shared across public and private services. It distinguishes services from any other product organizations may develop and deliver. And it is one of the reasons services are of central concern to public sector innovation. Once it is clear that policies directly relate to services while services directly link with people, we can look at services not as the end of the policy cycle but start new policy initiatives by exploring the service needs and opportunities first to inform the changes necessary on the organizational and policy level service. The moment policy begins to focus on human experience and human interaction we pay attention to services.

The role of services in policy

Services are key to successful policy making because, as we have explained already, citizens never experience policies *per se*. People experience services. It is services that bring policies to life. Policies and laws are words on paper. To apply and to implement them, to administer and monitor them, services are essential.

It makes services central to achieving and fulfilling a policy's intent. Services link policy intent with policy making and policy implementation. Figure 4.2 positions services in the context of policy intent, policy making and policy implementation. These relationships mean that services are directly affected by any policy change. It also clarifies that when a service fails citizens it fails the policy from which it originates, too. What we need is a greater awareness of services in policy design from the earliest stages of policy planning. But we also need to develop the capacity for policy makers and public managers to develop appropriate services that maintain the integrity of a policy.

Because services are central to policy intent, policy making and policy implementation but also central to how people experience government and interact with public organizations, they are a place from where we can start to innovate and transform the public sector around people. It is therefore time for services and the design of services to be included in policy research and policy work. Policy makers and policy-implementers eager to arrive

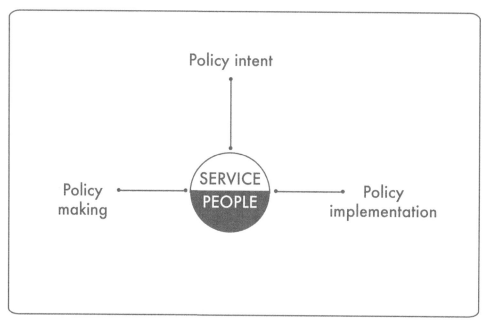

Integrated policy making and policy implementation allow for services that realize a policy's intent because they are meaningful and usable to the people they intent to reach. Design inquiries into services can generate actionable insights into what policies are needed or how a policy needs to change to achieve the desired outcome. Likewise, during the design of services, public managers and other staff can learn what internal changes can facilitate and improve a service delivery that is in line with the policy's intent and the organization's goals for efficiency and effectiveness.

Figure 4.2 Services are central to policy making and implementation

at citizen-centric policies and meaningful public services need to familiarize themselves with new design processes, design practices and design methods. Above all, they need to find ways to broaden their design thinking beyond the one they are currently applying. They will no longer think of a service as belonging to the tail end of policy making, external to their work but as a means to inform policy intent. For some, this can be an uncomfortable journey into new territory beyond traditional hierarchies, beyond the reassurance of one's own expertise. For others, it will be an opportunity to rethink their own role and practice.

There is also room for a shift in focus for policy scholars. For the better part of its history, research by social scientists into the relationship among public administration and society has been concerned with 'the possibilities for politicians to steer the bureaucracy according to their intentions', acknowledge Guy Peters and J. Pierre (2012, p. 403). They observe, though, that recent empirical research has become interested in a society-centered perspective. Either way, human experience and human interaction have yet to find their way into early stages of policy making and continue to be overlooked in implementation. Instead, policy makers still favor those aspects of a policy that help their own causes (Peters 2007). Other researchers conclude that a rationalistic approach has emphasized decision-making and problem-solving (Colebatch and Radin 2006) with the same effect: favoring theoretical abstraction over engaging with people.

Apple founder Steve Jobs gained recognition and respect for his intuitions and insights into user behavior and user expectations. He was a keen observer and never dismissed his own experiences and his own interactions with the world. He was an engineering expert and in many ways a genius. Yet, his most profound ideas derived from direct and personal experiences, from his own engagement with people and organizations. It is much more difficult for policy makers to echo Steve Jobs' approach. Their life circumstances and their everyday life experiences are often worlds removed from people they create policies for. It is not impossible, though, to take policy makers and civil servants into the field to get a glimpse into the everyday life of specific citizens. The Danish MindLab achieved fame for taking staff from SKAT, the Danish tax office, out onto farms where they spent a full day interviewing and observing a farmer one-on-one. The rationale is akin to that of Steve Jobs: understanding human situations and how products and services can improve them. Just like Steve Jobs began with the iPhone as a flawed product that ultimately revolutionized and revived an industry, we can pivot public sector innovation around the design of services that matter to people. One of the key motivations to invest time and effort in new ways of public service development is the promise that policies move from idea to real impact. In some ways policy makers share a problem familiar to designers: Imagination is necessary to come up with a good idea. But imagination needs to be informed and simply having an idea is not sufficient. What matters is to device ways to check reliably what this idea will do for people and how this idea can become a real product, be that an object, a service – or a policy.

Human-centered design and service design

To keep the focus on people, on the human experience and on human interaction, design thinking embraces principles and methods of user-centered design and human-centered design. Chapter 2 explained the differences between human-centered design and user-centered design. It is through the stronger interpretation of human-centered design that we can link public services and service design. It is through the efforts of understanding the needs and opportunities within the organization as well as the needs and opportunities outside of it that we can discover, invent, develop and deliver new kinds of services and service models. A service designer who disregards organizational operations and processes will not succeed in implementing a service design solution. Likewise, policy makers and public managers who do not grasp the role of services will also fail in their best efforts to improve this world.

A service perceived and developed around a human being depends on the integration of materials and function, organizational operations, and form. It follows that policy makers, public managers and anyone else involved in the design of services have to work hand in hand to create useful, usable and desirable services in a landscape of messy, ever-changing organizations and volatile politics.

One aspect that gets easily lost when we talk about human experience and human interaction is that organizations are also made up of people. When people in the organization do not understand the intent of a policy, and when they lack support for necessary changes to the organization's structure, procedures and processes, the resulting service may not be the one needed to achieve the desired policy outcome.

The moment we think of an organization as people making use of available resources according to agreed procedures following agreed structures to achieve a common goal or purpose, services emerge as central to organizational life as well. A service requires people who know how to provide the service in a way that fulfills the organization's purpose; it requires organizational structures and procedures that enable and support the service provision; and it requires appropriate and sufficient resources for the service to be delivered and maintained. Any change within the organization that develops and delivers a public service is likely to effect the service provision by that organization. When we make an effort to develop innovative and human-centered services, we also have a change to re-orient the organization around people.

Already, three of the largest management consulting businesses have each bought a major design firm with service design expertise to work on government projects. This shows growing interest in design practices and design methods as well as an understanding that public services offer a path to public sector innovation. The next chapter will talk specifically about design practices in public organizations.

Notes

1 Baxstrom, R. (2011). 'Even Governmentality begins as an Image: Institutional Planning in Kuala Lumpur', *Focaal, Journal of Global and Historical Anthropology*, Vol. 61: 61–72 (citation p. 65). (Italics in original.)
2 See Junginger, S. (2012). 'Public Foundations of Service Design', in S. Miettinnen and A. Valtonen (eds.), *Service Design with Theory*, Lapland University Press, Rovaniemi, Finland, pp. 21–26.
3 Kettl, D. and Fessler, J. (2009). *The Politics of the Administrative Process*, CQ Press, Washington, DC.
4 Junginger, S. and Sangiorgi, D. (2009). 'Service Design as a Vehicle for Organizational Change', *IASDR Conference*, Seoul, Korea 2009.
5 See for example: Sangiorgi, D. and Meroni, A. (2011). *Designing for Services*, Gower, Farnham, UK.
6 Junginger, S. (2012). 'Matters of Design in Policy making and in Policy Implementation', *Annual Review of Policy Design* [Online], Vol. 1 http://ojs.unbc.ca/index.php/design/article/view/542.

5   Organizational design
practices and design legacies

During my time at Lancaster University in England, I was able to introduce students to the complexities of designing with organizations. I was able to get permission from the university library to conduct a design inquiry. The students were initially seriously restricted in their research. They were told not to talk to library visitors or staff; not to take pictures and not to interfere with the operational life. In short, they were pretty much told off by the interim head of the library to engage in any sensible research. Neither the system nor the people seemed accessible. But the students were not deterred. They understood that part of their initial task was to develop a relationship with people working in the organization. We began to work together with the librarian responsible for design literature. She toured us through the building, explained the operations and the challenges the library currently faced in terms of purpose, resources and demands. She also introduced the student to the basics of library science. Though officially restricted, the students could visit the library in their role as 'students' and silently observe and take notes. Absent of permission to take pictures, they would document some observations by sketching.

One of the observations the students made early on was that the library had structured its information for people according to their university status. That is, the library addressed students, graduate students, faculty or visitors. What the design students realized by talking with people using the library on campus as well as with people who said they were not using the library was that the university status was not a useful way to develop products and services for library users. Instead, they found that it was much more relevant to understand why people were engaging with the library and what they were trying to achieve. The students ended up identifying eleven different user profiles for which they then developed new ideas for how to make use of the library space and for what kinds of new services the library could offer.

Among other things, the students managed to cut cost for the library because they could point out that this library printed almost fifty different kinds of flyers and brochures to get information out to people. Other comparable university libraries, the students found, got by with five to ten. But the most significant contribution of this project was to help the library better understand the people it engaged with and to shift its view of rank and status to action and objective. As one of the consequences, the library began to redesign its entry-level space according to suggestions from the students. Before the start of the project, the library still considered itself a space for reading and quiet time, for concentrated working and for people who arrive to look for some kind of book or information.

But the students could demonstrate that many people came to the library for social reasons and to do group work. Even people from the nearby city had developed routines to regularly come up to the library for socializing and reading the daily newspaper.

Indicative of the transformational thinking the students had triggered, the interim library head, initially unsupportive and disinterested in the student's work, stood up at the final presentation to express his sincere thanks and his appreciation. The students had helped him and his staff rethink the library's new place in a fast changing environment. The library was struggling with the digital revolution and questioned its relevance in a time when new places around campus sprung up that presented themselves as learning zones. Until then, the library was 'the' learning zone. The results of the projects presented the library with new paths forward and created links with these new learning zones so that it no longer felt a need to compete against them or be fearful of their impact. Instead, the library discovered new synergies that strengthened both the learning zones and the library itself to foster new knowledge and to make information accessible to everyone.

Being a public library, there still were no more resources available then before the project. However, the project had provided the library staff with ideas and actionable concepts they could systematically implement on their own speed. And they did so over the next couple of years, step by step.[1] How did the students succeed in their endeavor? They applied design research methods that centered on the human experience and on human interaction. But they did not stop at the door of the organization. They included staff in the organization in their research, they invited them to participate and made sure that whatever findings they had, they shared with any interested staff. For example, they brought staff into their project room and presented the research they had already undertaken. They explained what they did, how they did it and what they found. They shared the questions they had answered for themselves and the questions they still had. These interactions provided opportunities for the library staff to contribute their answers but also to help generate new questions they felt were relevant.

This was a way for the design students to constantly check if their findings concerning the organization's constraints and abilities, its stakeholders and its users were correct and complete. They were well aware that their ideas and their concepts depended on understanding how they would cope with the organizational context. Including and engaging the staff throughout this process helped build trust and convinced the staff that these 'design students' were not just out to have some fun and to come up with some outlandish design concept. Staff quickly realized that the students were sincere in learning about their organizational issues and struggles and that they were determined to develop solutions that benefitted everyone.

Dealing with a complex organization, the respect the students received from the library staff helped them overcome tough moments when the complexity and the intricacy of systems just seemed to stifle any effort at meaningful change. Working directly with members of the organization generated empathy for the situation of librarians. Students learned about problems they had to cope with, like that of the printers in the library: These printers, they learned were maintained by the IT department of the university. They held the key to the printers. This key was needed to restock the paper when printers ran out. IT staff did not work on Sundays. But librarians did. Students also worked on Sundays. Librarians, earning considerably less than IT staff at the university and working on weekends, got the brunt of dissatisfaction by frustrated students who had to print out their essays to submit them on time in class. Yet, the librarians had no way of fixing the printers.

It is a problem that seems easy to fix. We only need to stop and ask ourselves why we are doing it this way. This is the question that drives this chapter. Though the printer problem is not exactly a design problem, the situation is still a consequence of some kind of design thinking and an outcome of certain design practices. In this case, it is about keeping the design of IT services separate from the design of library services. The design thinking is segmented by organizational function, not guided by printing efficiency. This design thinking also ignores the experience of those students who depend on the printers on the weekend and of the staff that works there and gets yelled at without being able to change anything. A different view of design would enable staff and students to get their respective jobs done. A different kind of design thinking would lead to an integrated service that serves the organization, its staff and its users.

The question before us now is how to get to these different ways of thinking and doing. How do we become aware of other approaches and methods that exist and how can make use of these? For public organizations, this is an urgent question. Just like the library and also like the employment agency in the previous example, the way to do things and to go about developing and delivering services are rarely reflected on. We may criticize a service but we seldom invest time in finding out how that service came into being in the first place, what the design thinking was at the time, what design practices dominated and what design methods were used – or not. Dwelling on the past is not the objective here. Before organizations can transform their design practices, however, they need to articulate and assess their current approaches to designing. The objective is to create an understanding and awareness that we can do things differently. Before organizations can transform their design practices, however, they need to articulate and assess their current approaches to designing. Such awareness is a prerequisite for transforming organizations and the way they go about their business. For this reason, we have to look into how organizations, and especially public organizations go about designing.

What organizational design practices exist? In other words, what do people in organizations do when they have to develop a new service? What methods do they employ?[2] What design criteria do they set up and how do they arrive at these? How do they make sure that their design efforts lead to products and services that enable the organization to fulfill its purpose, mandate or vision? Since every organization has to develop some kind of product or service that is useful and relevant to at least some people, we can find methods and practices related to design within any organization. How representatives of each group are getting engaged in specific design efforts is an indication of organizational design practices. Organizational design practices are influenced by what an organization perceives to be its own design capability and by whom the organization views to hold the necessary or sufficient design expertise.

Who may participate in an organizational design activity?

Pelle Ehn reminds us that participatory design concerns 'designing before use'.[3] In public organizations, we tend to find three basic groups of people who may get involved and participate in product development. There are the internal *members of an organization*. Members of an organization may be managers, supervisors, front desk, administrative staff or all of the above. They may or may not be aware of their design activities and may therefore act as 'silent designers'. Steeped in and often hampered by organizational processes, structures and procedures, organizational members can easily overlook their own role in giving shape and form to products and services. *External experts* form a second, even more diverse group. External experts who get involved in the design of public services can range from a professional consultant to an academic researcher but would also describe an organization's external stakeholder. For government agencies, the needs, demands, and pressures of external stakeholders, such as professional trade groups, lobbyists, unions or other parts of government can pose enormous obstacles to any change or transformation. External participants tend to be more aware of their role as designers and shapers because they either make a living of it (as do design and management consultants), or they have a vested interest in the design outcome (as do lobbyists, unions, or industries). We can therefore refer to external experts more generally as external design experts. The third group of people that factors into organizational design practices are the people an organization either aims to provide for or has a mandate to serve. In business organizations, the term 'customer' is a catch all for this group of people. In public organizations, it is the *ordinary people* or *everyday citizen who may* have a role in organizational design practices. Ordinary people and citizens are individuals who are already engaging with an organization or who the organization would like to see engage with its services. I will use the term citizen to describe both non-citizens and citizens as we continue. However, I am aware of the difference and the distinctions they produce in public management and in policy work.

Choices: Designing to, for, with and by in public organizations

Who gets involved in the design of a product is indicative of the potential of an organizational design practice to promote or stifle organizational changes. It seems obvious that when the role of organizational members is minimized or even neglected, there are few opportunities to share knowledge and insights generated through the design activities with the organization. How then is the organization supposed to change? When we look at the range of organizational design practices, we do find many forms that create artificial barriers to collaborative and participatory practices with members of an organization. The reasons are manifold but many of them have their roots in what people who represent these three groups, think of their own role and that of people part in the other groups. In essence, they can each assume one of three roles: they can design for, design with or they can completely trust the design to one of these three groups. Organizational design practices follow directly from an organization's view of designing as an activity done by a group *to* or *for* people, done by a group *with* a group of people, or done *by* a group of people.[4] When organizational changes are intended to result from a design effort, members of the organization have to be conscious of their roles in the design process.

Designing for or designing on behalf of public organizations

Charles Leadbetter is among those who have begun to look into the distinct implications of design being done to someone (design for), design being done with and design being done by someone.[5] When one group is designing for one or both of the other groups, when the one group is expected to deliver something to or for another group, the opportunities for collaboration, co-development or co-design are very limited (Leadbetter 2009). He blames industrialization for creating a culture that seeks to deliver goods and services to and for people:

> Often in the name of doing things *for* people traditional, hierarchical organisations end up doing things *to* people. . . . Social services departments were created to help people

in need. Yet those on the receiving end of services often complain they feel they are being done to, processed by a bureaucratic machine.

(Leadbetter 2009, p. 1)

'Designing for' can also be understood as 'designing on behalf of' someone. This has implications for our understanding of organizational design practices. When internal organizational members design *on behalf of* citizens, they position themselves as the design experts in a design activity. They are the ones who know what needs to be designed and who know how to do this. The need to engage with either external design experts or everyday citizens is on a 'need-to-know' basis. For this reason, *designing for* reflects a rather paternalistic approach to product development, one that insists that 'we know best' and that pushes products out of the organization and imposes them onto people.[6]

If we stay with the idea of 'designing on behalf of someone', we can also imagine external design experts to take a leading role. For example, an organization can shift the responsibility for a design solution to external experts, thus paying them to design *for* or *on behalf of* the organization and *on behalf of* citizens. In this constellation, the burden to generate participatory opportunities rests mainly with the external design experts. It is up to them to decide how to involve organizational members and everyday citizens in the design process. Here, too, product development remains a one-directional activity because there is limited organizational interest in any actual engagement with the design task. More likely than not, the organization will lean back and wait for the result to be developed by other people. The on-going design work can hardly touch on any aspect of organizational life as it remains strictly separated from it. Learning and insights generated throughout the design process can therefore not be shared with the organization. There are not many opportunities for changing organizational design practices or for rethinking organizational design principles.

But cannot everyday citizens also design on behalf of an organization or on behalf of external design experts? This is a possibility that is increasingly being explored in a range of community projects in the UK by the conservative party. The Big Society, for example, was built around the idea that everyday citizens would or should know better what and how public services should be provided. Jane Suri suggests that when professional designers design for someone, they take their inspiration from people (Suri 2007).[7] Yet, in public organizations, the inspiration to *design for someone* is too often dominated by the internal organizational system and the organizational perspective. Rather than being inspired by people and how they experience real situations, it is political, legal, structural, procedural and economic needs that 'inspire' products and services. In such situations, the possibilities for new products and services are limited. Moreover, any new product or service is likely to reproduce and manifest the ways an organization goes about its business. In organizational literature, this aspect, though not understood in the design context, is considered to increase an organization's path dependencies. In very simple terms, path dependencies mean that previous decisions an organization makes limit the options for future decisions.[8]

It is the paradox of design that its ability to change can also be employed to stabilize existing situations. Sometimes people prefer to change back to how things are or were rather than venturing out into new areas. While designing always holds the potential for organizational transformation, organizations can choose not to take advantage of this potential. In the latter case, design activities may actually contribute negatively to organizational development by manifesting and further cementing existing paths, which makes future changes ever more difficult.

Exploring designing with public organizations

Members of an organization can also work with design experts, design experts can work with citizens and all three groups can engage with each other during a design activity. Charles Leadbetter explains the 'logic of with':

> A *with* approach to any issue or challenge has to be co-produced and negotiated. That means it cannot be planned out in detail in advance. *With* style campaigns and organisations have to emerge and develop.

In Leadbetter's view, 'the logic of with' allows for the co-creation of knowledge and learning from many sources. An organizational design practice that brings in external experts and/or everyday citizens should therefore have a better chance of achieving and realizing organizational changes. Suri explains that efforts to design *with* people designers depend on the ability and willingness of designers to learn *from* people (Suri 2007). If we apply the concept of *designing with* to public organizations, design can be used systematically and strategically to generate new organizational insights and new organizational learning. The design of a new product or public service can then encourage the participation of different stakeholders and different users. Their involvement in turn offers opportunities to inquire into existing organizational systems and practices that, once being questioned and reflected upon, can become subject to change inspired by people.

Leaving designing to citizens/population

Alternatively, an organization may delegate the responsibility for addressing a design challenge to everyday citizens. The burden to involve members of public organizations and external design experts rests on the shoulders of the citizens. Public servants dismiss this relationship between citizens and public organizations sometimes as 'citizen control', the top rung of Sherry Arnstein's (1969) 'Ladder of Citizen Participation'. They fear a loss of control and uncertainty about their own role when such powers are given to members of the population. But this is true only if we perceive of participation as a zero sum game (which Arnstein does).[9] Trust is a main factor for public servants to hand over design responsibilities to people who are not familiar with laws and regulations, politics and policies. How can they possibly produce anything sensible and manageable? Trust gets pitted against resources, though. With shrinking public budgets and payrolls, with rising social and demographic pressures, those in charge are increasingly forced to trust their population. More recently, we are witnessing how impatient and fed up citizens are self-organizing to provide services public organizations are struggling to offer. This situation is particularly coming to the fore in the current refugee and migration crisis.

Already, examples of 'citizen control' are emerging where public organizations allow members of the population to develop their own solutions to improve their living and work situations. Especially in Europe, we are bound to see this kind of design practice develop around migration and refugee questions.[10] The term 'citizen', it becomes clear once again, does not do justice to the range of people who may take on design challenges for organizations. Many of the migrants who will become engaged in developing new services to facilitate integration, for example, will not have been granted citizenship. Nonetheless, they are people public organizations have a mandate to support and work with.

How to begin a conversation about organizational design practices

One of the core challenges in the public sector is to start a design conversation around design practices within the organization. The other day, I sat together with a group in a ministry that had just been founded to improve this ministry's dialogue with citizens. The aim was to improve the relationship with citizens. My ears perked up when I heard the head describe her interpretation of this dialogue: it was about getting the citizens to understand what the ministry was doing and to communicate how the ministry worked. Sharing the background for decision-making and providing accessible information about the decisions that were made was thought to lead to better interaction with the citizens. It had not occurred to this group that their approach rendered citizens' to a passive audience in this 'dialogue'. For the ministry, it was already a proactive and progressive step to acknowledge the need for citizens to be informed. They were still stuck in their own thinking and they had not been able to look around at different forms of dialogue, at different forms of participation and engagements. They still knew only their own organization's perspective and needs. And they had no means to break out of their own mindset.

This is a common situation in the public sector. One way to initiate conversations about existing and possible organizational design practices is by explaining the range of possibilities visually. Figure 5.1 presents public servants with a landscape of design possibilities they may make use of. It is based on the ideas of designing for, with and by and tailored to the three groups I have identified above as possible participants in the development of public products

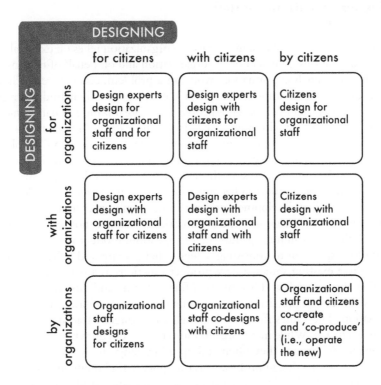

Figure 5.1 Common organizational design practices in government

and services. We end up with a three by three matrix that shows nine possibilities for how organizations go about designing. I will now explain how each approach relates to organizational change and organizational transformation. Doing so generates additional insights into design theory and its linkages to organizational matters. However, the transformative value of a visualization like this matrix is not found in the lines of a book. The transformative value of such a visualization is that it serves as a conversation starter and allows people in organizations to find 'their' place in a wildly confusing and still foreign design landscape. I have shown this matrix to different groups of policy planners and public managers. The reaction is always surprising: They hone in on one slot and begin a discussion for why they are in this place. They then cannot help but take a look at the other boxes in the matrix and begin to compare notes on projects they are aware of and of issues they are coping with. Transformation by design can take very subtle forms. But it is always concerned with people and with finding ways to create new relationships and new meanings.

Let me now explain the differences these nine design approaches imply for public organizations. The purpose of this exercise is to enhance the ability of public managers and others involved in public sector design to reflect on their own design approach and to enable them to examine if their current approach serves them well. Different situations, different circumstances and different problems benefit from a variety of approaches. There is, unfortunately, no 'one-size fits-all'. If there were, we would not need to worry about design and we would not need to think about how we might enhance our design capabilities.

Designing for organizational staff, designing for citizens

In this form of organizational design practice, an organization relies on external experts to develop design solutions on behalf of the organization and on behalf of citizens. External experts come in to analyse a situation, work on a problem, conduct research, interpret the results, and develop solutions. The external experts share their findings regularly in presentations to organizational staff, but people in the organization remain detached from any specific design activity, which may take place in near isolation from the organization. I am reminded of the design understanding displayed by the advisor to EU policy makers I have already mentioned in chapter 3. For him, design is about owning a logo that communicates his work to their clients. In this case, design experts develop visual communication that aids the organization to become more visible to citizens. This design practice does not foresee product development to have a role or an impact inside the organization. Introducing changes by design into the organizational system is not foreseen and difficult to achieve. Rather than inquiring into the organization, product development serves to affirm and give expression to consisting values, beliefs, norms and behaviors. As a manifestation of these existing values, a new product functions as a barrier to organizational change rather than a catalyst. This can be a fine outcome and satisfying to all involved. Nonetheless, this design practice remains among the most contentious forms of design in the organization. The causes for these tensions can be directly traced to issues involving organizational change. While many organizations turn to design when they seek to generate and implement changes, they often end up using design to avoid changes within the organization.[11] External design professionals can quickly find themselves stuck between a rock and a hard place: They have to change something (i.e., a product) without changing anything (i.e., the organizational system).

But it is not necessarily the organization, which renders this design practice less useful to organizational change. In some cases, the design experts intentionally limit the role of members of the organization in a design project because they view the staff as part of the problem–and unable or unwilling to change! In doing so, design experts deny people in the organization the ability to contribute to the solution to a problem. Ironically, the design experts themselves are mirroring the behavior and attitudes they are so critical of in organizational staff. By classifying organizational staff as 'the problem', design experts avoid the conversations necessary to reach into the organization. Simultaneously, they devalue and diminish the value of the experiences people have inside the organization. Similarly, design experts who focus too much on user-centered design can make the mistake to treat people as subjects, not as partners (Sanders and Stappers 2008).[12] Subjects are involved in a project but they are generally not assigned a participatory role. Instead, they are there to be studied. Liz Moor (2009) suggests that the demands of design management present additional obstacles for design consultants to engage people in participatory practices: The time spent to listen and learn from organizational staff is often difficult to plan, account and bill for: And yet, Moor points out that to design public services, designers will have to

> spend more of their time listening with various 'stakeholders' on the client side, getting 'buy-in' from these stakeholders, and devising accounting and measurement techniques that demonstrate outcomes and effectiveness.[13]

In a design practice where designing is outsourced to develop and to deliver a solution in near isolation of the organization, the prospects for organizational changes are slim. To introduce a significant change to a product or service that improves people's experiences, changes within the organization have to happen in parallel. If design experts see their role as determining what is good for the organization and the citizens, i.e., when they design for them, the situation can quickly get tense. The organization, unprepared and possibly unwilling to engage in any organizational change activity, is prone to resist if not reject these kinds of changes. The lack of trust in the organization can make designers feel unappreciated despite any evidence they may have generated through user research and prototyping. Designers complain about the organization and the organization complains about the designers. It is a cultural tension that has fed the development of the academic and professional field of design management.[14] Both the organization and the citizens may also react to paternalistic design approaches that are being imposed on them. This organizational design practice thus ranks among the most contentious ones and among those least promising for introducing organizational changes. When we talk about organizations, their procedures, products and services, we need to keep in mind that there are people inside the organization as well as outside of it. Organizational changes by design remain evasive unless an organizational design practice recognizes and involves citizens and organizational staff alike.

Design experts, as we shall see in the case study of the IRS Tax Forms Simplification Project, can consciously or unknowingly create barriers to organizational change when they are designing products and services on behalf of organizational staff for citizens. Yet, this remains a dominant organizational design practice and we should therefore pay attention to the pitfalls it poses. The approach to design for the organizational staff and for the citizens can be read as design experts designing 'in place of' organizational staff and citizens. It can also be read as design experts focusing on the needs of citizens and on the needs of the organization alike. When design experts are brought into a public organization to design something for organizational staff and for citizens, public managers seldom seek organizational changes. External design experts are hired as part of an on-going organizational design effort but their activities are not expected to reach beyond the boundaries of a product in question. Any change is limited to the size, form, and shape of the 'logo'.

Designing for organizational staff, designing with citizens

This design practice is similar to the above in that the organization relies on external design experts and their relationship with citizens to generate and develop solutions. Citizens are likely to be directly involved and engaged with the design team. Organizational staff may either decide to watch from the sideline and jump into the design process as it sees fit. It may also be pushed aside by the design experts who might view them as obstacles to their change efforts. Just as likely is that the design team is mindful of its role as 'consultant' and therefore feels it needs to deliver to, rather than involve the organization in any design work. In the context of organizational change, this design practice can function as a 'door-opener' in the sense that the organization gets to learn something about the people it serves and about the problems they experience which otherwise they would not become aware of. However, there is no commitment and no plan to act upon any recommendations that result from the design activities. This has the advantage of being uninhibited by any organizational constraints. But it also means that the findings may not be developed for implementation. Mindlab in Denmark shows that it is possible to make strategic use of this organizational design practice to build a case for people-oriented organizational changes.[15] This innovation lab continuously produces data and evidence to challenge the status quo of policy making and policy implementation in various government agencies.

Designing for organizational staff, designing by citizens

In this organizational design practice, the organization approaches citizens as external design experts. The organization trusts citizens with the design of relevant products and services. Citizens are directly involved in the design of products and services that are relevant to them. The Big Society concept in the UK sought to develop this design practice. As the official UK government webpage stated: 'The Big Society is about helping people to come together to improve their own lives. It's about putting more power in people's hands – a massive transfer of power from Whitehall to local communities'.[16] Although there is no emphasis on design experts, design experts may be involved as mentors and supporters. It may still sound odd to some ears but there are indeed first instances where citizens are brought in by a government organization to re-design a product the organization uses to communicate with citizens.

Experimental approaches along these lines have emerged in Denmark. Thus, it may not surprise that one example for this organizational design practice comes from the Danish Tax Office: Two Heads of Sections at the Danish Ministry of Taxation realized that the letter they sent to taxpayers about their property tax duties caused distress and confusion among taxpayers. They invited taxpayers to re-design this letter for the tax office. This organizational design practice bears a great potential for transformative organizational change when the organization is committed to enacting the kinds of changes generated by citizens. The organization, by inviting citizens into their organizational life, already makes a statement that it is willing and ready to reach into and review its organizational practices, its structures and procedures as part of any re-design.

Designing with organizational staff, designing for citizens

In this organizational design practice, the organization encourages its own staff to co-design with external design experts to better understand their own internal design approaches and opportunities. Here, staff learns from and with designers who specialize, for example in participatory design methods, user research, idea generation or prototyping. Citizens themselves are not directly involved in such a design efforts because the focus rests on understanding, changing or integrating organizational design processes. This design practice appeals to organizations that seek to develop their internal design capabilities and acquire new methods before they design concrete products and services with citizens. This approach to changing organizational design practice is now emerging in the policy making realm. Both the Australian Tax Office and the United States Office of Personnel Management can be looked to as examples of public organizations that have embraced this approach.

Designing with organizational staff, designing with citizens

In this constellation, the organization all but depends on external design experts that can lead and facilitate this effort. The role of design experts is to introduce participatory methods for co-creating or co-designing products and services but also to steward and guide the on-going design process.[17] Members of the organization, external design experts and everyday citizens are all contributing in one way or another in understanding a situation and in generating a solution.

Designing with, as Leadbetter and Suri explain, creates many opportunities for organizational change because organizational staff is encouraged to review and discuss organizational structures and organizational resources in light of the products and services they lead to and in light of the experiences they provide for citizens. The Domestic Mail Transformation Project by the United States Postal Service illustrates both the benefits and the drawbacks of this design practice. In that project, the aim was to design with postal service members and with mailers but also by inclusion of all relevant stakeholders, be they from the mailing industry or from the postal union.

Designing with organizational staff, designing by citizens

The organization collaborates with citizens to co-design products and services. Organizational staff is in direct contact with citizens. However, here citizens determine how, when and for what reason organizational staff is involved in the design process. They also make the design decisions. This design practice shifts the responsibility to citizens and assigns organizational staff to a role of support. What is important here is that the organization works directly with citizens, no external design expert mediates between citizens and the organization. It is a design practice we see currently emerging in the public sector.

Designing by organizational staff, designing for citizens

The least salient yet most common design practice in public organizations is for organizational staff to design procedures, products and services for citizens. In this design practice, members of the organization assume the role of design experts. They identify and define a design problem based on their expertise. Citizens are often referred to as 'clients' or 'customers'. This assigns organizational staff the responsibility to design *for* their clients, not *with* them. This design practice reduces the chances for individual citizens to become involved in the design process. In fact, it is not unusual for organizational staff to avoid any participation by citizens (Bason 2010).[18] For the same reasons, knowledge, experiences and insights from citizens cannot easily cross into the organization. Products and services emerge in an organizational bubble and may or may not be useful, usable and desirable to people outside this bubble.

When organizational staff designs products and services for 'clients', the possibilities to introduce changes through their design activities exists. However, organizational staff may not use the development of products and services as a vehicle for organizational change.

There are three obvious explanations for the difficulty to connect designing with organizational transformation when members of an organization are the sole design experts: First, organizational staff may perceive a change as an interruption of their own workflows and procedures, which bears the potential of more work and in the least, temporary uncertainty. Hence, managers and staff are more likely to develop and deliver products and services that fit their current way of doing business. Second, products and services designed 'for clients' further manifest the role already assigned to people. Product by product, service by service, the relationship gets cemented, expectations harden and change becomes ever more difficult. Thirdly, opportunities for organizational changes may be overlooked because organizational staff may not dare to envision anything that does not fit with what already exists, what already is known. All this limits the potential for significant changes on a product and service level. This in turn reduces the chance of changes that reach into the organization and may affect its structure, resource and vision.

Designing by organizational staff, designing with citizens

In this organizational design practice, the organization relies on its organizational staff to design products and services with citizens. Importantly, in this design practice, the organizational staff is aware of its role as designers and reaches out to citizens to learn about becoming better in developing and delivering the products and services that aid people in accomplishing the tasks posed by the organization. The example of tax compliance in chapter 11 shows this design practice at work and the potential it has for lasting organizational change. In this example, the organization made an effort to educate its own staff in human-centered design and to embed a human-centered design approach within the Australian Tax Office. This is a design practice where the organization seeks to develop new knowledge and new skills to advance its internal design capabilities.

Designing by organizational staff, designing by citizens

In this emerging organizational design practice, the organization sees its role in providing a platform for citizens to design and implement their own solutions. The public organization perceives itself as part of wider network of communities, resources, structures and shared goals. But rather than the organization imposing design onto the community, it is the community that takes ownership of the design. We can think of this organizational design practice as a conscious de-coupling of the organizational design expertise from the design expertise of citizens. The Australian Centre for Social Innovation (TACSI) and their family-by-family program can serve as an example of this organizational design practice.[19] The family-by-family program aims to help families with social and economic problems to improve their own lives with the help of other families who 'made it' – families who successfully moved up the social and economic ladder, overcoming the troubles that held them back. The organization emphasizes that it is not religious, not governmental and not judgmental. TACSI receives government funding for this program in a kind of acknowledgement that this programs supports families when all other public services stop and when often the real problems for families are just beginning.[20] For public organizations, this is an interesting approach, albeit one that is rather unconventional. A former government official now working with TACSI confided: 'I first laughed at these methods. . . . We are recruiting hair dressers and visual artists, that was not possible in my previous job!'[21] Furthermore, the official shared how they go about engaging citizens: 'We knock on doors, meet them at supermarkets. We come to them we don't wait for them to come to us.'

Design engagement in policy work

We can think of a similar matrix to depict the design engagements of people who are involved in law-making and policy development. We could leave the public organization in the left column but replace the citizen in the upper column with policy maker or lawmaker. We could map cross-ministerial co-designing as well as co-creation efforts by public organizations involved in the early stages of policy making. The aim would remain the same: to map possible approaches to policy making and law-making and to explore the benefits and drawbacks of each of these for the design task on hand. This is an urgent and emerging area where design thinking and design methods are now being revisited. Law-makers, for example, are increasingly coming under scrutiny for how they go about designing laws. The official in charge for de-bureaucratization in the German Chancellor's office has great understanding for the constraints and pressures lawmakers are under when they are tasked with developing a new law. For each new law, they have to check how it matches against 37 different aspects that guide law-making more generally in addition to four aspects specific to the latest governments coalition contract. At the same time, they have to follow between 20 to 40 guidelines (Leitfäden), each of which may range from 20 to 300 pages. All this adds to a politically charged high-pressure environment and can zap energy from even the most energetic designer. Yet, design they must and the result, for better or worse, is what citizens have to live with. For the official concerned with improving citizen experience by making laws meaningful, accessible, understandable and usable, new designing approaches and new forms of design thinking offer hope for transforming some of these legal design practices.

The collective ownership of specific values, or ethos, of an organization is driven by an organization's habitual adherence to certain goals and practices, states Angela Meyer (2011). This is another reason why organizational design practices matter and why we need to address them. 'Ethos embodies knowing what's important and what we care about as an organization' (Meyer 2011, p.187). Habits have been identified as a problem for public as well as for individual action. John Dewey, for example, connects the public with 'long-established habits' (Dewey 1927). Later, he observes, that 'unless one takes intermediate acts seriously enough to treat them as ends, one wastes one's time and effort at changes of habits' (Dewey 1930, p. 35). This very much applies to organizations. Lucy (2010) suggests that the idea of 'Design-as-practice' allows us to explore professional design practices as 'habitual, possibly rule-governed, often shared, routinized, conscious or unconscious' practices, which are 'embodied and situated'.[22] I would just like to point out that when we refer to organizational design practices, we should not limit ourselves to designing-as-practiced by professional designers. This would lead us to overlook a whole range of influential design practices that shape our world and that need to change in order to affect transformation.

Organizational design practices and transformation

I have identified three groups that can get involved in the design of products and services in the public realm. They include members of the organization, external design experts and ordinary citizens. We were able to see how organizational design practices are formed around the idea of design experts and the question of what is considered to be relevant and valid design expertise. Organizations trust members of the organization when the focus is on content concerning laws, rules and regulations. These design experts are found in the organization. They design for citizens or with citizens. When organizations focus on improving processes, forms, beauty and interaction, organizations trust professional external experts to bring in their design expertise. They may design for the organization or with the organization. They may also design for citizens or with citizens. If the focus rests on radical innovations to improve usability, meaningfulness and desirability, organizations increasingly seek out ordinary citizens as design experts. When citizens assume the role of design experts, citizens may even design products and services for an organization. In all this, we must never forget that staff within organizations are people, too. Any change in organizational design practices affects their work directly and we need to consider organizational structures and organizational resources as we seek to enable people to accomplish their respective tasks confidently and satisfyingly.

Paying attention to organizational design practices brings to light the interactive nature of the activities of designing, changing, organizing and managing. Taking on its own, designing always presents opportunities for changes within the organization. But when the design activities are not managed well and when they fail to consider the organizational context, change remains elusive or superficial. Articulating organizational design practices prevents external design experts from getting trapped or stifled by existing organizational practices. At the same time, it offers new avenues to connect with and engage with the people within the organization who are already designing. A successful design approach will have to address these boundaries and be able to engage the organization, reaching out to people and into its structures, resources and purpose.

The Lancaster University Library, by the way, has just undergone a major refurbishment, which has taken on many of the concepts for more interaction and improved services.

Notes

1 This student-led project took place in 2008. Beginning in 2009 and up to 2012, library staff continuously returned to the student concepts to make incremental, small-scale improvements to the library space. The 2015 library refurbishment, however, realized several of the ideas developed in 2008, including new spaces or group work and social spaces, a need the students identified through their research.

2 Organizational design methods have been looked at as methods to create government organization's structure and decision-making hierarchy. In his review "Army Construction Policy: A Historical Analysis", Lieutenant Colonel Walter J. Cunningham, Jr. from the United States Army uses the term 'organizational design method' to describe how government organizations go about creating "the necessary conditions at the top that will enable leaders at the lower levels to reduce their organization without retaining endless bureaucracy". In this sense, organizational design method is the method that leads to an organizational whole. The methods themselves are not "design methods" but rather methods of play (cf: Bree 2011).

3 See specifically Ehn, P. (2008). 'Participating in Design Things', *Proceedings of the Tenth Anniversary Conference on Participatory Design 2008*, Indiana University Indianapolis, USA, pp. 92–101; as well as Ehn, P. (1993). 'Scandinavian Design: On Participation and Skill', in *Participatory Design: Principles and Practices*, CRC Press, Hillsdale, NJ, pp. 41–77. Also see Binder, T., de Michelis, G., Jacucci, G., Linder, P. and Wagner, I. (2011). *Design Things*, MIT Press, Cambridge, MA.

4 Charles Leadbetter's original thoughts on this topic are captured in 'An Original Essay for Cornerhouse, Manchester Draft March 2009', available online at charlesleadbetter.net [accessed August 2012]. Published under a Creative Commons License.

5 Based on Leadbetter, C. (2010). 'For, With, By and To', published online at http://charlesleadbeater. net/2010/05/for-with-by-and-to/ and Leadbetter, C. (2009). 'The Art of With', An Original Essay for Cornerhouse, Manchester, Draft March 2009'. http://charlesleadbeater.net/wp-content/ uploads/2010/05/The-Art-of-With-PDF.pdf.

6 The limits of designing for people have been explored across different design disciplines and have positioned designing in open systems (Garud, R., Sanjay, J. and Tuertscher, P. (2008). 'Incomplete by Design and Designing for Incompleteness', *Organization Studies*, Vol. 29 (3): 351–371).

7 Suri, F.J. (2007). 'Involving People in the Process', *Keynote Delivered at the 2007 Inclusive Conference*, Toronto.

8 See Sydow, J. and Schreyögg, G. (2009). 'Organizational Path Dependence–Opening the Black Box', *Academy of Management Review*, Vol. 34 (4): 689–709.

9 Arnstein, S.R. (1969). 'A Ladder of Citizen Participation', *Journal of the American Institute of Planners*, Vol. 35 (4): 216–234. Arnstein's ladder of citizen participation deserves a close look by anyone interested in citizen participation in government. As I explain elsewhere, she has explained very vividly how policy makers and public managers may view participation. For a design relevant discussion, see Junginger, S. (2012). 'A Human-Centered Design Perspective on Participatory Government – And Its Implications for the Practice and Education of Design Management', *Conference Proceedings of the 19th DMI Academic Conference*, London, 2012.

10 An example of how designing for, with and by works in community projects is provided by DiSalvo, C., Clement, A. and Pipek, V. (2012). 'Communities: Participatory Design for, with, and by Communities', in J. Simonsen and T. Robertson (eds.), *The International Handbook of Participatory Design*, Routledge, Oxford, UK, pp. 182–209.

11 It is at this point that both designers and managers tend to express fatigue with promising concepts like Design thinking, Massive Change, and the Power of Design.

12 Sanders and Stappers (March, 2008). 'Co-Creation and the New Landscapes of Design', *Co-Design*, Vol. 4 (1): 5–18.

13 Moor, L. (2009). 'The State and Design, in Design and Creativity', in J. Gulier and L. Moor (eds.), *Design and Creativity: Policy, Management and Practice*, Berg, Oxford, UK, pp. 23–39. Ironically, these kinds of logistical arguments echo the arguments public managers put forth to avoid participatory design methods (cf: Bason 2010).

14 Walker, D. (1980). 'Two Tribes at War', in M. Oakley (ed.), *The Handbook of Design Management*, Blackwell Reference, Oxford, UK, pp. 145–154.

15 See www.Mind-lab.dk.

16 Source: http://www.cabinetoffice.gov.uk/big-society [accessed July 2012].

17 See Boyer, Bryan, Cooke, Justin W. and Steinberg, Marco (2013). *Legible Practices: Six Stories about the Craft of Stewardship*, Sitra 2013. http://www.helsinkidesignlab.org accessed January 2016].

18 See Bason, C. (2010). *Leading Public Sector Innovation*, Policy Press University of Bristol, Great Britain.

19 http://tacsi.org.au [accessed January 2016].

20 http://www.tacsi.org.au/who-we-are.

21 Comment made during presentation of the family-by-family project at the *How Public Design Conference* at Mindlab in Copenhagen, 2011.

22 Kimbell, Lucy (2009). 'Design Practices in Design Thinking', *Proceedings of the European Academy of Design* 2009, presented at the European Academy of Management, Liverpool, UK, May 11–14th 2009. http://www.lucykimbell.com/stuff/EURAM09_designthinking_kimbell.pdf.

Section II

Three examples of transforming public services to re-orient government around people

6 The USPS domestic mail manual transformation project[1]

The Postal Service shall have as its basic function the obligation to provide postal services to bind the Nation together through the personal, educational, literary, and business correspondence of the people. It shall provide prompt, reliable, and efficient services to patrons in all areas and shall render postal services to all communities.[2]

This first case study looks at the *Domestic Mail Manual (DMM) Transformation Project* by the United States Postal Service. This project demonstrates how the design of a product affects all elements of the organizational system described in chapter 2: people, structure, resources and vision and how this allows for transformation by design. For this project, the organization explicitly recruited external designers willing and capable to work together *with* the organization on a difficult organizational problem.[3] Design methods and design thinking were brought into the organization to redesign – that is to change – one of its core products. But this was not possible without considering the organizational system at large.

In 2001, then Postmaster General John E. Potter described the United States Postal Service as 'a massive organization'. He underlined this with numbers:[4] 'In roughly one week the Postal Service matches the annual volumes of United Parcel Service™ and in two days, it delivers what FedEx™ delivers in a year'. Translated into numbers, the Postal Service delivered more than 680 million pieces of mail to more than 135 million addresses in the United States that year. To do so, the organization maintained 458 mail processing facilities, 38,000 post offices (including stations and branches) and operated the largest fleet in the nation with 205,000 vehicles, ranging from trucks to carrier vehicles. All in all, the organization employed nearly 900,000 people to ensure it could fulfill its constitutional mandate, to provide universal service to all Americans: 'Everyone, Everywhere, Every Day.'[5]

Even today, the USPS maintains boats, planes, trucks, and horses to get a letter or parcel to its intended recipient. From Benjamin Franklin to Jack Potter, the Postal Service has had a crucial role in weaving the American fabric in social, commercial and economic terms as well as in terms of personal freedom and liberty – the right to live anywhere without losing access to society. In many rural communities, the local Postal Office is a treasured institution, and it is difficult to imagine US streets without mail vehicles or letter carriers. The Service in this sense has always provided a certain kind of comfort to people that they are connected with other people. But this relationship is not without woes. Electronic mail and private competition have cut into its operations. The circumstances under which the Postal Service operates are unique among government agencies. It is not funded by taxpayer money but relies on self-generated revenues.[6] At the same time its status as a member of government prevents it from accumulating operational profits. In other words, the Postal Service needs to make money to operate but cannot make more money than is needed for its operation.[7] Despite this challenging business model, the United States Postal Service, with a history of more than 200 years, has outlived many traditional businesses. But this struggle for survival is getting increasingly more difficult.

As in private organizations, procedures, rules and regulations exist to govern the use of the Postal Service. These rules and standards are contained in the Domestic Mail Manual, also referred to as 'the DMM'. For both mailers and employees, the DMM holds the ultimate truth to any mailing question. Indeed, staff throughout the USPS refers to the book as 'our bible.'[8]

> The DMM is the bible of the postal service . . . it impacts many departments and most of the employees in the organization at one time or another have looked at this book.[9]

A book that holds such weight within the organization can be expected to be substantial, and the DMM does not disappoint: more than once had the heavy six-inch binder been successfully used as a doorstopper or bookend. These non-intended secondary uses had become symptomatic of a bigger problem that plagued the organization. Because people were not paying attention to the standards and rules of mailing, they were also not preparing their mail appropriately. This led to more and more interruptions on the processing level. Every single interruption was costly.

> People quit looking at the standards: they just go by, went by, what they remember, what another customer did. And so over the years, we have just been going way, way, way, way down a slippery slope in terms of verse versus standards and when I hear people talk that there are issues with this, I am thinking everybody has gotten away from the standards. They are making this up in their head. This is not logical and I think the reason this is not is because they quit looking [at the rules and standards in the DMM][10]

In early 2001, the head of the division had enough and decided 'We need to fix that book.'[11]

A brief introduction to 'the book', the Domestic Mail manual

The DMM is a legal document that is citable in court and changes often. Ignoring the DMM is not an option: 'Everything that happens in the United States Postal Service depends on the DMM'.[12] The DMM is the axis around which all continental USPS mailing operations turn. For anyone in the mailing industry, from the small print house that bundles customer mail for better rates to the technician who develops new mail processing equipment and on to the software developer who works on a computer program for small business mailers, the DMM is just as relevant as for those people who actually do the mailing: Parents sending care packages to their college students; small business owners promoting a sale; medium businesses strategically targeting select customers and markets and large mailing companies that build much of their enterprise around their ability to get things in the mail, quickly and reliably. For USPS employees, the DMM represents the law on which they rely when they make decisions about customer services and complaints.

For anyone mailing anything, for people in the mailing industry and for employees of the United States Postal Service, the DMM holds all the answers to their mailing questions. Want to know the maximum size of a postcard? Or how many mail classes there are? Want to find out what you cannot mail with the United States Postal Service? Or what your rights are as a mail recipient? Want to know how to write software for mail applications? Or are you more concerned about how to pallet your periodicals correctly? In any event, the source to turn to for an answer is the DMM.

By the time the DMM Transformation Project started, the DMM had already undergone two major makeovers. First there was the 'Green Book'. Named after the forest green color of its plastic covers, the Green Book organized the USPS rules and standards first by mail class (for example, *First Class* or *Priority Mail*), then by topic (for example, *addressing* or *eligibility*), and finally by shape (for example, *letter, flat* or *parcel*). It may well have been the most densely printed rulebook the USPS ever published. To keep the printing cost manageable and to keep the weight of the book feasible (both for reasons of distribution and handling), the pages of the Green Book were very thin and the print size chosen was very small.

Many postal employees romanticized the Green Book. Though it was very difficult to read because of poor layout and visual design, it offered employees a familiar pathway into the information organized around *classes* of mail: *First Class, Express Mail, Standard Mail*, etc. These were concepts most employees were familiar with. However, when the Green Book finally became unmanageable, two staff members involved in issuing, maintaining and enforcing standards and rules were asked to simplify this booklet. They were explicitly instructed to cut down the number of pages of the document. In only six months, they did as told and carefully weeded through the document to remove any redundant information. Sentences and paragraphs were taken out and the document was reorganized around relevant mailing *topics*. In the minds of the Postal Service, *Eligibility* was a topic as was *Addressing*. Each topic contained information sorted by mailing class and mail shape. Just reading through this paragraph offers a glimpse into the language and concepts at work. We get a sense for the difficulties people had trying to relate to these.

Nonetheless, that team presented a new version of the DMM with fewer pages and more 'white space', that is bigger margins around the text. The new DMM showed typographic improvements and a clear visual layout to make the document more appealing to the eye and more legible. In many ways, this first attempt at simplification of the DMM is comparable with the *IRS Tax Forms Simplification Project* described in chapter 10.

Over the design of the 'thing', the actual document and its pages, the organization, however, had lost sight of the needs of those people relying on the DMM who were not experts. The rigorous elimination of pages had inadvertently created a disconnected system of twelve arbitrary sections. Confused customers and employees now had to piece together information about a mailing topic by themselves in a detective-like mode. Among DMM users the 'five-finger-search method' became popular: researching the answer to a mailing question, they would find one part of the answer on page five, but this page referred them to a rule on another page, that rule again referred to another section and another section in the document, and so on and so on. The reader ended up 'bookmarking' every page with another finger as they needed to flip back and forth to reassemble all elements to their mailing question.

Since every rule and standard was stated only once within the document, the responsibility to piece together relevant information to a particular question fell to the person searching for an answer in the DMM. In their hunt for a complete answer, people often forgot their original question by the time they had pursued three or more of these references. Reading through difficult legal language added to their frustration and fatigue. The unintended result of eliminating redundancy in words was a dramatic increase of redundancy in work. Customers and employees alike continued to complain about the book, and, instead of using it to guide them in their mail preparation, they simply avoided the rules altogether.

Recognizing this problem, the Postal Service initially developed a series of 'children documents', add-ons to the DMM that sought to offer compact information on at least some questions. These 'Quick Service Guides' were often printed in color and included illustrations. However, they, too, were written from a postal perspective and organized around mail topics that required and assumed previous knowledge of the rules and standards. Knowledge few mailers had.

Even those mailing experts who over the years had come to be quite familiar with the DMM and who actually set out to find the answer to a mailing question themselves often reached for the phone to confirm their own interpretation with someone at the post office. They soon found out that the answer changed from one post office to another. The postal clerk, say in California interpreted the same rule differently than his counterpart in the state of Maine or in Louisiana.

Organizational project background

Since the creation of the modern U.S. Postal Service in 1971, the organization operated under a business model built around the assumption 'that continuing growth in mail volume and revenue would support continued infrastructure growth'.[13] But changes in technology and general business climate proved this business model to be outdated at the end of the second millennium. U.S. congress had followed the developments at the Postal Service and continuously voiced concern over its viability (as it does today).

In early 2001, the Comptroller General of the United States, David M. Walker, effectively added the Postal Services 'transformational efforts and long-term outlook' to the High-Risk List maintained by the General Accounting Office. He justified this measure 'so that we and others can focus on its financial, operational and human capital challenges before the situation escalates into a crisis where the options for actions may be more limited'.[14] While the report commended the Postal Service for steps already taken, it also pointed to factors that effectively have prevented much needed changes in the past; including postal unions and the Postal Rate Commission but also 'statutory and other restrictions' that require the Service to honor existing labor agreements, maintain binding arbitration requirements, pursue a cost-based rate-setting process and impose facility closure restrictions.

The Postmaster General needed an opportunity to show that the impossible can be done. Remaining relevant to the American people also meant to provide a value proposition that the Postal Service had never made directly addressed to the mailer. What was the value of mailing to the everyday American and to an American businessperson?

The search for creative thinking generates a vision, a commitment and a strategy

It was not the first time that the DMM was perceived to be the source of many troubles. But it was the first time that the organization devoted time and resources to find out what exactly the problem was and how a redesign could resolve this. It called for a design approach that would involve the organization. 'We need creative thinking about a very unusual problem. We would like someone to take on to make the document accessible.'[15] Previous attempts by internal experts had failed to achieve this goal. In fact, the strengths of the experts and their detailed knowledge of the DMM content had proved to be part of the problem. But simply handing over the project to an external consultant was unthinkable because of the complexity of the rules and its central role within the organization. The manager of the DMM group expressed the concerns in an interview as follows.

I knew that for this project to be a success, we had to work very closely with whoever was working on it. And I also knew, and I think [my manager] knew too, we do not have the expertise here to design something. But what we do know is, we know about all those rules and we know all the legislative history and regulatory constraints that we are under and the legal restraints and the organizational constraints, so we knew how to navigate all that and write good rules – but the other part we did not have. . . . And I did not want to work with anybody who wanted to take it entirely, either.[16]

Among several design schools and universities approached with this problem, the School of Design at Carnegie Mellon University promised to have the theoretical foundation, the methods, and the people needed to approach the problem. The school's reputation as a leading force in human-centered design principles and its continuous emphasis on a participatory design process convinced the USPS manager and her superior to sponsor a first pilot study on the subject. Working closely with the organization, five students and one professor conducted initial research into the organizational system, the DMM itself and engaged with people who already used the DMM. Based on the findings and insights of the initial pilot study, the CMU team and the USPS team agreed that the vision for this project was to make the DMM system accessible to all mailers.

It was also agreed that the project would follow an iterative and evolving process based on participatory design approaches and human-centered design principles. Furthermore, the redesign would begin by addressing the least complex mailing questions of everyday mailers. From there, it would gradually move towards the more complex and specific rules and regulations relevant for experienced mailers. From the start, the *DMM Transformation Project* was perceived as a co-design activity for design students and USPS staff. Unusually though for the organization, it granted the design team the lead in this effort. Figure 6.1. links developments in government with the project timeline.

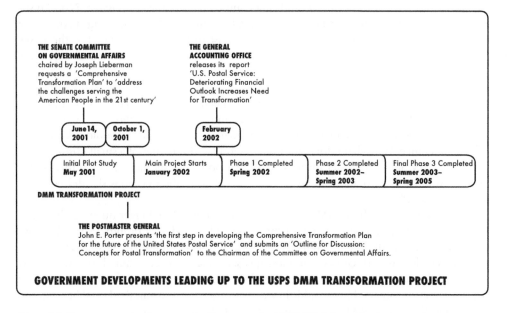

Figure 6.1 Government developments leading up to the USPS DMM transformation project

Design thinking and design methods: Participatory design and human-centered design principles

> This is not a document design project. We don't do document design. Our design process is evolving and iterative. We research people extensively. We want our clients to participate in the design process. We emphasize team participation.[17]

This description provided by the principal investigator summarizes the key elements of the human-centered design approach at the heart of this project. The design methods and activities focused on the needs of people and on involving the Postal Service in the research and design for their own new DMM. User research soon identified four different kinds of customer groups for the postal service: household mailers; small business mailers; large business mailers and specialty mailers. Each group distinguished itself from the other in the purpose and the methods of mailing. For example, household mailers were mainly interested in getting things from point A to point B (a letter to a friend, a check to an insurance company, a care package to a son in college). Especially household mailers were left to their own device when they tried to find out about the best service for their specific situation. Instead of making informed choices about which service to use, they had to rely on the recommendations made by the window clerk who accepted their mail piece.

For the window clerk, this meant more work; for the other mailers in the post office this meant a longer wait time; and for the customer it meant leaving the post office without a sense of closure as he or she would not know if the chosen mail service was the right one until the mailpiece arrived or was returned to sender. Clearly, household mailers were in need of mail information, but did they need to read through the whole DMM? What information was really relevant and useful for them? How, when and where would they need to learn about mailing rules and mailing options? And it was not only household mailers who struggled with mailing options. In one case, a small business mailer would regularly buy 1,000 stamps and manually adhere them to 1,000 postcards because she did not know that she could use meters and other automated options for postage. Nor did she understand that she could cut her mailing cost by using a different mailing method. For this businesswoman, the result was unnecessary cost in time and postage. For the Postal Service it was a missed opportunity to establish a relationship with a potentially growing business.

This initial user research led to the first design criteria for the new DMM: It would have to serve three purposes simultaneously: it would need to educate mailers and employees about the products and services available so they understood their choices; it would need to provide tools that enable mailers to execute mailings and finally; it would need to be a reliable reference. But what information was useful for this owner of a small business who was clearly trying to grow her business? At what point did she need more information? Where would she learn about these services? What were the questions she did not even know how to ask?

As the functions of the DMM became more and more clear, bigger questions began to emerge. What real value did mail offer businesses? How did mail fit into a larger business strategy? And how did the different services and products support these strategies? Soon, the project identified three basic business goals: business owners wanted to acquire new customers, business owners wanted to grow their operations and they also wanted to retain their current customers. How could they achieve their goals using the Postal Service and how could the new DMM mediate and contribute to this relationship?

Moving from product to service and into the organization

Around this time, senior managers from other USPS divisions were invited to join in the project, bringing insights from marketing, product development and customer service perspectives. Several staff members that had paid little attention to the first project initially – because it concerned customers not visible to them and because they were not involved in writing the DMM – suddenly began to pay attention. They sensed that the design team was beginning to reach into the organization and challenged organizational design practices as well as organizational design principles. They also realized that the DMM redesign would advance with or without their input. Resistance to the project grew as the design team began to challenge employees' perception of their own customers and start to inquire into their established ways of going about their work. These staff members were organizational experts who had dealt and struggled with DMM issues every day, and in many cases, had done so for decades. How could a team of young students from a private university possibly understand the enormous complexity and intricacies in which rules and standards were written, issued and maintained? What did they know about the history of rules and the plight of their customers?[18]

As interest and anxiety grew, the ring of design participants grew wider, too, and now included external stakeholders. As a result, information began to flow in several directions: the organization learned more about its customers, its employees and its stakeholders; the stakeholders learned more about the organization and their customers; and customers learned more about the organization and mailing services. Designers also learned more about the work and responsibilities of the DMM staff. By the time the second design result went into print, employees and customers alike had developed a shared understanding of the larger project vision. They also understood why this second design outcome represented yet another major step towards re-designing the whole system along human–centered principles. Nonetheless, design students and DMM staff remember the second product development project as a period of tensions and turbulence.

It was during these activities that the organization, and especially the DMM group, openly struggled with the new vision and its implications for their own work. It was also during this phase that the participatory design approach pursued by the design students seemed to have reached its limits. A change in project leadership within the DMM group at USPS headquarters was one of the consequences. The new project leader, familiar with the project but not as convinced and motivated to see through changes, took organizational participation in a different direction and was less articulate about the vision than his predecessor.

From the beginning it was clear that in order to identify and resolve the larger issues that ailed the DMM, the USPS team would have to be on board with the vision and play an active role. It was the organization's staff that possessed the knowledge and the expertise with rules and standards, but this was also the team that issued the current DMM with all its weaknesses. The initial concern that the design students did not have the mailing knowledge and the organizational skills needed to succeed in the redesign was indeed widely shared. Several USPS team members pointed out in conversations that a serious cultural gap separated the design students from the postal employees, at least in their minds. The students were acutely aware of this and employed a wide range of methods and design activities to keep the staff engaged and the project on track.

Key design methods and activities employed in the DMM project

Visualization methods

Visualization techniques served to explore issues, to share insights, and to clarify concepts that were difficult to grasp in words alone. Visualization aided the project on two levels: it directly supported work on the prototypes and it facilitated communication with USPS staff members and stakeholders. Among the many purposes of visualization served during the course of this project were exploration, clarification, description, expression and communication. The project relied particularly on Diagramming (Affinity Diagrams, Pathway Diagrams), Sketching, Modeling (Concepts and Process), Concept Mapping, and Visual Story Telling.

Research methods

The variety of methods and techniques used by the design team over the course of the project is elaborate and indicative of the need to align research efforts with the research participants and their situation while not losing sight of the research question. The project distinguished between research in the field, analysis of gathered and existing data, historical research, experimental research and methods of recording and documenting data as follows.

> *Field Study Techniques:* Role Playing, Site-Visits, Workshops, Document Review (Prototype Review), Interview, Artifact Collection; SME Expert, Conversation; Participant Observation; Online research; Anecdotal Collection, Shadowing; Immersion
> *Analysis:* Modeling (Process and Concepts); Heuristic Evaluation
> *History:* Document Analysis; Online Search
> *Experimentation:* Storytelling; Story Boarding; Scenario Development, Prototyping
> *Identifying and Recording Data*: Research Protocols; Card Sorting; Questionnaires; User Testing

Team methods

These methods and techniques ensured that individual learning and insights from ongoing research activities came back to the team, thus creating an effective feedback-loop. But they also contributed to keeping the team dynamic and functional. The team listed the following activities: Role Playing, Critiquing, Review and Reporting, Discussion, Debriefing, Presentations, Brainstorming, Scenario-Building (generative, speculative, exploratory, exemplary), Task Analysis, Improvisation, Role Assignment and Rotation, List Reduction and Iteration.

Project management and stewardship

These methods and techniques came to be referred to as 'Project Stewardship', as they aimed at keeping the project on track and in sync with the organization. Five items were listed under 'Project Stewardship': Strategic Planning, Project Planning, Relationship Maintenance, Documentation, and Participant Recruiting.

Methods across all areas of the project

The team listed the following methods separately when it discovered that they were activities that concerned every aspect of their project. These included *Concepts, Making, Expressing,* and *Comparing.*

The diversity and multitude of the methods and techniques surprised the team. In line with human-centered product development, the design students had always focused on exploring the problem, never on a particular method. Working with people meant that the method had to be appropriate for the people the team was working with at a given point in time in order to elicit the information the team needed to move on with the product development. For example, a protocol aimed at postal employees had to ensure that participants felt safe to share their views and experience without the fear of repercussions from superiors. It also had to take into account the environment in which the research would take place. And it would have to provide a task – if this was part of the protocol – the participant could relate to.

The project required continuous adjustments to existing methods and at times demanded the invention of completely new research methods and techniques. One gap in methods emerged when students searched for a method to understand how the information architecture, the basic structure of the document, needed to look like. They ended up developing a research protocol supported by hands on materials to test hypothetically the logic of pathways that were still in the making. The point of the project was to create and establish these new pathways. Thus, they did not exist yet![19]

The above list of employed methods generated by the design students is helpful in understanding the multiples facets of human-centered product development. Another reflection is needed that provides insights into the relationship between the organization and the design team. The ability to affect changes in this project within the organization depended on the opportunities both the design students and the staff members were able to create for mutual learning. The design students and the USPS team pursued this effort with a number of parallel strategies. These included a shared vision, an evolving and iterative design process, the development of scenarios, user research with mailers, user research with and within the organization, stakeholder buy-in, user-testing, oral and visual presentations, written reports and documentation, and a project website to enhance communication. Below is a detailed description of these activities.

A shared vision

The vision was generated early on by the design team with the organization and it was carefully guarded and continuously shared so that the purpose of the redesign task was always in the minds of all participants. At crucial points in the project, the design team could remind the project members of the overall purpose. This vision allowed for the DMM200 and the DMM300 to emerge as the project went along and the audience became more and more defined.

Evolving and iterative design process

While the vision, the modular strategy and the commitment to human-centered product development were agreed on early on, most aspects that concern the form of the design outcome remained unspecified. The design team and the organization knew it would be something that could be printed on paper, but neither the physical format, nor the content of any of the modules, nor the number of the modules, nor even the general appearance was fixed. All of these aspects emerged over the course of the project.

Scenario development

The design students developed and tested scenarios for a variety of purposes. The team distinguished between scenarios that generated ideas, scenarios that formulated concepts, scenarios that speculated about an issue and scenarios that served to evaluate a proposed solution. These scenarios were double-checked with USPS staff in the field to ensure that they were accurate and likely scenarios.

User research with mailers

The design team identified and recruited individuals and businesses to participate in the user research and user testing. This effort was supported by the organization in that it sent out letters to existing customers explaining the purpose of the project and calling for their participation in improving the DMM. The design team developed trust relationships with these participants, allowing the design team to come back for more information or specific research tasks. Over time, the DMM Transformation Project touched more than 600 people involved in mailing one way or the other.[20]

USPS employees occasionally sat in when user research was conducted by the design team, both with external clients and internal employees.[21] At some point, USPS employees desired to conduct their own user tests and user research, guided and supported by the design students, using protocols prepared by them. In an interview, the DMM group manager commented on the impact this continuous user research had on the project and its viability.

> And all this time while we are developing this document for consumers [the DMM100], we continued to talk at every opportunity with the customer base that the DMM today is really focusing on and that is more commercial type mailers. Carnegie Mellon has been to every single forum and going to other events where customers are. So we have been in this discussion with customers about re-designing this book for a couple of years now. So it is not like it is a foreign notion to our customers.[22]

User research with and within the organization

Beginning with the pilot study, the organization participated in the inquiry. It provided the design students with access to people in post offices and mail processing facilities. The team met with individual employees on all levels across the nation for interviews, conversations, scenario testing, card-sorting exercises, document reviews and user tests. In addition, the organization routinely sent senior staff to participate in design sessions and had the design team come out to its headquarters. The organization conducted a series of stakeholder meetings that involved members of the design team. These meetings often took the form of workshops to generate insights from different stakeholder groups while it provided an opportunity for sharing the vision.

In most of these sessions, the manager of rules and standards or someone standing in for her presented current prototypes and shared the issues the design team was struggling with at that point. This gave employees an opportunity to understand where the design team was coming from and put the work in perspective. It also communicated that the changes were driven internally and that the design students merely aided in this effort.

Directly interacting with managers, senior officials, and field employees alike, allowed the students to test their understanding of the subject matter. Their questions, in turn, contributed to the realization among USPS members that they were not communicating clearly and effectively with their customers. A senior USPS manager reflected on this issue in a conversation about the project.

> What happens within any large organization I believe is that you become myopic. You understand what the rules and regulations are, you understand what needs to be done. What I thought was a fresh perspective was that interfacing with the Carnegie team is that people were reading what we wrote, ok, and saying, well what does that mean? And we would say, why don't you understand what that means? And the team was engaging enough so that it was not just an issue of, you know, that they would get you into a dialogue about words, terms what it could possibly mean, whatever.[23]

Stakeholder buy-in

From the very beginning of the project, the organization undertook the difficult task of generating buy-in from other divisions of the USPS headquarters but also from the industry, the Postal Rate Commission.[24] This signaled commitment and created visibility.

> And we also took it to the opinion leaders – associations who represent mailers – in Washington there is an association for everything. So while we are doing this early part of the project aimed at consumers who really do not have a whole lot aimed at them, we are also beginning the conversation with the larger mailers and the more complex aims.[25]

User testing

User testing occurred throughout the development of each module and was conducted by the design students. The purpose of these user tests was to ensure that particular components or sections of a module in development were in line with the logic applied by users. Final user tests occurred after a final module went into press. These user tests sought to determine the overall integrity and usability of a module and the redesigned DMM system.[26]

Oral and visual presentations as opportunities to share the vision

The CMU team went to great lengths to present and report on ongoing project work to customers, stakeholders, and members of the organization. In addition, the design students prepared presentations and reports on the project for USPS members to facilitate their communication about the vision and the goals.[27]

Written reports and ongoing documentation

The design students delivered written reports with visual documentation at the end of each project phase. Early on, the design team realized the importance of communicating its findings from user research in a form that is easily accessible and understandable by the USPS team. For each interview team members conducted, they produced a written report that summarized the findings and observations for a participant. In addition, the team documented participant's feedback often onto the prototype itself, producing a valuable artifact, which together with the interview questionnaire provided valuable insights into the obstacles and opportunities for the redesigned DMM. These research results were then captured and visualized using a power point template that also contained a brief description of the participant, their business function and experience in mailing as well as background on their organizations. During meetings and presentations, these slides were displayed prominently for staff to see.

A project website

A project website was maintained by the CMU design team and accessible to the USPS team at any time. It provided information on team members, research activities, and project schedule. It also included photographs of prototypes, diagrams, and essential findings. The website was a core element in the initial communication but became secondary over the course of the project.

In combination, these methods and principles of human-centered product development turned into common strategy for the organization and the design team to generate and implement fundamental changes. We will now turn to a phase-by-phase discussion of the project to see how the strategy unfolded.

Notes

1 Mission of the USPS as stated in 2012.
2 The *Domestic Mail Manual Project* funded several PhD students at the School of Design at Carnegie Mellon who actively participated in the research and development activities for this project. I was one of these students and studied the project as Participant Observer and received funding from the DMM Transformation Project.
3 The difference between working with and working for the organization, as we have seen in chapter 5, is significant because it defines the relationship of the two parties as either partners or clients. At the time, the organization struggles to find a design team that was willing and capable to take on this project.
4 These numbers have of course changed since, but the 2001 numbers formed the context for this design project.
5 See *Outline for Discussion: Concepts for Postal Transformation*, p. 19. Submitted by the *United States Postal Service* to the Chairman of the *Committee on Governmental Affairs* on October 1, 2001, p. 19. The numbers of addresses have increased since, as has the number of people moving about the country and for whom the Postal Service tracks mail and forwards it to their new locations. At the same time, the home page of the Postal Service lists the number of employees for 2015 as 750,000. (www.usps.gov).
6 Stamps and other forms of postage are the main source of postal revenues.
7 This unique status is a result of the 1970 Postal Reform. There was a time when the Postal Service was fully tax-funded.
8 The term "bible" was used independently by several interviewees in reference to the DMM. The term also came up several times during the project work.
9 Author's note, statement by senior USPS manager, May 4, 2004.
10 Author interview with senior USPS member, May 4, 2004.
11 Ibid.
12 Author's notes, taken during the summer 2003 orientation for students of design project (June 1, 2003).

13 Statement of Postmaster General John E. Potter, on the Establishment of a Postal Presidential Commission, December 2002.

14 United States General Accounting Office, GAO-01–598T, page 2. April 4, 2001.

15 Author notes of comments made during Summer 2003 student project orientation by manager in charge of the DMM group.

16 Author interview with manager of DMM group, May 4, 2004.

17 Author notes of statement made by the principal investigator during the summer 2003 student project orientation.

18 Credibility issues among USPS team about CMU research work lingered throughout the project. One team member expressed concern about "how people's responses were tainted by their personal interactions" with students from CMU. He wondered how the designers would discount people's responses for the possibility that people were merely doing the nice student a favor by saying positive things. But the same person also pointed out that the CMU team might be getting "better" results because employees would be less concerned about internal sanctions and he cited an example in which a postal employee was "definitely distressed" by being asked to participate in a user test that was partially conducted by managers from headquarters.

19 See Hanington, B. (2003). 'Methods in the Making: A Perspective on the State of Human Research in Design', *Design Issues*, Vol. 19 (4), pp. 18–26.

20 This number includes participants from workshops, user testing, BMEU visits, National Postal Forum events and stretches from the pilot study to the final DMM300. The number is actually higher since it does not include the participants of the final testing rounds in Spring 2005. BMEU stands for Business Mail Entry Units, the locations at which business mail has to be dropped off.

21 This was eyed carefully by the CMU team, as they worried both about their own ability to conduct valid research and even more about the impact the presence of senior officials from headquarters might have on individual, typically subordinate USPS employees. But could the design students deny the DMM staff to participate in the research? Would the benefits of the DMM staff learning about design research outweigh the risks? What code of ethics needed to be applied? It turned out that the DMM staff developed a good sense for when their presence could interfere with the research goals. Without prompting from the design students, the DMM staff often left the room to take pressure off participants.

22 Author interview with manager of DMM group, May 4, 2004.

23 Author notes of comments by former manager of market development specializing on small business. May 6, 2004.

24 Examples include PCC Meetings, the report to the Postal Rate Commission, and the Postage Meter Workshop in Boston during the National Postal Conference in Fall 2002. Also see DMM Transformation Project Report Internal Stakeholder Interviews, July 3, 2003, reporting about interviews with stakeholders June 23–27 in Washington DC.

25 Author interview with manager of DMM group, May 4, 2004.

26 Only once was user testing separated from the ongoing research. This was the case when USPS hired a focus group to test the already published DMM100. It offered a great opportunity for the design students to study the strengths and weaknesses of focus groups as a limited number were allowed to sit in behind the mirrors. The study was sponsored by the Deputy Postmaster General to find out if the DMM100 did affect mailer's behavior.

27 Of course, USPS members would review and edit these materials to make them fit their needs.

7 What do people know about an organization?

Pilot study summer 2001

The heat was on in Pittsburgh. Somewhere on the university campus, five students stared at thousands of pages of mailing rules and standards. The book stared back. Instead of an internship in a fancy design consultancy, they had decided to earn some money working on a rather unusual project. 'What is our task here?' challenged their professor. The task was to find a new organizing principle that would help the Postal Service to re-orient itself around people.

In this summer project, the students visited local mail processing facilities and local Post Offices. They immersed themselves in the activities involved in mailing by sitting in classes that teach about mail preparation and by visiting regional mail processing facilities and local post offices. They talked to window clerks and mail specialists in larger mail facilities and they traced how mail got from here to there. In addition, they gathered information about mail related services and issues wherever and whenever they could.

These techniques of immersion and role-play helped the students empathize with mailers and postal employees. The three USPS officials who oversaw and guided the project at the time for the Postal Service arranged for access to physical facilities and provided contacts for local employees the students could enlist in their research. Beyond that, the USPS officials personally worked with the students, sharing information regarding organizational context, problems the organization is experiencing with the DMM. They also worked through particular questions that emerged in the student's ongoing research. During the duration of the pilot study, the student team had direct access by phone and e-mail to these managers, and vice versa.

The results of the pilot study produced four key insights into people who were using the DMM: DMM users were either novices and new to the DMM and its rules, or experts familiar with the DMM standards. DMM users were either members of the Postal Service and had some understanding of their organization, or they were external without knowledge of how the Postal Service worked and operated. The pilot study further revealed four kinds of mailers: household mailers; small business mailers; large business mailers; and specialty mailers.

For each of these mailers, mailing served a different purpose, and for each mailing group the learning curve and entry point into mailing differed. Based on these findings, the design team recommended to redesign the DMM in a way that tailored relevant mailing information to each group of mailers: The team suggested a DMM for household mailers;

a DMM for small business mailers; a DMM for large mailing businesses and another one that addressed the sophisticated and unique needs of special mailers (those who shipped life bees and life chickens, for example). Together, these modules would constitute a new and easily accessible DMM. Its key advantage over the current DMM would be that it would reorganize the information around the pathways of the respective user and make the DMM accessible, user friendly and usable.

This was a departure from the previous approach that ensured all and every information was contained in one document, leaving it up to the mailer to find the information like a needle in a haystack. It was also a departure from the way the Postal Service previously generated insights into mailers and mailing behavior.

> One of the things that came out of the summer project was sort of a loose kind of a plan that began with a document for consumers. And we did not have a document for consumers in this office. The office that really talked to consumers was consumer affairs or retail.[1]

Another thing that came out from the pilot study was that the development of such a document would require the commitment both from the organization and the design team to work hand in hand. The restructuring of the DMM around people depended on research into people and into the organization. This research could not be outsourced to a third party but had to involve members of the organization. To understand how they worked with the DMM, how it worked for them and how not made it clear that user research would have to include employees across the different postal functions. At the same time, the design team would have to spend time with current and potential mailers: people who already were comfortable using the services and others who were not. Beyond user research inside and outside the organization, a close collaboration with headquarters was necessary. The re-structuring and re-designing of the DMM had to include the content experts to ensure that the rules and standards remained intact but also because they needed to be able to work with the redesign. It would be their job to maintain the new DMM, just as it was their job to maintain and update its current version. It made clear that going forward would demand full commitment and active participation from the organization on all levels.

The design team suggested an incremental approach and to begin Phase I with the design of a retail document centered on the questions and experiences of everyday people. This first part of the project would tackle the largest group of mailers – private, or 'house-hold' mailers. This would allow the design team to identify and understand the basic issues concerning mailing. Subsequent project phases could then address ever more complex mailing questions and mailing situations, for example those of business mailers. For the design team, this approach had the additional advantage that the scope of Phase I could produce a first output in a short amount of time. That would turn out to be crucial for the organization and project.[2]

After the design team established that people who used the DMM included novices and experts who were either internal or external to the Postal Service, they began to look for what all mailers had in common. Soon, they discovered the shape of mail as a point of entry for all mailers into the Postal Service. They found that every mailer knows *what* she wants to mail, even though she may not know *how* to mail it. Mailers may or may not know about a particular mailing rule or standard but they do know what they hold in their hands. With this discovery, the pilot study identified the shape of mail to be the organizing principle for mailers. A DMM that would be easy to use by non-experts and experts alike within the Postal Service as well as outside the organization needed to be organized around questions of shape.

The pilot study finished with a sample page spreads for a potential document for household mailers. This prototype demonstrated that a human-centered approach to the DMM provided different avenues to think about mailing and to learn about mailers. Above all, it showed that it could be done, that the DMM could look and feel different and that tackling the complexity of this task posed a design problem for which human-centered design principles and methods applied. It also showed that the previous organizational design practice and the previous organizational principle around classes of mail had run its course. The vision and strategy developed during the Pilot Study persuaded the USPS management team to invest in Phase I. It presented the Postal Service's first commitment to a human-centered product development. Soon thereafter, the manager to whom the DMM group reported and who wanted to 'fix that book' was promoted to the position of Vice President of Marketing. Her new position enabled her to create visibility for the project and its fundamental role in transforming the organization. Just three months later, in October 2001, John E. Potter, the Postmaster General listed the redesign of the DMM around the needs of customers as one of the strategies employed to transform the Postal Service in his *Outline for Discussion: Concepts for Postal Transformation*, submitted by the United States Postal Service to the Chairman of the Committee on Governmental Affairs.[3]

Making change possible: Inviting the organization

Phase I, spring 2002

With the start of the Phase I in January 2002, the small group conducting the initial six week pilot study was joined by five additional masters' and doctoral students from the Carnegie Mellon School of Design.[4] These student researchers received either credits or tuition assistance in return for their work on the research project. They were also encouraged to reflect on their insights and their work for academic purposes, at conferences, and portfolio presentations. For some students, this project was one among several they had committed to that semester. A recent graduate of the School's Master Program in Communication Planning and Information Design, who had a key role in the pilot study became the fulltime project manager.

She coordinated her efforts closely with the Principal Investigator, the former head of the School of Design who had initiated the project and lead the early strategic conversations. Throughout the project, he led and guarded the project vision, oversaw the project's direction and progress and also ensured that the project environment continued to offer an educational opportunity for students. He reminded everyone of the key problem: to organize and to present mailing information in a way that people could make sense of with the knowledge and experience they had. He liked to refer to 'his mother', though it could really have been anyone's mother:

> Let me tell you about my mom. She knows nothing about the Postal Service. She wants to mail this jar of homemade pickles. How does she get it done? What are her worries? What does she need to know? Where will she find this information?[5]

Students easily identified themselves as 'household' mailers, customers who mostly sent letters or received packages from friends and family members. They visited local post offices and traced their own steps – literally by redrawing their own footpaths around the facility and figuratively by explaining their own experiences as they set out to accomplish a mailing task they had set for themselves. They noticed and documented the questions, issues and obstacles they encountered. As part of this research, the students split into three different groups one day to visit different local post offices. Of the three teams, one explored the mailing experience for a foreigner with limited English skills while another team sought to find out what it took to mail a unique and fragile portfolio with a high personal value. Everyone else was carefully studying their mailing experiences and their interactions with the post office environment, postal employees and even other customers, too.

To get different perspectives, students gathered information about mailing activities and mailing experiences from people around them: neighbors, classmates, friends and others. They analyzed and discussed their findings and visually shared these with everyone else in the design team.[6]

As the first prototypes for a household mailer document organized around shape emerged, the students enlisted participants to review mailing scenarios and to act out realistic mailing scenarios.[7] The design paid attention to include diverse groups of mailers across demographic groups like the elderly or people with lower educational backgrounds, as well as different gender groups. Participants typically spent an hour or less with the research team. In most cases, the research team consisted of two students, one conducting the interview and the other ensuring the documentation by taping the session and taking detailed notes. Each research session with a participant was carefully documented. The protocols and questionnaires were transcribed with the answers and comments provided by the participants. Marked-up prototypes and videotapes helped capture information. Together, they formed the basis for analysis of how participants interact with the DMM and how they went about mailing.

During this stage they were reminded that 'reading' meant different things to different people. Some of the participants scanned the table of contents of the pages they were handed; others flipped through the pages until something caught their eye. Yet others diligently moved from one page to the next, careful not to miss a single word. With no uniform point of entry to the document, the new information architecture had to allow for flexible navigation and respond to all kinds of different reading styles, if it were to serve as many people as possible. After establishing shape as the organizing principle, the search was on for what these different entry points into the document might be.

While the students' research inquired into questions about the information architecture, they were working closely with the organization. The Postal Service, at this stage continued to support and facilitate the ongoing inquiry. Headquarters provided access to regional employees and permitted independent interviews with employees in local facilities. The design team was able to conduct research with window clerks and other postal employees in the field who directly dealt with retail (i.e., business) mailers. The USPS project manager and her superior, the manager of the DMM group, were in regular contact. The Vice President of Marketing returned to campus for project update presentations. Simultaneously, the students became more familiar with the rules and standards, the DMM's core content. As they were reading through the legal wording, they engaged with the content and began to ask headquarters questions about their meaning and relevance.

The collaboration was not without its difficulties. A trust relationship still needed to be developed. This was not an easy task given that the design team, in the eyes of the senior postal employees worked very differently from what they were used to and familiar with.

The design team was aware of this. To demonstrate and communicate the characteristics of the iterative and evolving design process they employed to the DMM staff members in Washington, D.C. and to draw them in, the CMU design team decided to present their first prototype as a work in process, on brown (lunch bag) paper. Instead of professional print outs, they prepared hand drawn illustrations and concepts. This came as a shock to the DMM staff at headquarters used to polished 'professional' presentations by external consultants they usually worked with. But the design team was not interested in consulting the Postal Service. It was looking for a collaboration to support their own internal efforts at transformation. For that to happen, the staff had to become part of the team and to engage in an open participatory design approach. The brown bag paper presentation served this purpose as comments and feedback from the staff in the meeting were immediately noted and captured on the prototype. This was initially confusing to the staff. As one staff member put it, 'There is always a danger in showing your house before it is cleaned up'.[8] The design team was oblivious to that danger because they did not want to build 'a house' on the wrong assumptions, however nicely it would look like. The redesign had to get the structure right and the only way to ensure this was the case was to build and test as they went along. They depended on testing and discussing their current findings with the USPS staff.

For many members of the DMM staff, this was the first time they learned in detail about the redesign project and the collaboration with the student team. It was also the first time they met with the design team in person. It is fair to say that the first project presentation immediately challenged the staff's expectations. Many had spent years in an organizational culture were preliminary work would be judged as not sufficient or lacking. Not all of them trusted that the design team was ready to work with legal rules and standards.

As the design students refined the concept, developed several more prototypes that were reviewed with the DMM staff, they impressed with their eye for detail and their concern for the accuracy of the content. However, some members of the DMM group did not feel very involved in the research and development activities at that stage. A senior staff member recalled: 'we all looked at the prototypes but we were not so involved.'[9] Skepticism about the need for a DMM for everyday mailers loomed large among the DMM staff. There was also skepticism about the design team's ability to produce a result. Several DMM experts remained convinced that it was impossible to introduce significant changes to the complex and continuously changing document. In their view, the design team was doomed for failure.

In the end, however, the students, supported by the leadership of the DMM group, succeeded. Slowly, they unfolded the story of mailing. They had found out that the only thing people knew when they arrived at the postal service was the very thing they held in their hand. Accordingly, they began to organize the information of the DMM around the four basic shapes of mail: Postcards; Letters; Flats; and Parcels. They identified the rules and standards mailers needed to know about when they were mailing one of these shapes. Soon, the students discovered the basic pathway for mailing anything: What are you mailing? What service is the right one for you? What extra services can help you to have proof, get protection, or confirmation? How do you address an envelope? How do you prepare a package? What other sources of information are there about mailing? This pathway presented the outline of the first redesigned document of the new DMM.

The final product was a 24-page document that communicated all mailing regulations that applied to household mailers. In contrast with the 'old' DMM, it made use of illustrations and graphics. In its first edition, the Postal Services released seven-and-a-half million copies of the document to post offices nationwide. In a further gesture towards becoming customer-centered, the brochure was immediately translated into Chinese and Spanish. These versions were made available to regions with a pronounced Chinese respectively Spanish speaking population.[10]

Around that time the DMM project received another boost from the Postmaster General Potter who described in the *United States Postal Service Transformation Plan* what the *DMM Redesign Project* would achieve and how these achievements would link back to the organization.[11] In doing so, the Postmaster General publicly adopted the project's vision and its human-centered design principles. In the words of Postmaster Potter, the DMM redesign would . . .

> . . . articulate the key decisions that different customers must make when doing business with the Postal Service, then connect those decisions to the procedures required to transact the mailing; . . . create a system of information that will support Postal Service marketing efforts by providing consistent, clear information that employees can use to explain Postal Service products and services to retail and business customers; . . . reduce redundancy in the Postal Service workplace by creating an information system that is easy to use and understand, thus eliminating the need for information subsystems; . . . increase customer confidence in the mail by making it clear which mailing alternatives will best suit their needs and provide the most value for their business; . . . protect revenue by helping customers make the right decisions about the level of service they need and ensuring that customers pay the correct postage rate for that service; and . . . identify mailing standards or Postal Service procedures that can be eliminated or improved.[12]

With that, the Postmaster General effectively provided a framework for success against which the efforts of the *DMM Transformation Project* can be objectively evaluated. Of the three criteria he mentioned, two specifically address a change in relationships between customers and the organization ('greater convenience and clarity, particularly for consumer and small business customers'; 'Improved communication between Postal Service representatives and customers') whereas the third one calls for an operational impact, 'expecting higher efficiencies to result.'[13] Also at about this time, the *DMM Redesign Project* begins to be referred to as the *DMM Transformation Project*.

Measured against this criteria, the DMM100 succeeded in all three categories. With the release of the first product, the Postal Service for the first time ever in its 200 years of existence directly addressed the concerns of everyday mailers. Until then, anyone sending a parcel or letter had little opportunity to find out why the postal service was a good choice, what values the service provided, what services were available and how they differed or where to look for examples of making wise decisions about mailing.

John E. Potter signed a personal copy of the DMM100 for every design team member. It was an encouragement to move into Phase II to address mailing for people who were relying on the Postal Service for business purposes. Their problem, too, began with shape. They also followed the basic pathway of mailing. But for them, mailing was part of a business strategy. What would the DMM have to do for them?

Notes

1 Author interview, May 2004.
2 Author interview, May 4, 2004.
3 *Outline for Discussion: Concepts for Postal Transformation*, Submitted by the *United States Postal Service* to the Chairman of the Committee on Governmental Affairs on October 1, 2001.
4 Two of the original pilot study members, having graduated in May 2001, had left campus after the summer 2001.
5 Author meeting notes, spring 2002.
6 A task analysis is an important method applied in human-centered product development. Essentially, it is an investigation in which designers scrutinize what it takes to accomplish a particular goal. In a task analysis, designers pay attention to what kind of knowledge people are assumed to have who are trying to accomplish this task. This includes a look at what decisions need to be made and the kind of support – or obstacles people can count on and what point in time and under what circumstances. I like to give students in product planning and product development courses this simple task for their analysis: On campus, go to building x and get a bottle of water out of the soda machine. Then return and describe your steps and your experience to your classmates. What appears to be a simple thing to do, reveals its complexity when students do not know where building x is, when the soda machine is broken or has been moved, or when they do not have the right change to retrieve the bottle of water, and so on. A task analysis reveals the kind of assumptions that are implicit in achieving a particular goal.
7 To ensure that a mailing scenario is realistic, students drew on real stories shared by private mailers and postal employees.
8 Author's notes of interview with senior DMM staff member, 2004.
9 Author's notes of interview with senior DMM staff member, May 5, 2004.
10 Statement by CMU's project manager taken from "Meeting a Big Challenge for a Mass Audience," http://www.adobe.com/education/gallery/cmu/postoffice.html. The Adobe company watched the project carefully as it pushed the boundaries of document design and single source system.
11 *United States Postal Service Transformation Plan*, K-14–16 Appendix, APPENDIX K–Growth- and Value-Based Strategies: Promote Greater Ease of Use, April 2002.
12 Ibid.
13 Ibid.

8 Engaging the organization

Project II, summer 2002–spring 2003

Motivated by their success with the DMM100 for household mailers, the design team quickly entered into the next phase and moved on to develop the second module, the DMM200 for small to medium size businesses. They built on the knowledge and experience of the first project phase, and added new team members for this larger project. New issues emerged as the students gradually waded deeper into the complexity of mailing rules and tried to match them with the mailer's logic of going about mailing. They still concentrated on clarifying the tasks and factors that enable mailers to achieve their mailing goals.

Project Phase II once again began with an introduction to the Postal Service by the USPS project manager. This was important since new students had joined the team. It provided a background for all those who were not part of Phase I. Further information on the organization and its needs was provided by the USPS manager of the market development group who had brought along a staff member. Roughly a week later, the manager of the DMM group joined the students for a research meeting with a local representative of the Business Mail Entry Units, which produced additional insights into the current relationship between employees and customers.

Document analysis over the summer of 2002 saw the design team reading through rule after rule. One of the findings was that rules, standards and rights have co-existed historically. Another discovery was that new and complicated rules often resulted from the introduction of new technologies. The technology issue was a complicated one indeed: Rules driven by technology could result from technological upgrades the Postal Service introduced to its own mail processing facilities. But just as often, such new rules originated from new technological capabilities of a large mail client. As a result, technology constantly undermined the mail class-based system the Postal Service had established. In some instances, rights and privileges changed for each mail class and for each mailer.[1] How was a mailer to find out about which rights and privileges applied to his or her situation?

Another round of extensive user research was conducted to include different kinds of business mailers.[2] It was the design team that recruited research participants. They identified and contacted businesses with the request for participation in user research for the Postal Service. Participants ranged in diversity from small Mom-and-Pop stores to large regional grocery chains and include non-profit organizations as well as mailing service providers. Participants agreed to voluntarily review prototypes, execute mailing scenarios using prototypes or other tools the researchers presented them with. In addition, business employees volunteered information about their use of the DMM and allowed students to observe them as they did so, asking them questions. These research sessions generally lasted an hour or less. Often these prototypes used for testing became part of the documentation when participants commented on particular pages, which were then marked up by the student interviewers.

Most of this user research involved two students visiting the participant on the business premises. One student led through the research protocol while the other student observed, took notes and videotaped the participant's interaction with the prototypes and/or the DMM.[3] Typically the work environment of the mailer was also documented and photographed.

Through their conversations with different business mailers, researchers learned how organizations went about mailing, where and when mailings happened in their organization, how often and for what purposes. Of particular interest at this stage of the research was how people found out and learned about mailing options or mailing procedures and how they went about finding rules and standards that applied. Findings in this phase allowed the design team to disproof the prevailing views on mailing at headquarters. They developed visual diagrams that began to document 'the circle of pain' many business mailers found themselves caught in when they tried to take advantage of services and products offered by the Postal Service. The Postal Service, it turned out, did not have a lot of information on the 'five to twenty million' customers who used their products for business purposes.[4]

> There are so many ways to define the mailers. Even the [organization] doesn't have a very good grasp of who their audience is. Or rather, their audience definition is based on marketing (i.e., how much revenue the business generates for the [organization] while that lends nothing to help these businesses. It is important to develop a way to define the audience not only for ourselves, but also for these small and medium sized businesses. They also need an understanding of where they fit in and what type of business and mailing habits they have. Some ways to define small business include: geographic (local vs. national), # of mail pieces, frequency of mailing, # of employees, and level of maturity. We have realized for a while that we have only touched on a small segment of potential 200 users: the novice and beginners, the small business. Now we must examine the semi-experts and more frequent users that characterize medium businesses. This includes businesses such as [supermarkets], [radio stations], insurance companies, letter shops, local banks. From interviews with these, we hope to gain a better understanding of their needs and mailing habits (and find out from them what we didn't from the previous interviews last week). Then we can also better understand where 200 mailers stop and 300 mailers begin.[5]

The investigation into the document and into mailer behavior and experience was complemented by further research into the organization itself. For this purpose, the design team interviewed USPS employees on all levels, in mail-processing facilities and at different distribution points. They engaged with managers from different USPS divisions and worked with them in project rooms on campus and off site, running through scenarios, discussing rules, and system requirements.

Gaining insights into the what, how and why of business mail emerged as the key for a successful redesign of the DMM for business mailers. The business aspect of the DMM200 (the DMM module tailored to this group) had to speak directly to people's motivation for business mailing. For the DMM staff, this meant they now needed to reach out to other functional areas across USPS' organization and to bring in their marketing and new product development representatives. For the students, this meant additional learning about the organization in an effort to provide business mailers with the material and the tools to arrive at the best mailing decision for their business.

During the development of the DMM200, the design team intensified its engagement with DMM staff members. This interaction took different forms and served distinct purposes. All fifteen members of the DMM group were now included. The DMM project leader, often accompanied by two regular staff members and the DMM group manager held weekly phone conferences with the design group and visited regularly.

When members of the design team joined a retreat in Washington to present the first prototype of the DMM200, the roughness of the brown paper format was no longer a topic for the DMM staff. This time, a few new participants from the organization's market development and sales department participated, too. Once again, the intentional unfinished state of the concepts presented provided the members of the organization with an opportunity and an invitation to help shape these ideas and concepts. Nonetheless, the ever-changing prototypes began to confuse the DMM staff. Intended as opportunities to elicit comments and suggestions regarding the broad information architecture that was evolving from the user research with customers and field employees, the majority of DMM experts fell back into their habit of line-editing. This proved problematic at the following prototype review because these prototypes were not ready for line-editing reviews. For this reason, they also still contained spelling errors, misplaced rules and other elements that the design students had merely thought of as place-holders 'for the time being.' For some members of the DMM staff, this was an indication that the design team was not up to the task. A staff member shared this 'imaginary hall talk' at the time among the USPS team.[6]

> *T1:* Carnegie Mellon? I mean they are going to design this?
> We have had people do this, all the time . . .
> *T2:* Yeah, but they did it poorly.
> *T1:* So now we have *these* 'professionals' doing this?

Here was a group of Master and PhD students from a private university; there was a group of postal employees, several of whom had started in the Postal Service as letter carriers. How could these young, preppy academics possibly understand and remedy what the practitioners had struggled with for so long? Aside from professional matters, personality issues emerged. 'There were people in the CMU group that came across as abrasive.'[7]

In a further escalation of the tensions, DMM staff members expressed dissatisfaction about the process and frustration over not seeing the changes they had suggested during the previous meeting. The DMM staff did not understand that their comments and insights were part of the ongoing design research and that their feedback often entered the document in subtle ways.

At the same time, the DMM staff appeared to be struggling with the freedom the organization allowed the design students in redesigning the DMM. This was confusing to some members of the organization who were accustomed to follow hierarchical lines. A DMM staff member made the following comment:

> CMU in this project has been given a lot more latitude than most design contractors would on most projects, primarily based on that. In general, a group at a lower level would be working with – other than the advertising agencies which usually get sort

of this leeway too – on most projects the relationship would be a little tighter than it had been in this project. Which is actually in some regards there is a lot of give and take with CMU more so than there may be in some other relationships.[8]

While the design team felt it needed to share as much of its process as possible with the members of the organization, a good number of DMM experts felt that the open process caused more problems than it solved. They felt particularly uncomfortable showing people from other organizational divisions the rough phases of the project. Traditionally, the DMM group interacted with these other departments when they were preparing a rule change. Their effort generally aimed 'to give them a final draft that looks as closely as possible to the final rule'.[9] The participatory and iterative approach by the CMU design team changed that. DMM staff members reflected their struggle with the iterative design process as follows:

> From their [DMM staff's] perspective, when they saw earlier prototypes they were used to be doing what they were doing in the past. Bad grammar, sentences cut off. They just thought the CMU team was incompetent and going down the road.'[10]
> 'They [other departments] were brought in on a conceptual phase. It did not work it was upsetting to them. We changed that. It was even too early to bring in our own department to such an early prototype phase. We are not used to working in an evolving kind of way. This organization is used to a core group developing it. Working through the issues with the industry and then present it for the others to review. That was difficult.[11]

DMM staff also experienced difficulties in catching up with the ongoing changes in the prototypes themselves and the changes in the systems architecture. There were DMM experts who preferred to maintain the current system, as this quote shows.

> In some respects, for some of the people, it has been very negative. There has been too much change, or [it] was not sort of explained or developed enough. There were people who were very comfortable with the way things were and really did not see a need for change or thought that change could come about a different way.[12]

Despite the rough beginning, the joint work sessions and the participatory design approach fostered mutual respect and instilled a sense of shared accomplishment. One DMM staff member noted the progress in an interview.

> He [a design student] really wanted to know what is behind the standards so he could understand it because it made no sense to him. So here is a standard that somebody could look at and say 'who came up with this !#' Who could have ever written this it makes no sense. And he did not have this attitude at all. So I felt we worked really well when we were out there [at the retreat].[13]

The physical prototypes acted as medium for members of the organization to discover and discuss the problems of their existent system. The prototypes highlighted issues and generated discussion points around which conversation could begin. Throughout the development of the DMM200, the design team kept pointing to the overall vision of the

DMM Transformation Project and to the specific goals of this second DMM module. It was the overall vision, established and agreed early on, that allowed the design students to explore these different aspects. This vision was kept in view by the Principal Investigator who reminded the organization that, they, too, had to guard and foster that vision. More than once he asked, 'Who is guarding the vision?' He did so during a visit by the USPS team in the presence of the DMM project manager and the manager of the DMM group;[14] he also posed the question for design students when the project appeared to be at a crucial junction.

There were moments when either or both the design students and the organization were in danger of losing sight of the vision. Towards the end of the project, the DMM staff, dealing simultaneously with a *Rate Case*,[15] was beginning to get distracted and was no longer pushing hard on the redesign. There were other moments during which the vision was questioned, for example, if it was broad enough for the task at hand. When everyday details about rules and concerns about implementing and maintaining the new DMM system threatened to cloud the vision and bog down the DMM group, the design students understood this as a challenge to the vision.

A usable and easily accessible DMM for mailers could not become a burden to people in the organization. The design students believed that a failure to provide a solution that was unsustainable in organizational terms, equally failed the vision. For this reason, they expanded their research activities to inquire into technical issues related to the implementation of the new DMM. They formed a technical team to explore the possibilities and implications in detail. Again, they worked closely with the USPS project leaders on clarifying their concerns and their needs. Subsequently, they approached a software company to bring in additional expertise and information. They shared their findings with the DMM group. Unfortunately, the preferred solution by the DMM staff was not technically feasible.

In addition to these new research and development activities, the design team began to offer support to USPS leaders in their communication of the vision and state of the project to stakeholders and customers. When the DMM200 was introduced to customers at the National Postal Forum in New Orleans, the manager of the DMM group used a Power-Point presentation prepared by the students. When a staff member needed visuals for a public relations event in New York, the students prepared a poster presentation. These extra efforts contributed to the visibility of the project and ensured that the vision was being communicated consistently. They had benefits for the design team, too: they expressed care and concern for the needs of the organization and strengthened the relationship with organizational members. Often, these project presentations resulted in additional volunteers for user research.

In line with the iterative and evolving design approach, the form and shape of the DMM for businesses and organizations changed over the course of its development in significant ways. Most notably, the design students saw the DMM for business mailers to consist of two components: a path that guides mailers in making a decision about the method of mailing most appropriate for them; and a subsequent, second path to conduct and execute a discount mailing. Thus Phase II began with a concept for a DMM200A and DMM200B.

The design students began to work on the DMM200A, the decision-making document. It was envisioned as a general introduction to mailing for businesses and organizations. Its function was to explain the value of mail and match it to the business mailer's situation with that method of mailing that is most efficient and effective for their purpose.

To do so, the DMM200A provided information and examples of the different kinds of methods. Though the DMM200 did not provide step-by-step procedures, the document did provide an overview of procedures relevant to making a decision. This allowed a sense of closure for mailers who sought to find out about the best method for their situation. The DMM200 aims at eliminating the sense that 'there is always another pub[lication] to pick up, another DMM regulation to look up', a major source of frustration for many mailers.[16]

All along, while developing the DMM200A, the design students were researching and conceptualizing the DMM200B, in their view the second half of the DMM200. However, the phase ended without a 'how-to' document. The idea of showing the 'order of play' for a discount mail never caught on with the DMM project manager and his team. In the end, the DMM200A (which ultimately became known as the DMM200) offered far more instructions than any other DMM publication ever did.

Despite this clear setback, the DMM200 achieved several breakthroughs. It identified and explained the three 'methods' of mailing the Postal Service offers: Retail Mailing, Online Mailing Services, and Discount Mailing. Never before did the USPS differentiate methods or think of its products in these terms. Nor did it acknowledge Online Mailing Services as a distinct mailing method. In fact, this mailing method was still in its pilot phase when the DMM Transformation Project began. And at the time, the design team was discouraged to even mention it in the document because the general sentiment was that the product did not do well and was likely to be discontinued. But user research showed that customers liked the product and had great interest in the online service.[17] Only, they had never heard of it before. Similarly, it turned out that few USPS employees knew of the service or could explain it to their customers. Following the findings from the user research, the organization established Online Mailing Services as a product and a method. This demanded an internal decision to commit to a service still in its infancy. The DMM200 thus directly affected the development of a new product by the organization.

The DMM200 achieved consistency in terms and concepts that are consequential for the organization and the further development of the DMM. After much internal struggle, the organization agreed to 'Discount mail' as the accepted and official term for anything that had previously been loosely referred to as bulk mail, standard mail, presort mail, direct mail, or business mail. Similarly, the organization committed to the term 'Online Mailing Services' as the official term for online mailing methods. Agreeing on these terms was no easy task for the organization but it was a major requirement for the development of a consistent system.[18]

In general, the DMM200 moved one step closer to clarifying the overall language for mailers, offering glossaries, definitions and explanations in the context of use. It was yet another demonstration that the complexity of mailing for business mailers could be tackled by business mailer's pathways to mailing and not by the USPS' concern for rules and regulations (though not neglecting the latter).

Finally, the DMM200 dealt with the delicate issue of Mailing Service Agencies, those industry players that greatly contribute to the efficiency of the Postal Service since they prepare mail professionally before it enters the mail processing facilities. Mailing Service Agencies benefitted from the perception that mailing is too complicated to 'do it yourself'. Initially, the USPS tried to steer mailers towards using such mail services for more sophisticated uses of mail. The design students, however, argued that in order to make an informed choice, mailers needed to know and understand what sophisticated mail options were and how to use them. Rather than alienating Mailing Service Agencies, the industry turned out to be grateful that someone was finally spelling out the services they provided. In the words of the representative of a large mailing service agency: 'The DMM200 makes our life easier as we finally have a way to communicate to our customers what it is we do for them.'[19]

Expanding on the paths the DMM100 has laid out, the DMM200, too, began with the one thing every mailer knows no matter how much she knows about mailing: the shape of their mail piece. The DMM200, like the DMM100, contains information that does not change very often and is considerably stable. Thus, the maintenance for the DMM staff is held to a minimum for both documents. It provides a core introduction to the purpose and the methods of business mailing and simultaneously serves as reference, tool and educational resource.

For the first time, the DMM was communicating directly with small and medium size business mailers the value of the USPS. User research into this group the USPS once estimated to range between five and twenty million customers has not only generated a better understanding of the needs and purposes of the small and medium size business mailer but also contributed to a better understanding of those mailers generally thought to be DMM300 mailers. In line with the incremental development approach, the DMM200 turned into the second stepping-stone for the redesign of the DMM. It prepared the ground for the third phase of the development, the DMM300.

Notes

1 Author notes taken during the early work on the DMM200, July 8, 2003.
2 Previous research for the DMM100 had focused on individual household mailers but also included small businesses in an attempt to identify the point at which a household mailer turns into a business mailer.
3 Documentation of this user research focused on capturing the participant's interaction with the information to reveal reading styles, important sections, etc.
4 Numbers provided by several senior USPS officials.
5 Author's notes, June 20, 2002.
6 Author interview with DMM staff member, May 5, 2004.
7 Author interview with DMM staff member, May 2004.
8 Author interview with senior DMM staff member, May 2004.
9 Author interview with project manager for the DMM group, May 2004.
10 Author interview with DMM staff member, May 2004. Interestingly, the interviewee distinguished himself from the other team members, referring to them as they. The same interviewee stated that he had almost no role in the project. This is true if the involvement is measured in overall project hours. When the involvement is measures by impact, this staff member made significant contributions.
11 Author interview with senior DMM staff member, May 2004.
12 Author interview with senior DMM staff member, May 5, 2004.
13 Author interview, with DMM staff member, May 5, 2004.
14 Author team meeting notes, 2003.
15 A *Rate Case* is a formal request by the United States Postal Service to increase the rates for its services and products. A Rate Case may concern all classes or just First Class Mail. For example, a recent Rate Case raised the price for a First Class stamp to 39 cents.
16 Author notes on self-immersive scenario, January 30/31, 2003.
17 Author notes from user research, July 24, 2003.
18 For example, the term "work share" emerged early as a term that intuitively referred to the need for mailers to share in the work of mail preparation if they were to save on mailing cost. But there was concern among senior staff that encouraging customers to share in the work would alienate union members who might fear that this would mean less work and thus less employment for them.
19 Statement made by the mailing liaison for a large mail service provider during customer interviews conducted by the design students at the National Postal Forum in New Orleans, 2003.

9 Reorganizing around users, pathways and shape

Phase III, summer 2004–spring 2005

With the quiet death of the DMM200B, the document that would have shown small and medium business mailers how to execute a discount mail, and the vanishing need for a DMM400 for special mailers, the design students' efforts began to concentrate on the design of the DMM300. Though the student team still felt that the 'how-to-document' would be of great benefit to business mailers, they were consoled by the fact that the redesigned DMM200 accomplished most of the goals it set out to achieve.

Perhaps the most important one remained invisible for people picking up the document: the development of the DMM200 aligned members of the organization with the design students around the project vision. By the end of the second project, the systems architecture has become clear: There would be three modules. The DMM300 was the only one left to develop. Finally, this provided some certainty for the DMM staff about the new DMM system. They were relieved finally to know how and what the system would look like. By June 2003, members of the design team conducting research with the organization in Washington, D.C., observed: 'Generally, there is a positive attitude of the project. Only one [staff member] felt the project is overrated and not needed.'[1] The DMM project manager attributed this change in attitude towards a change in how and when he involves other departments in the redesign.

He felt that his team had taken 'a beating' in the prior two phases for sharing prototypes on a conceptual level. There was now a core group of five DMM experts working very closely with the CMU design team. They held weekly phone conferences and met for several days at various times to work out particular issues. But there were no longer detailed discussions of prototype spreads to elicit comments and feedback from the whole group. Instead, the status and the vision of the project were presented in broad terms. The manager for the DMM staff reflected on these changes.

> We changed this process. I could see the pain from CMU's perspective with holding these meetings but these were more from a political perspective to show people what we were doing to bring them into the fold to tell them that what we are doing is meaningful to them.'[2]
>
> 'We changed the process to give them a very high level perspective. Not even prototypes. No examples really just a very high level perspective.[3]

Despite the new and welcome calm, new worries set in. Among them was an increasing concern among the design students that mailers may have come to expect too much. The DMM100 and the DMM200 so radically departed from the old DMM that this had raised expectations about what the third product could do, look and feel like. The designated content of the DMM300 were the rules and standards the other DMM modules linked to. And neither the rules nor the standards could change, however complicated they were. Would users be disappointed if they were provided with easy and intuitive navigation only to arrive at a piece of law difficult to read and understand? How could information be presented differently and more intuitively without changing the rules? The students introduced graphics and visual displays to illustrate rules and to communicate standards.

How may information be structured in this document that would hold all the rules and standards and that would most likely be used by people with a need for citation and reference? This was a completely different user pathway than the one people pursued when they sought to prepare mail or wanted to make an informed decision about a mailing service. Also, how could people find a particular rule even if they did not know much about the USPS rules and standards to begin with? How would experts, trained and skilled in the old citation system, find their way around?

How would the design students ensure that all the rules and standards would make the transition into the new document? Leaving out even one rule or standard could have a ripple effect throughout the mailing industry. Finally, how did the organization plan the transition from the old DMM to the new system? What and who needed to be prepared for the change? And how could the design students support their efforts?

Increasingly, the organization's attention shifted towards the rule writing process. While students were told during the development of the DMM100 that rewriting was not part of their task of re-redesigning the DMM, now the organization encouraged the students to explore how the rules could be written differently. This posed a new challenge to the design students but the opportunity to make the organization rethink its approach to communication was welcome. Two notes from a student caught this movement.

> Develop Illustrations and Diagrams (long-term changes to book, in spring [2005]. We work with the USPS to rewrite rules, redesigning, redrafting, 'can a picture replace words?' 'Can pictures have a legal standing same as text?' Drive to make the organization think differently about communication . . .[4]
>
> Promised for spring [2005] to provide a model for how to write rules (how to conceive of a rule and structure a rule so it is understandable, meets legal requirements, giving precise guidelines, language.[5]

Towards the completion of the DMM300, the design students explored the possible implications of the transition to the new DMM. In many ways, this task was perceived to be changing drivers in a moving car. The design students wanted to let the DMM staff know that they were interested and willing to support their efforts in switching over to the new DMM system. They prepared a Transition Workshop and invited the DMM project management to participate. The workshop was facilitated by two members of the Australian Tax Office who had personal experience with organizational change in large bureaucracies and who had a leading role in introducing human-centered design principles in their Australian government agency. That case is described in one of the next chapters.[6]

A successful project

The project succeeded in the design of a DMM that is accessible to all customers. It did so by generating a vision, a commitment and a strategy. Figure 9.1 illustrates how the redesigned DMM would create new customer pathways. The dotted lines show the previous paths for mailers before the redesign of the DMM. Neither household mailers nor small business mailers had direct access to the DMM information.

Although the DMM100 was intended to provide basic mailing information to household mailers, it turned out that the simplicity and clarity with which it discussed mailing issues were widely embraced by customers and employees who were not thought to be interested in mailing information on that level. A DMM expert at the D.C. headquarters has found it surprisingly useful: 'a lot of times, customers call and I can take the [DMM]100 and read a simple piece in there that explains what is in my head'.[7] At its introduction at the National Postal Conference in New Orleans, the head of the Division calls the DMM200 'a breakthrough project.'[8]

Among the major mailing clients, the DMM100 found use in internal training of new employees but also as free handouts to employees using their corporate mail system for sending private mail. User research revealed that business mailers engaged in mailing activities all across the board and that the new modular DMM provided them with a tool to provide information to their customers and employees in the right form at the right time. One such example is a company that processes credit card data, a business that centers on mailing out or receiving information. This is a firm for which an increased awareness about mailing among its employees translates into smoother operations.

For most business mailers, the DMM200 contains all the information they ever want to know. Only rarely do they need to look up a particular rule for citation or referencing. Generally, they want to know what options they have for mailing and what option works best for them in their given situation.

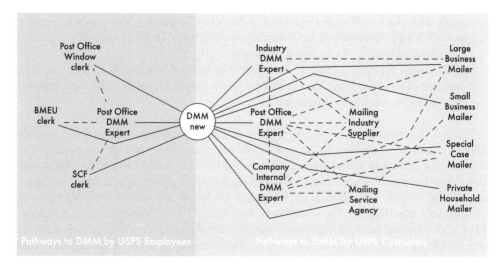

Figure 9.1 Internal and external pathways to the DMM before and after the DMM transformation project

Early tests of the new DMM300 showed that within twenty minutes of working with the new reference book, both experts and novices felt comfortable working with it. This showed that the project achieved a major milestone of bringing in people with little experience without losing the experts. Rather than alienating this group of people – a fear the DMM staff harbored – this customer group welcomed the ease of use the new DMM modules provided. Even mail and print businesses commented positively on the new documents, going as far as to say 'That makes our life easier. Now we can explain to our customers what we do for them!'[9]

Vision, strategy, design approach and leadership as factors in the outcome

Most people who worked with the DMM found comfort in knowing that all the rules and standards were there, somewhere. But few of them were able to cut their own path through the rules jungle. The way the rules were organized followed the logic of those people who wrote, issued and maintained them. The complexity of the information was overwhelming and assumed pre-existing and extensive knowledge about mailing processes. Mailers who knew little about the organization, the origin of its rules and the way it was structured, were at a loss when they tried to find out how best to mail something or how to comply with all the rules and standards that applied to their mail situation.

The complexity and difficulty to 'get it right' created a need for mailing experts on all levels. These experts, many who had spent decades working with particular sections of the book, had become quite adept in finding and interpreting certain rules. Over time, these mailing experts effectively created a layer around the Postal Service, as Figure 9.1 shows. And because internal experts mostly dealt with expert customers – those who already knew how to ask questions – few saw a need for redesigning the DMM.

> . . . They [the postal experts] have spent their entire career learning and knowing and understanding those rules and the way that they are written, and they are written from the point of view of the postal service, and they are written for our convenience in publishing and maintaining them, because the current design is extremely efficient in terms of writing and publishing to it. We publish basically the entire book twelve times a year or once every four weeks and we have got that huge Framemaker-based system that does it and it goes up on the Internet. Your power users, the people who know it, know how to use the book love it because it is always updated . . .[10]
>
> . . . Look, we have this big book. It is called the Domestic Mail Manual and contains all our rules for mailing. . . . A lot of people have trouble working with it. We don't. But a lot of people do. . . .[11]

A core document that is not easily accessible to customers and employees cannot serve the organization either. If the goal of redesigning the DMM were to make the rules and standards accessible to all mailers, the current role of these internal experts might change. In addition, it would affect a whole mailing industry that was built around the perception that it is way too difficult to deal with the Postal Service directly (see Figure 9.1 above). Changing the DMM, therefore, would have profound implications on the organization itself and possibly on the industry. The more people knew about mailing, the more they could see value in the Postal Service, and the more the Postal Service could benefit financially and operationally. In an era of increased competition from private companies and digital forms of communication, the latter is a major concern. Could the DMM be redesigned in a way that changed people's behavior?

It is no small accomplishment to maintain, issue and update a document that is central for an organization of 900,000 employees and a surrounding industry of nine billion dollars. The rules and the standards in the DMM ensure that millions of letters and packages reach their intended recipients on any given day. Any change to this book would have ripple effects throughout the organization, internally and externally. The small group that tackled the task of writing new rules, maintaining the document and reinforcing the standards was skeptical. Every day, these staff members amended or changed an existing rule or wrote a new one. Every four weeks, the group reissued an updated DMM. Any mistake could result in millions of dollars of damage for the organization. On average, the DMM staff members had worked on a particular content issue for fifteen years. It is through this technical expertise that they were able to deliver the required changes and write the new rules in the short time they were allotted.

The task for the manager was complex: All elements of the organization had to be part of the answer. If the goal was to change people's behavior, the vision of the purpose of the DMM had to change as well. With that, the structure of the document was in question, and, since the document took on such a core position within the organization, these questions led right into the organization and its ability to commit resources.

As we shall see, the promise of the *DMM Transformation Project* to reorient the organization around people aided its visibility within the organization and generated support from the highest management level. Human-centered product development, involving people, resources, structures and purpose, provided a gradual path to implement organizational change.

Beginning with the most basic mailing needs and mailing issues in the first project, the DMM100, the product development turned to a more sophisticated use of mailing in the second project, the DMM200. For the third project, the DMM300, the efforts concerned an even smaller group of people who use the DMM for referencing and citation. This incremental increase in complexity allowed for an equally incremental increase in involvement of the organization's experts and other stakeholders. These questions did not concern detailed knowledge about particular rules and standards but centered on identifying the key concerns of mailers.

This created many opportunities for internal organizational learning, as information gradually moved from the outside in – from customers, business partners and field employees to USPS headquarters, especially the marketing, consumer services and of course, the rules and standards division. Among other things, the project offered the organization a welcome opportunity to 'clean house' and to identify elements of the DMM that are no longer relevant or needed because technology or law has rendered them obsolete. The head of the DMM group understands this: 'Sometimes we realize that there is text in there that nobody has looked at for a long time because we have not had a reason to do so'.[12]

Another example of clarification concerns the amazing range of additional services mailers can purchase. The students' visualization of these services organized them according to the mailer's purpose (proof, protection, or confirmation), listing the options that are available in each mail class (Express Mail, Priority Mail, etc.). The resulting table surprised even some seasoned mail experts: For some services, three different products were being offered with only slight differences. The table thus identified opportunities for new product development and product revisions that had gone unnoticed up to that point.[13]

A third example involves a product that was being pilot tested by the USPS at the time. User research identified 'Netpost' as a viable and welcome third method of mailing – alternative to retail mailing (using stamps) and discount mailing (preparing mail for discounts) for business mailers. The response and feedback USPS had gotten internally was rather disappointing and the new product was in danger of being cancelled. User research revealed that customers and employees saw value in this product but that neither had heard about it or knew how it worked.

Organizational engagement was key. Figures 9.2 and 9.3 below show how members of the organization became more involved with the design of each new DMM module. The figures also demonstrate how each subsequent module narrowed the audience, as the mailing questions became more specific. The more specific the topics, the more interest a module generated among mailing experts (inside and outside of the organization). For example, many DMM experts in the organization did not pay much attention to the development of the DMM100. Some, in fact belittled the 24-page document aimed at regular household customers.[14] At the time of the development of the DMM100, these experts did not understand that the document was the beginning of a fundamental shift in the vision of what the DMM could be for mailers.

However, after the successful distribution of the DMM100 in Post Offices nationwide, the brochure effectively established the new vision for everyone to see. It set a new standard internally and externally. People began to look at the DMM and thought: Why could it not be like the DMM100?[15] The incremental approach allowed for many different contact points between the designers and the organization. The two figures also represent the reach the design project had into the organization.

The success of the DMM Transformation Project can be linked to the overall vision and the incremental strategy that had been laid out during the Pilot Study. Equally significant was the steadfast commitment to human-centered product development, marked by an iterative and participatory approach to the redesign of the DMM. Without leadership, however,

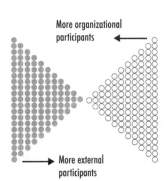
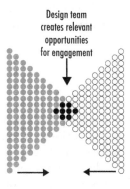

The butterfly approach to organizational participation in a design process: Just a few members work on the design project inititally but organizational involvement increases over time as the complexities and the issues reach deeper into organizational structure and processes. The design team creates opportunities for relevant engagement and meaningful contribution by all stakeholders.

Figure 9.2 Butterfly diagram I

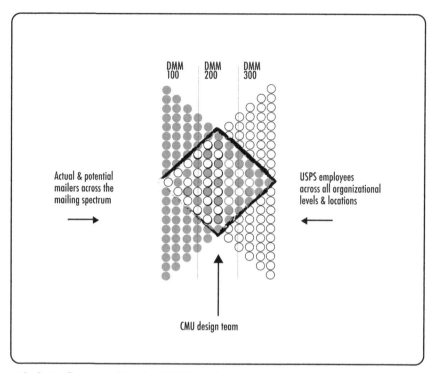

The butterfly approach for the DMM Transformation Project: The design team created continous opportunities for engagement and involvement of USPS staff and external customers, including potential and actual mailers

Figure 9.3 Butterfly diagram II

the project would not have been able to withstand the storms of the second part of the project. Without leadership, participation on the side of the organization might have been difficult. Making the project a priority for the organization was an important factor.

The vision

In face of increasing resistance, especially during the development of the DMM200, it would have been tempting for the organization to abandon the project. But the project had become a high priority within the organization all the way from the Postmaster General down. In fact, it had become a cornerstone of the official Transformation Plan. The purpose was to have a 'book speak to people' and to reorganize the DMM around shape.[16] Because that was how people could access mail.

The strategy

Generally, it can be said that the first deliverable product, the DMM100 raised the expectation among customers and employees about how information about mailing can be presented. For the manager of market development, seeing the DMM100 energized him to participate in the development of the DMM200.

Now one of the things that the 100 did for me though is that it gave me a perspective about how – because I had looked through the 100 – it had given me a perspective about how to display information and data in a much more inviting way.[17]

For people who needed to see to believe that something can be done or is possible, holding the new DMM100 in their hands delivered the 'proof'. The following comment by a staff member confirms this:'But when the first DMM100 hit the market, people were saying: O man, this is nice. Sometimes you need to see the finished product'.[18]

The response from customers to the DMM100 was immediate and overwhelmingly positive. Included with every brochure was a survey postcard that invited readers to submit their comments on the redesign. Analyzed by Gallup, the results showed that a big majority of the respondents perceived the document as valuable and as easily accessible.[19]

The development and delivery of the first product, the DMM100 thus served to establish the new vision among customers and employees and showed that it can be done. It played a key role in the organization's effort to transform and represents a core element of the strategy of changing the DMM and transforming the organization and its services around people.

The participatory approach

The character of the participatory design changed several times over the project. While external customers and field employees were equally involved throughout the three module developments, the involvement of the organization varied. Reasons for this can be found in different leadership personalities that headed the project for the United States Postal Service. For example, the change in USPS' project management in the second project phase had a profound impact on the project dynamics, as the new project manager felt the previously pursued participatory approach had resulted in sharing too much information too early.

> [The design professor] would say you have to understand our process. That was fine for the core team. The core team began to get a feel for the process. But bringing in other people from other departments and trying to tell what they are looking at just did not work. We are giving them too much information at too early a stage in the project.[20]

Thus the open and iterative process was considered appropriate for the design team but inappropriate for dealing with the organization.

> The process that is good for designers was not a good process for bringing in those groups of people. Project manager and team are bearing the cost, not the design team.[21]

Those design students who returned frustrated and disillusioned from a two-day meeting in September 2002 with stakeholders in Washington D.C. argued the opposite: 'We took a bullet for the team'.[22] The student reporting for the group continued:

> The first day went well but the second was tough.[23]

So tough indeed, that they had wondered if the project had arrived at a breaking point. During the meeting, they had been confronted with the tensions that were building within the USPS team.

To their surprise, the DMM group manager and the DMM redesign project leader had a completely different view of the very same meeting. The USPS managers, equipped with a better sense of the personalities in their group, found the overall outcome positive and members of their team to be generally thankful and supportive.

> Some participants expressed their thanks that they were talked to in advance. There was a sense that 'that's the way people do things at the Postal Service'.[24]

This incident shows how the participatory design approach that involved members of the organization in the design activities provided opportunities for the organization to come to terms with the need and the purpose for changes. It also shows that, at times, the design meetings and workshops were less about the design of the prototype than about the restructuring of the organization.

Just what 'participatory design' means in the context of a large and complex organization was not always clear to every participant, and it was a debate even among design students who ran continuously into new challenges. For example, what does it mean to 'provide comments and suggestions', as the DMM staff was continuously encouraged to do? There are several occasions on which the DMM staff members balked at the prototypes because they failed to show the changes that had been made at a previous review session.

> Feedback we got from [DMM]100 [was that] while we asked for feedback from all the departments we never listened to them. [We got] extremely negative feedback even after the book was published. Our department took a few hits for that. That hurt the [DMM]200 process because people were being asked to come back and [provide more feedback.][25]

This sentiment lingers in the first project, during which DMM staff involvement was minimal and surfaces powerfully over the course of the second project, when students actively seek and need the input of the experts. In September 2002, a scheduled prototype review with the DMM staff turns into a confrontation between the design team and the experts. Frustrated that they could not detect the changes they had suggested previously, the DMM staff first critiqued the spread and then the design team.[26] As the manager of the DMM group observed: 'Integrating design into a complex organization is a challenge for both, designers and the USPS.'[27] Difficult it was, but the DMM Transformation Project succeeded in redesigning the Domestic Mail Manual, the 'bible' of the Postal Service and it did so by insisting on human experience and human interaction as organizing principles. This led to the DMM being reorganized around the shape of mail; around considerations of mailers (speed and cost) and around the methods of mailing.

Leadership plays a pivotal role in the DMM Transformation Project. The manager who initiated the project and who supervised the DMM group manager almost immediately moved up to the top executive level. From there she was able to keep the project a priority and ensure visibility within the organization and among customers. She oversaw and supported the work of the design research, endowing the design team with credibility and authority.

Somewhere caught between the demands of the day-to-day operations and the challenges of a dynamic research project was the head of the DMM group. On her shoulders rested the responsibility to get her staff to share in the new vision and to support the design students by participating various workshops, exercises, and document reviews.

Much of the initial success can be traced to the energy the first project manager brought to the table. She had joined the DMM staff just recently and unlike most of the other staff members, had not risen through the organization's internal ranks. She was the one reaching out to other departments, like market development and customer service, thus raising the profile and the participation level within the organization.

But for some in the organization, this approach felt too radical and too fast. There were doubts that someone who did not move up through the ranks understood all the implications. Just a few weeks into the second project phase, the original project manager for the Postal Service resigned and shortly thereafter left the organization. Responsibility for the project was handed over to a senior DMM staff member who generally enjoyed greater acceptance among his own team and within the organization.

Impact on the organization

After reviewing the factors that played a role in the outcome of the project, the question that remains unanswered is the impact the *DMM Transformation Project* had on the organization itself. How did the project touch and change the organization?

Changes involving organization's structure

1　Experts are no longer the gatekeepers of important information, mailing knowledge is accessible to everyone. The DMM Transformation Project has changed the flow of information within the organization.
2　The impact includes a new emphasis on user research and user testing in the process of writing and changing rules.
3　There is a renewed effort to pair internal experts at headquarters with field employees familiar with the problems 'out there' when new rules have to be written.
4　The project's participatory design activities have at least temporarily led to an increase in teamwork among the DMM staff. Redundancy in information reduces redundancy in work for many USPS employees. However, the redundancy also complicates the life and work of the DMM group.
5　The creation of the 'Small Business Marketing Council to serve and address the postal needs of the country's 20 million small businesses' can be interpreted as a direct result and consequence of the work on the DMM200.[28] As with the household mailers, the small business mailers were a group previously not addressed directly by the organization. As Figure 9.1 showed, their pathways typically led through gatekeepers.
6　The restructuring of the Domestic Mail Manual around the needs of customers, beginning with shape of mail, mailing methods and mailing purpose, is now reflected in other USPS communication, most visibly its official website (usps.gov).

Changes involving the organization's vision

1　A major shift occurred as the organization moved the purpose of its activities from one of enforcing and imposing legislation to one of offering tools for customers that enable them to pursue *their* goals using the Postal Service.

2   The project generated a new vision for the DMM. This vision influenced the vision of the overall organization. This is evident from the integration of human-centered design principles into the *USPS Transformation Plan*.
3   Evidence of the new vision taking hold is provided in the invitation to the design team to participate in an ongoing, actual case of rule writing.
4   Mailing as value and the need for the Postal Service to communicate this value to its customers were clarified and became part of the process and result.
6   The project leads other departments within the USPS to envision a rewriting of their own rules and procedures.

Changes involving organizational resources

1   The DMM itself became a resource for the USPS for marketing, customer service and product development purposes.
2   The organization itself turns into a resource for mailers.
3   User research and usability testing turn into resources for future product development and rule writing.
4   The organization adapts human-centered product development as a strategic tool to re-orient the organization around people.
5   Strain on manpower: The project at times 'was inconvenient' for employees. For example, employees resented the notion that the project took priority over other tasks that employees considered even more important. One employee recalls that 'people actually loose friends during a rate case'.
6   Attrition of long-term employees: four people left the DMM group because they did not agree with the project or ran into issues because of the project.
7   The *DMM Transformation Project* freed organizational resources. The new DMM modules, particularly the DMM100 and the DMM200, function as proxies for postal employees, as it reduces contact time with customers, provides consistent answers and satisfies answers to inquiries.

Even DMM staff members who were in favor of the vision and the project had moments during which they doubted the approach. Especially when the project interfered with their other duties and responsibilities, many of which the DMM staff ranked higher in priority, the demands by the project team were viewed as inappropriate. A member of the DMM staff talked about this problem with the author in an interview.

> So sometimes being called upon to answer questions about the project or have input in the project was very inconvenient because of other things that were going on. I remember one particular instance when we were working on a rate case we were talking about FED EX standards that are going to affect the nation when it comes to the postal service. There were times when the project was given precedence over those things. And I sort of had a problem with that.

For the organization and its members, it would have been much easier in the short-run to allocate all of its resources to ongoing routines. Yet, the focus remained on changing the DMM, even at the cost of some short-term gains. This, too, represents the impact the *DMM Transformation Project* had on the organization.

Changes involving people linked to the organization

1 Lower ranked employees were brought in from the field to participate in the project.
2 Longstanding employees left the department because of resistance to the change.
3 Project participants received recognition and promotions.
4 Employees acquired new skills in user research and product development that allow them to write rules for people.
5 Experts learned about the needs for non-expert customers, but they also discovered new opportunities to serve their existing expert customers. The DMM200 surprised the Postal Service with the attention it received from its most sophisticated clients. Those clients were thought to be only interested in topics beyond 'basic' issues of business mail.[29]
6 Employees perceived differently the role and function of the DMM.
7 Employees perceived differently the function and form of communication.

One specialist at the DC headquarters shared how he uses the 26-page DMM100 – the very same book that was belittled by many experts – as both a source for quick information and as an inspiration to better communicate what he has to get across to the customer. In one example he provided, he had received a call from a USPS specialist in rates and classifications.

> And he said: [name] 'Can you just tell me, can you just give me two words?' and I said 'No!' 'No.' 'No.' But the point is, I was going back in history to these customer support rulings that just totally confused the situation. And I could not explain it to him. I was trying hard but it was this, all this old stuff was in my head and I just could not get it across. A lot of times customers call and I can take the [DMM] 100 and read a simple piece in there that explains what is in my head.[30]

The same headquarters specialist points to the organizational implications of improved customer service and more efficient use of employee's work time.

> But if I can break those complex conversations down to something that you under-stand, our conversation is much better, it is shorter, the customer leaves with a good taste in his or her mouth. Right? So the [redesigned DMM] 100 does that.[31]

Figure 9.4 summarizes how research into people, structure, resources and vision progressed from the Pilot Study through the three projects to produce the DMM100, the DMM200, and the DMM300. The figure shows how each project was part of a systematic approach to transform the DMM and with that the organization. In retrospect, each project had a different function in relation to organizational change. The first project invited the organization, the second project engaged, and the third project enabled the organization to complete the changes it sought. The fourth project thus represents the one project the organization and the design team set out to accomplish in the first place. To get there, both the organization and the design team had to diligently and systematically work with people, resources, structures and the vision.

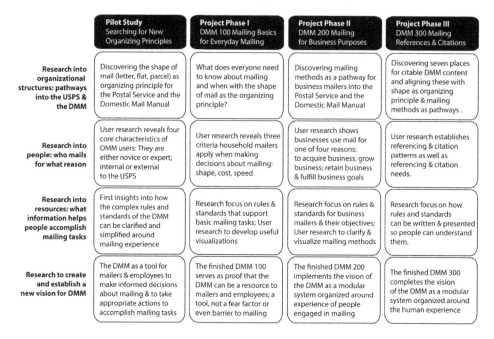

	Pilot Study Searching for New Organizing Principles	**Project Phase I** DMM 100 Mailing Basics for Everyday Mailing	**Project Phase II** DMM 200 Mailing for Business Purposes	**Project Phase III** DMM 300 Mailing References & Citations
Research into organizational structures: pathways into the USPS & the DMM	Discovering the shape of mail (letter, flat, parcel) as organizing principle for the Postal Service and the Domestic Mail Manual	What does everyone need to know about mailing and when with the shape of mail as the organizing principle?	Discovering mailing methods as a pathway for business mailers into the Postal Service and the Domestic Mail Manual	Discovering seven places for citable DMM content and aligning these with shape as organizing principle & mailing methods as pathways .
Research into people: who mails for what reason	User research reveals four core characteristics of DMM users: They are either novice or expert; internal or external to the USPS	User research reveals three criteria household mailers apply when making decisions about mailing: shape, cost, speed	User research shows businesses use mail for one of four reasons: to acquire business; grow business; retain business & fulfill business goals	User research establishes referencing & citation patterns as well as referencing & citation needs.
Research into resources: what information helps people accomplish mailing tasks	First insights into how the complex rules and standards of the DMM can be clarified and simplified around mailing experience	Research focus on rules & standards that support basic mailing tasks; User research to develop useful visualizations	Research focus on rules & standards for business mailers & their objectives; User research to clarify & visualize mailing methods	Research focus on how rules and standards can be written & presented so people can understand them.
Research to create and establish a new vision for DMM	The DMM as a tool for mailers & employees to make informed decisions about mailing & to take appropriate actions to accomplish mailing tasks	The finished DMM 100 serves as proof that the DMM can be a resource to mailers and employees; a tool, not a fear factor or even barrier to mailing	The finished DMM 200 implements the vision of the DMM as a modular system organized around experience of people engaged in mailing	The finished DMM 300 completes the vision of the DMM as a modular system organized around the human experience

Research into People, Structure, Resources and Vision: The DMM Transformation Project

Figure 9.4 Research into people, structure, resources and vision: The DMM Transformation Project

Conclusion

In the *Domestic Mail Manual Transformation Project*, re-organizing the rules and standards of mailing around the experience of customers and employees allowed the organization to move from enforcing and imposing legislation to offering customers and employees a useful tool that enables people to make informed decisions and take appropriate action to use the mailing services of the US Postal Service. The final modular system offers education while it constitutes a reliable reference for citation. The project demonstrated that designing around the human experience and around human interaction implies changes to the organizational system. Changes in this example can be seen in regards to people, structure, resources and vision, though the extent of these changes differs.

This case study illustrates how an organization recognized the redesign of one of its core documents as an opportunity to inquire into the organization, its own organizational design practices and its purpose. The organization made a conscious decision to approach their redesign from a human-centered perspective and to employ design research to turn 'that book' into something customers could use and understand without having to become experts in mailing rules and standards. From the beginning, the idea of creating clear pathways for mailers to accomplish their mailing tasks dominated. The DMM100 and the DMM200 served as milestones and way posts along the path being built.

Three key factors can be identified in the project's successful outcome: A shared vision; an incremental strategy; and a commitment to human-centered product development that emphasizes a participatory design approach. Sharing in a vision that did not specify particulars of a product but that provided general guiding characteristics (making mail easy to use) proved crucial in this effort.

Opportunities for participation in the development were opportunities used to find a common ground of values and vision. Initially these workshops were small and included only the core team at the agency. Over time legal, marketing, product development and other departments were included and thus the 'circle of change' (Rousseau 1995) was increasingly widened.[32] The total number of people involved changed over time. During the Pilot Study, three DMM experts and five students worked together. For the first and second project phase, a total of 22 students (distributed over several semesters) worked with a DMM core team of four experts from headquarters. Workshops, exercises, informational meetings and research sessions at headquarters included all members of the DMM staff (a total of fifteen experts) and about a hundred experts from different departments across the organization.[33] Fifteen design students worked with a core team of five DMM staff on the third project phase. At times, the DMM experts received support by up to five additional members in their group. More people from the Postal Service participated in the second phase of the project than did in the first. In the final third project phase, again fewer members of the Postal Service were involved.

Design research in the organization

The project pushed the frontiers of design research in more than one way. For one, it redefined the concept of co-designing. Traditionally, 'co-designing' or 'participatory design' has been used to describe the involvement of people for whom a design is intended. In a typical product development situation, these people are potential buyers or otherwise external to the organization. Co-designing in the organizational context of this project required the involvement and personal engagement of internal and external people, customers and employees alike. And while co-designing with external customers often means learning from the customer, in the *DMM Transformation Project* it was equally important that employees involved in the designing activities familiarized themselves with design thinking and design methods.[34] This could not have happened without the encouragement and the support of the organization's leadership. But it also required the design team itself to be open about their thinking and doing, and to include organizational staff in their ongoing research activities.

About a year into the project, the USPS project manager and another senior staff member involved in the project from the beginning asked the student team for research protocols and questionnaires so they could lead and conduct their own user research in Washington, D.C.[35] In this case, participatory design required the design team to support the USPS team in conducting their own research. They were eager to employ user research methods they had just acquired. But this also meant risking that the lack of experience with these research methods and their interpretation might lead them to evaluate their findings differently than the design team. Moreover, the design students wondered about the ethical implications and the research validity if senior staff of the organization were to interview lower ranked staff about organizational issues. After one of the first sessions in which DMM staff participated, the student reporting back to the team complimented the professional behavior of the DMM staff members and their ability to elicit valuable information for the project.[36]

Interviews went well, S1 and S2 were very helpful, polite and appropriate in their manner. S2 left the room during interviews with P1 and P2. Both S1 and S2 assisted the [student] interviewers with interpreting questions or teasing out details about projects the interviewers would not know about. They sat quietly in the background and waited until the end of the interview for follow-up questions.[37]

The *DMM Transformation Project* shows that human-centered product development suggests a vulnerable designer. A human-centered designer does not seek to impose a design solution but engages in an inquiry with clients, stakeholders, organizational staff and end-users. As the design methods and the design thinking guiding this project illustrate, the tools designers employed to this end ranged from traditional to innovative but are always thoughtfully selected and applied.

The design way

This example as well as the two following stories of the IRS and the Australian Taxation Office raise questions about the views both the organization and the designers have of designing and how this affects the ability for design to instill changes into the organizational system. Differences become apparent that might help explain the project outcome.

1   Who can and who cannot design?

In the *DMM Transformation Project*, everyone could participate in the design activities. The term used in this case study to distinguish the CMU design team from the DMM group is 'design students'. But not all of the students were members of the design school. In every phase there were members from the English department. It was also a characteristic of the School of Design at Carnegie Mellon to take on graduate students with diverse backgrounds. Not everyone had background in classic design disciplines, like graphic design or industrial design. Students may have possessed previous education and experience as writers, engineers, computer specialists or in crafts. This diverse background ensured a range of talents within the CMU team and also made it easier to relate to members of the organization. The CMU team encouraged the DMM staff and other members of the United States Postal Service to actively participate in the design process. Teamwork did not distinguish between designers and non-designers but between people who engaged with the subject and those who did not.

2   What can and what cannot be designed?

The laws alone, the rules and standards, did not change in this project. Without the support of the organization and its openness to pursue research into areas that emerged as trouble spots, the result would have looked very different. The organization, however, did believe that the experience of the mailer could and should be designed and it understood that experience is shaped by the kinds of products with which people interact.

3   What is the perceived purpose of the design outcome?

The stated and the perceived purpose of the design outcome was to effect and to communicate a change in the relationship between the organization and its customers. From an organizational perspective, the purpose of the DMM Project was to support an ongoing transformation effort. The Postal Service turned to design in an effort to relate people to people. 'We want to have a book that speaks to people' is how the manager of the DMM group explains the purpose of the DMM redesign to a group of managers of business relations, USPS members who are DMM experts.

4 *What does it mean to design?*

Design offers a purposeful research into the organization. The *DMM Transformation Project* turned every stone that seemed to block the intuitive path for users. It questioned particular rules and ended up proposing guidelines for writing rules that people can understand. It questioned the organization around topics and ended up restructuring the book around shapes that people can relate to. It questioned the need for people to know about all rules and ended up delivering a system that tailors the information to specific customer groups. It questioned the value of mail to customers and ended up generating a value statement. It questioned the inconsistent use of terms and ended up generating consistent terminology. The organization and the design team understood designing as an iterative and participatory activity that inquires into people, structure, resources and purpose of the product in development, the DMM.

A decade after completion of this project, the *DMM 100: A Customer's Guide to Mailing* is still available online and continues to serve the organization as well as everyone who seeks to make use of its services. This indicates that the design inquiry led to a substantial and fundamental alignment of the organization's purpose and its services. Designing for and with people inside and outside the organization has been crucial in this outcome.[38]

Notes

1 Author notes from the general team meeting held on June 30, 2003.
2 Author interview with USPS manager of DMM project, May 4, 2004.
3 Ibid.
4 Author notes from team meeting, early fall 2004.
5 Author notes from a PhD team meeting, September 3, 2004. In addition to general team meetings and specific project group team meetings, doctoral students and their professor met to discuss the project and to reflect on ongoing design research.
6 In fact, the two facilitators were key participants in the Australian Taxation Project undertaken by the Australian Tax Office. This project will be discussed in chapter 11.
7 Author interview with DMM staff member, May 5, 2004.
8 New Orleans, April 2003.
9 Author notes of comment made by a 300-level customer during the National Postal Forum in Boston. The customer made the comment after reviewing the first print issue of the DMM100 and after providing feedback on a prototype of the DMM200.
10 Author interview with senior USPS official, May 4, 2004.
11 Member of the group that issues and maintains the DMM, May 4, 2004.
12 Author interview with manager of DMM group, May 4, 2004.
13 See "Adding Extra Services," *DMM 100: A Customer's Guide to Mailing*, p. 8.
14 Author interview with DMM staff member, May 4, 2005.
15 Author interview with DMM staff member, May 5, 2004.
16 Manager DMM group explaining the purpose of the DMM Transformation Project to a group of USPS Managers of Business Relations from New England. September 23, 2002.
17 Author interview with former manager of market development. May 6, 2004.
18 Author interview with DMM staff member, May 5, 2004.
19 In 2004, Gallup sent out 100,000 surveys with a 10% response rate. See Mtg. Minutes 2004 Mailers' Technical Advisory Committee October 27–28.
20 Interview with senior DMM staff member, May 5, 2004.

21 Ibid.
22 Team meeting notes on D.C. stakeholder meeting, September 13, 2002.
23 Ibid.
24 Ibid.
25 Interview with senior DMM staff member, May 5, 2004.
26 The incident occurred on September 23, 2002.
27 Manager DMM group, September 23, 2002.
28 USPS marketing executive Anita Bizzotto, who was the leading force behind the *DMM Transformation Project* and PostCom President Gene Del Polito were introduced as chairs of the council. PostCom Bulletin, July 1, 2005.
29 Interview with manager of the DMM group, May 4, 2004 who said: "And then we went to customers who are not super sophisticated but customers who do more than just retail type business, like your e-bay type customer. And we did one [DMM Guide] that was aimed at small to maybe medium size customer and what we found there is that even the very large customers usually will have customer service groups within their own organization, so they found that book helpful."
30 Author interview with DMM staff member, May 5, 2004.
31 Ibid.
32 Some USPS members brought a keen understanding of the role of prototypes with them. One DMM staff member shared: "The prototypes were great because it is just like writing a song. I have never written a perfect song first time out. I have a very interesting way of writing a song. I have a flip chart at home, an old flip chart with paper, and I actually write the concept out, and I think about that concept and what kinds of sounds I hear from that concept. And basically I go over to my computer hear a couple of things, just to generate sounds to see . . . it always changes, sometimes to the point it is a totally different song from what I started out with."
33 This latter number counts workshops and other sessions with managers of business mail relations, legal experts, market development group and RCNC, etc.
34 Research by Katja Battarbee and Ilpo Koskine also explores the boundaries of co-design and participatory design, See Battarbee, Katja and Koskinen, Ilpo (March, 2005). 'Co-Experience: User Experience as Interaction', *CoDesign*, Taylor and Francis, Vol. 1 (1): 5–18.
35 January 13, 2004: User research undertaken by the postal design team.
36 Notes from team meetings, January 2004.
37 June 30/31, 2003.
38 The latest version is available at http://pe.usps.gov/cpim/ftp/manuals/dmm100/dmm100.pdf.

Reference

Yriö Engeström and Virginia Escalante (2001). 'Mundane Tool or Object of Affection? The Rise and Fall of the Postal Buddy', in B. Nardi (ed.), *Context and Consciousness,* MIT Press, Cambridge, MA, pp. 325–373.

10 The Tax Forms Simplification Project[1]

For the IRS to do its job well, it must start from the perspective of what government is about – namely, it is of the people, by the people, and for the people. The government is funded by taxes paid by the people. Therefore, the future state vision of the IRS needs to be designed around the needs of the people.[2]

To this day, filing and paying annual taxes remains one of the most, literally, 'taxing' tasks citizens and residents face every year. From Denmark to Germany, from the US to the UK, many governments have begun to seek ways to reduce the burden involved in reporting taxes by citizens and businesses. And many have put pressure on their tax administrations to make tax compliance easier. Improving tax services reduces cost for tax administrations, increases the flow of revenues and contributes to greater satisfaction of citizens with their governments. Likewise, well intended tax policies, like any other public policy, depend on services people can access, understand and use to achieve their aims. None of this happens when the government agency responsible for these services lacks the capability and knowledge to develop such services.

This chapter provides insights into the story of a remarkable public sector innovation project. The following pages detail how the *US Internal Revenue Service* (IRS) was instructed by the US Congress to hire design expertise to make life easier for tax payers. Known as the *Tax Forms Simplification Project,* this project demonstrates the need for a broader design understanding in the public sector. In this case, external designers brought with them a limited perspective on design, which effectively excluded members of the organization from participating in developing a solution. Moreover, the design team, despite its cutting edge methods at the time, was not prepared to connect their own work with existing design practices in this organization. The fact that this project was undertaken nearly 40 years ago points to the continuous relationships and role of design in the public sector. In addition, the case provides lessons and insights into issues of designing for, with and by that have particular relevance for today's efforts at public sector innovation by design.

A brief introduction to the IRS

In the US, the Internal Revenue Service, or short, 'the IRS', was founded in 1862 to enforce current tax laws. The agency is a bureau of the Department of the Treasury. Today, the U.S. government relies on the IRS to ensure that all individuals and businesses are paying their fair share to keep the government operational and to fulfill their social obligations. The numbers the agency has to cope with are staggering and growing every year. In 2014, the agency collected more than three trillion dollars in revenue and processed more than 240 million tax returns.[3] Because the US tax system is based on voluntary compliance built around trust, confidence in the IRS and in the tax system – as well as in government more broadly – are essential for public life.

How much people trust the IRS is directly linked with how many people report their taxable income. A high compliance rate translates directly into income for government. At the 2016 Budget Request Hearings, IRS Commissioner John Koskinen explained the financial consequences of even minor increases in non-compliance for the US: 'A 1 percent decline in the compliance rate costs the government 30 billion annually.' Clearly, the IRS serves a key role in American government and in American society. Its responsibility for achieving compliance and for fulfilling its role in the US government depends on services people can access, understand and use. IRS services include information that helps taxpayers calculate the amount of taxes they owe, as well as when and how to pay their dues. For every tax season, the IRS prepares tax forms and instruction manuals that reflect and explain all changes in the tax law. Another service the IRS provides to the public is statistical information about taxpayers, tax income and tax spending. The IRS may be one of the most scrutinized government agencies. For every step of its operations, it remains accountable to politics and the public.

There is general agreement that the US tax code is too complex. What is often overlooked is that it is not just too complicated for taxpayers. It is just as complicated for staff, which sometimes has to cope with more than one change to the tax laws *per day*. For example, there were 579 changes in the tax year that ended April 15, 2015.[4] Every change had to be incorporated in the materials taxpayers receive. Every single change has consequences for certain taxpayers and how they report taxes. Most changes require an adjustment or update to an existing tax form.

Despite its significant role and work, the IRS continuously faces pressure to spend as little as possible on collecting taxes so that the bulk of the tax revenue remains available to government for investments in the nation's infrastructure, economic and social programs.[5] New technologies, especially electronic filing, have seen the agency reduce its workforce significantly over the past decades. According to the *Transactional Records Access Clearinghouse,* a non-partisan research center at Syracuse University, the number of IRS staff has continuously declined since 1988 while the returns the agency processes annually have steadily increased over the same period.[6] Between 2010 and 2014 alone, the IRS has lost over thirteen thousand employees.[7] The situation was exacerbated after an internal scandal in 2013 when the IRS faced an accusation of targeting specific political groups.[8] With fewer staff, changing expectations and more demands, the IRS has to look for new ways to enable citizens to fulfill their obligation to society in an easy and simple way. Once again, this involves the development and delivery of services. To report income and to calculate taxes, the IRS prepares forms individuals fill in. But it does way more than that: it designs pathways for taxpayers to accomplish the task of paying taxes. For the IRS, the challenge is to create clear pathways through the tax jungle that enable everyday people to fulfill their tax obligations in a way they can understand. But the design practices and design methods employed by the IRS over time failed to produce this outcome.

Design under scrutiny at the IRS

From the 1940's, printed forms were the only means for government to collect information from anyone required to comply with US laws. The designs for how to go about collecting data from citizens where the responsibility of each government agency. Since the staff at the IRS was responsible for gathering tax relevant data, it was also in charge of designing everything that was needed to accomplish this task. In this pursuit, staff developed and designed forms around the needs of their organizations. Little attention was paid to the needs, knowledge, circumstances or experiences of those who had to fill in information. Empathy with people reporting taxes, while not completely absent, rarely figured into organizational design decisions. Few tax experts comfortable with technical terms thought it necessary to adjust their language to that of tax layman. Most applied technical language out of habit, because they did not know what else to do. Others took pride in their expertise and thought of it as a mark of distinction.

By the late 1970s, complaints by individual citizens, businesses and associations about requirements to provide information to government reached a new high. In addition, a 1975 study revealed that four out of ten American adults struggled to perform the 'typical computational tasks of daily life'. Yet, the income tax forms at the time confronted people with complex calculations. Eventually, this led to the demand for new income tax forms that were easy to read and use across a spectrum of income and educational levels.[9] In 1977, President Jimmy Carter issued an Executive Order to the effect that all government agencies ought to be 'cost-effective and easy-to-understand by those who were required to comply with them.' Earlier, in 1971, President Richard Nixon had already called for the *Federal Register* to be 'written in layman's terms'. There was also a conference held in 1978 on Tax Forms Simplification.

The IRS was an easy and obvious target when it came to complaints about paperwork for citizens. For years, the agency had struggled to provide taxpayers with tax forms they could understand. The General Accounting Office (GAO) acknowledged these efforts in its 1978 report on the Internal Revenue Service's efforts to provide simpler tax forms to the American people.[10] For example, the readability of the most common tax forms and instructions had been reduced to an eighth grade level, and the explanation of specific tax items had been redrafted with a view towards simplification. But the GAO also concluded that any further simplifications that were 'needed and possible' to reduce the burden on taxpayers required expertise the IRS did not have within its own ranks. As a consequence, the GAO demanded the IRS seek external design expertise to 'further simplify' its tax forms.[11]

About a year later, in September 1979, the Department of Education funded research into document design in the public sector. Aptly named the *Document Design Project*, its task was 'to study the problems in public documents and to get help for Federal agencies that wanted to implement plain language.' The Project's goal was to increase the knowledge and skills of people who produce public documents. The *Document Design Project* had three tasks: Its first task was to conduct theoretical and applied research studies on language comprehension on 1) the ways in which skilled and unskilled writers work; on problems associated with different document features; 2) to bring research into practice by working directly with government agencies as they produce materials for public use and 3) to bring research and practice into education by developing courses on writing and design for graduate students and under-graduates.[12]

The *Document Design Project* eventually ran for three years, from 1978 to 1981, and involved 19 US government agencies. It was run as a design research project where design professionals from the New York design firm Siegel & Gale collaborated with language experts from Carnegie Mellon University in Pittsburgh, Pennsylvania and the not-for-profit *American Institutes for Research* in Washington, DC, to develop improved government forms and along with instructions people could understand and follow. The researchers weeded through regulations as well as agency guidelines and legal notices. In addition, they reviewed a wide range of government publications, such as booklets, brochures, and patient labels to identify opportunities for improving legibility and accessibility. Various workshops and seminars introduced government employees to principles of plain language, easier layout and better writing. A seminar that taught 150 tax law specialists about clear writing provides a sense of the magnitude of the Document Design Project across the 19 government agencies. Among the many outcomes of this project are the *Federal Communications Commission Rules for Marine Radios*, the *Housing & Urban Development Rules for the Privacy Act*, and forms and instructions for student financial assistance.

In retrospect, the *Document Design Project* set the stage for the Tax Forms Simplification Project. It presented the IRS with a first opportunity to revise documents (for example, its Spanish language tax publications) and provided a glimpse into the possibilities of rewriting publications (such as the one on Individual Retirement Accounts, or 'IRAs'). For the research team, reviewing the tax forms and to 'work with staff to rewrite instructions for Forms 1040, 1040A, 4684, and Schedules A, B, C, E, R, and RP' offered an opportunity to pioneer new research methods (i.e., field testing for form design) and to practice design in an area where design has consequences for millions of people. The scope of the *Document Design Project* and its significance for design research in the public sector is evident in the summary provided by the design team after its conclusion. In its own words, the design team

- performed linguistic analyses and critiques of all types of documents, diagnosing problems and making recommendations for revisions. In doing this, we took into account the audience for the document and the system which created the document and in which the document functions.
- edited and helped rewrite documents of all types according to our research-based guidelines for clear writing.
- worked directly with agency staff on specific documents to build their capacity in clear writing.
- performed graphic analyses of forms, brochures, and other documents, providing recommendations for redesign based on research-based guidelines and sound graphic principles.
- helped agencies to redesign public-use forms and other documents, taking into account the audience and the system.
- helped agencies to evaluate their documents to find out how usable and understandable they are.
- helped agency staff design studies, create test instruments, analyze data and interpret results.[13]

This summary reveals that the Document Design Project, undertaken several decades ago, foresaw the need and opportunities for designers to engage with the public sector and vice versa. Moreover, the project already identified participatory design ('working with staff') and their impact on the organization ('capacity building') as key to improving tax forms for citizens. Nonetheless, the focus remained on the forms and the design of the forms. That is, capacity building focused on education about graphic, visual and cognitive skills. Though the *Document Design Project* produced valuable *Guidelines for Document Designers,* these guidelines specified the role of design at the IRS to be concerned with the four core principles for clear writing: 1) Principles for Organizing Text; 2) Principles for Writing Sentences; 3) Typographic Principles; and 4) Graphic Principles (Locke 2004).[14] Figure 10.1 provides a timeline of these.

A new law calls for further action

The IRS was keenly aware that the way it interacted and engaged with taxpayers would not be tolerated for much longer. Alerted and reprimanded by the GAO to make changes, the IRS had already sent the call for tenders for the Tax Forms Simplification Project when President Jimmy Carter signed the *Paperwork Reduction Act* December 11, 1980. The original Act defined burden imposed on citizens by government

> . . . as including the time, effort, or financial resources expended to generate, maintain, or provide information to or for a federal agency. Paperwork burden is commonly measured in terms of 'burden hours', reflecting the amount of time agencies estimate it will take nonfederal entities to comply with their information collection requirements.[15]

The *Paperwork Reduction Act* had far-reaching implications across all government institutions. It illustrates how a policy change puts new demands on government agencies that are charged with developing and delivering the kinds of services necessary to achieve the policy's intent. Language emerged as a first line of attack to improve cumbersome forms marked by technical and legal terms few people outside the IRS could make sense of.

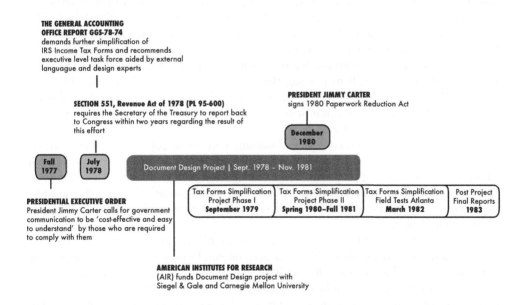

THE IRS TAX FORMS SIMPLIFICATION PROJECT: DEVELOPMENTS IN DESIGN & GOVERNMENT

Figure 10.1 The IRS Tax Forms Simplification Project: developments in design and government

The *Plain English Movement* had already sprung up in English language departments within universities. 'Plain English' aims to remove or in the least reduce linguistic barriers for people. Sometimes referred to as 'Plain Language', it is a call to express complex ideas and procedures in words and sentence structures people can understand without being experts in a given area. To achieve this, 'Plain English' avoids legal wordings and acronyms.[16] Moreover, it had demonstrated its potential in the *Document Design Project* and had become a cornerstone of the *Document Design Guidelines*.[17] 'Plain English' can be viewed as an early attempt at human-centered product development within Federal agencies. Its impact on government over time is well documented by Joanne Locke (2004).[18] The principles and methods of Plain English continue to apply to all areas of communication and information design today. Figure 10.1 offers a timeline of these developments.

A task force and a call for proposing design improvements

In an effort to satisfy the GAO recommendation, the IRS set up an Executive Level Task Force. This Task Force, referred to either as the *Tax Forms Simplification Control Group*, or the *Long Range Tax Forms Simplification Group*, was led by the Tax Commissioner and involved all senior IRS officials at the time. Its first duty was to issue a *Request for Proposal* (RFP) that invited external potential contractors to analyze, restructure, and simplify the tax reporting system used by individuals.

The RFP emphasized the need for a comprehensive overhaul of the entire system – not simply cosmetic changes of the most frequently used forms.[19] It called for proposals 'to mount a comprehensive evaluation and redesign of the entire system of individual tax forms and instructions'. This system included not only the 1040 'long form' and the 1040A 'short form' with their instructions, but some 60 ancillary forms and schedules that could be filed together with both 1040 forms.

Siegel & Gale had just demonstrated their competences as participant in the *Document Design Project*. The design firm put together a design consortium design that included Deloitte, Haskins & Sells, a tax consulting firm as well as a previous client; Yankelovich, Skelly, and White, a market research firm also with previous ties to Siegel & Gale and J&F, experts in usability and readability.

Usability experts focused on the general usability needs of taxpayers. Readability experts brought cognitive skills to the team. For the IRS, this expertise gave the consortium an advantage over competing proposals. The easier a form could be read, the faster someone could fill it in, the better the IRS could comply with the *Paperwork Reduction Act*. In addition, language, usability and readability were testable and measurable, unlike visual aspects of document design.

The team tackling *Tax Forms Simplification* for the IRS thus consisted of cutting edge experts in language, cognition, visualization, and content. Its proposal called for simplifying the *entire* system of income tax forms. This comprehensive approach was novel, as it brought in all different facets of how people approach, read, and fill in income tax forms. In addition, the consortium's proposal addressed the need for measuring and evaluating the developing forms with extensive usability tests and user research. For the IRS, already in a tough spot with taxpayers on the one hand and the General Accounting Office on the other, the elements of testing were reassuring because putting out any new form without knowing that it would be better than the previous version was a risk too big to take.

Members of the Design Consortium for the IRS Tax Forms Simplification Project

Figure 10.2 Members of the design consortium

In September of 1979, this design consortium received a two-year contract.[20] Figure 10.2 provides an overview of the consortium, its members and their respective expertise.

The IRS was acutely aware of the difficulties – or the 'perceived difficulty' as some IRS executives insisted even years later – of its tax forms that prevented many people from filing their taxes themselves.[21] The IRS knew that many people preferred to hire a tax expert whom they trusted more with their tax situation than the IRS itself. In the words of a former IRS official: 'U.S. taxpayers tend to be suspicious that the IRS only tells them what is good for the IRS but holds back with information that is beneficial to the taxpayer.'[22] Referring to people's actual difficulties merely as 'perceived' difficulties, however, exposes a view within the IRS that taxpayers are at fault for failing to understand tax forms and tax procedures. For many IRS members then, the citizen was the problem. Poor design of tax forms or confusing tax procedures, all of which IRS staff had the powers to change, were rarely recognized as culprits. Instead, IRS staff simply did not trust taxpayers to have the ability to understand tax laws and tax forms. No design in the world would remedy that!

The design team immediately proposed three 'broad phases' for the original two-year contract.[23] Each phase centered on a distinct project task. *Phase I* was to conduct research into and identify problems with existing income tax forms. *Phase II* would see the development of alternative approaches to income tax form design. *Phase III* would be dedicated to the development of actual system components that the IRS could implement *if it so chose to do*. After completion of *Phase III*, the new tax forms would be tested and evaluated by independent experts from the design and taxation industries.[24] The intent of the project structure was to enable the consortium to conceive of and to develop an 'entirely new, totally integrated system of tax forms, schedules, and instructions to be used by individual taxpayers.'[25]

Figure 10.3 maps the participants and their roles in the project. It also maps the primary interactions among the different participants. The graph shows that the project assumed a prominent role within the organization early on and involved IRS staff on many levels.[26] Given this situation, the project provided a possibility for systems–wide organizational

STRUCTURE OF IRS TAX FORMS SIMPLIFICATION PROJECT & TASKS

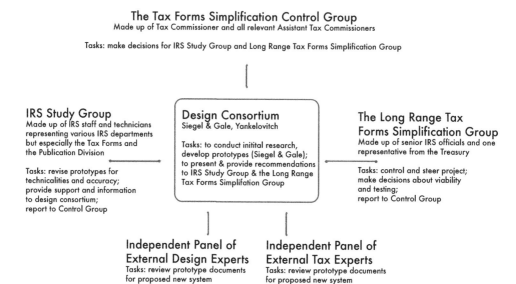

Figure 10.3 Structure of IRS Tax Forms Simplification Project and tasks

change. However, this possibility was not realized and the question is why not. The answer involves organizational design practices and a disagreement over the meaning of simplification, which I will explain below.

Vague success criteria and differences in interpretation of task

The design team understood that the IRS had entrusted the consortium with the investigation into a new system for tax forms. As the design team saw it, the purpose of the Tax Forms Simplification Project was to 'permit all taxpayers to prepare their taxes efficiently and accurately, while availing themselves of all the tax benefits to which they are entitled.' It was to do so while accommodating the 'statutory complexity' of the Internal Revenue Code and respecting the printing, distribution, and processing requirements for IRS documents. It further had to take into consideration that the newly developed system 'be cost-effective to administer and be superior enough to the existing system to justify change.' But being 'superior enough' to 'justify change' are like moving targets in the absence of clear articulation of success. This oversight would come to haunt the design team and the project. The fact that the IRS had not committed to implement any of the solutions resulting from the project – but could 'choose to do so' – posed another foreseeable problem.

From the beginning, the IRS held a radically different view about the purpose of the project and the meaning of the task: simplifying tax forms. The IRS, 'simplification' was mostly concerned with achieving internal goals: First and foremost, the agency sought to comply with the GAO recommendations and the *Paperwork Reduction Act*. This was important politically. Second, the redesign of tax forms promised significant operational benefits. Every error made by taxpayers filing the 1040 and 1040A income tax forms resulted in cost and/or a loss for the IRS. The more errors taxpayers made in their returns, the more work had to be done by the agency to correct them. Inaccurate calculations kept IRS staff busy figuring out the error, reporting the error to the taxpayer, providing information about how to appeal the IRS finding, and possibly engage in the appeal process. Error management absorbed capacity at the IRS that prevented it from tending to other important issues.

The Tax Forms Simplification Project promised improvements on both levels. Thus, simplification in the eyes of the IRS staff was a matter of numbers: a question of reducing the number of lines and the number of pages for each tax form. Less paper would translate into cost savings on material resources, printing and distribution costs, and the like. It was from this internal organizational perspective that the IRS approached the issue of simplification and perceived the role and task of design. In the mind of at least some IRS staff, 'simplification' meant to 'idiot proof' the complexities of the tax forms. IRS staff remained focused on its internal needs and experiences.

This constitutes a very different approach to arrive at easy to read and use tax forms, than, for example, an attempt to clearly communicate complex rules and laws to a user with average intellect. Barnett makes this very point in his 2003 essay 'How Do You Know If Your Forms Fail?'[27] The design team, in contrast, interpreted the task of *Tax Forms Simplification* as one of restructuring if not re-orienting the tax form system around taxpayers. Simplification for the designers derived from the ease of use experienced by taxpayers filing their returns. Once the design team realized the two different interpretations at work, it made great efforts to challenge the IRS' notion of simplification and to argue for a different understanding.

'Simplification does not necessarily mean fewer or shorter documents. A common misperception about language simplification is that it always results in less paper. But briefer doesn't always mean simpler. The simplified short form, for example, has two sides instead of one, and the tax package itself is somewhat longer than the one currently issued by the IRS.'[28]

Disagreement over the meaning of simplification would not form the only point of contention. Even the issue of who should get credit for the final accomplishment, the 1040 EZ – the shortest and simplest income tax form even today – remains in dispute. Both the design team and former IRS members continue to claim it as their respective intellectual property.[29] In defiance of the GAO, which had judged the IRS as incapable of designing simpler tax forms, the IRS staff developed the 1040EZ secretly in-house. IRS staff did so without consulting or informing the design team. Not even the sole staff member in charge of the project for the IRS was in the know. Yet, senior IRS members encouraged by the (new) tax commissioner had begun to develop their own competing version of a 'simple' tax form.

This situation points to the lack of co-design and participatory design methods in the Tax Forms Simplification Project. Instead of creating synergies with staff in the IRS, the design consortium and especially the designers worked in ways that promoted an atmosphere of 'us' against 'them'. Both the design team and the IRS are using these words when they talk about the project. To this day, IRS staff involved in the development of the 1040EZ feel they never received due credit for the contributions they made to the final design. At the same time, former members of the design team insist that the resulting 1040EZ tax form could not have been built without their research and design work. In a sign that designing tends to have an organizational impact even in cases where this is not understood or admitted by staff, the scale tips towards the design team: When the IRS staff justified its preference for their self-generated in-house design solution over that developed by the external design consortium, it argued that this final solution considered and addressed all of the design team's research findings.[30]

Advanced design methods, user research and user testing

Given that the Tax Forms Simplification Project took place nearly four decades ago, the wide range of cutting edge methods employed in this project may come as a surprise to some designers today. The design consortium built on the insights generated and lessons gained during the Document Design Project. In addition, it adhered to an iterative design process and continued to expand its use of user research methods, field tests and other novel approaches to design. Here is a brief summary and discussion of these methods and approaches:

- *Adhering to an iterative process:* Product development began early and continuously underwent evaluation and testing.
- *Conducting user research within the organization:* One of the first things S&G did was to interview stakeholders about what they thought were the strengths and weaknesses of the existing forms. This included a survey of the IRS's previous simplification efforts and interviews with IRS personnel. It also included visits to District Offices and Service Centers whose staff had direct contact with taxpayers.
- *Conducting user research with regular tax filers:* The consortium recruited testers by making phone calls and screening potential testers nominally to ensure that the participants were indeed 1040A users (which meant that they had very little knowledge about taxes and little experience with forms in general).
- *Scenario development:* The consortium, together with its liaison in the IRS, developed simulation test scenarios that were then used in tests with common taxpayers. These tests were conducted by Yankelovich and Partners, using existing and proposed instructions to compare their ease of use.
- *Stakeholder buy-in:* In the summer as forms were being mocked up, tax preparer groups received confidential packages so they were seeing what changes were coming in and to allow them to train their people on the new forms.
- *User testing:* The prototypes were tested regularly with regular tax payers and tax experts. Sometimes these tests took place in malls with people recruited there. There were focus group testing and simulation testing session in San Francisco and Denver. A large field test ('live-tests' during tax season) was conducted for the new 1040 EZ in Atlanta.
- *Oral and visual presentations to the organization:* Siegel and Gale presented their work with overhead transparencies and brought in people from design expert panels to evaluate, comment on, and discuss the findings for their client.
- *Written reports:* Much of the project communication occurred via written reports on the status, developments and background of the project addressed to different organizational levels. Since the design methods and activities did not include the direct involvement of the organization, the role of the IRS was to control the cost and steer the course of the project and make decisions about the recommendations

and proposals brought forward by the design team. Thus the interaction between the design team and the IRS project members was a formal one with few points of contact.

The division of labor proves problematic

Despite efforts and opportunities to collaborate more closely throughout the project, all indications point to a lack of engagement between the organization and the design team. Methods compiled from documents and personal accounts of former project members from both the design team and the IRS paint a picture of a clear 'division of labor' (Smith 1904) that creates and maintains boundaries around the product (tax form) and the organization.[31] The design team was happy to focus on what it considered to be 'designerly' work: the redesign of the tax forms. While it planned and conducted design activities around taxpayers it did not involve users in the organization once the initial round of interviews was completed. The purpose of these interviews, it appears, merely served the design team to answer some of the questions it had. The interviews were not intended as part of relationship building or meant to involve staff in the design work. Instead, the design team treated the organization mostly as a client. This client was presented with findings, recommendations and a solution. Assuming that solid arguments and rational evidence would speak for themselves, the design team expected to persuade the organization with the final design.

In contrast, 'evidence' for the IRS leadership meant a demonstration that the organization could handle the shift, that the new design would not put any more demands on already shrinking resources, overloaded structures and hardly manageable processes. It was these criteria the IRS was looking to evaluate the final solution.

In the beginning, this division of labor offered a comfortable way to work for both sides. The design team was left to focus exclusively on its cutting edge design research. Likewise, the IRS was able to concentrate on organizational matters and political aspects. However, it was a set-up that was not suitable to achieving the objectives of this project as the following phase-by-phase review illustrates. With both sides unprepared to work together on this design task, the process was fraught with frictions and misunderstandings. The outcome, though presentable, remained far from fulfilling its innovative potential. When design concerns public services and public organizations, the loss is not limited to those involved in the design process. It has direct consequences for the people, here taxpayers.

Discovering tax filing status as organizing principle

Phase I, analysis and recommendation (September 1979)

The design consortium started its work by conducting 'a variety of developmental and research efforts.'[32] This research produced findings about the core problems of the two income tax forms, the 1040 and the 1040A. During this phase, Siegel & Gale delegated much of the user research tasks to team members from Yankelovich, Skelly and White. Thus personal conversations with taxpayers and tax experts, including interviews with IRS staff at headquarters and in local Service Centers took place in isolation from the analysis of current tax forms. Siegel and Gale meanwhile applied their graphic and Plain English expertise to analyze the existing tax forms for their strengths and weaknesses. In addition, the design team studied the general IRS and technical tax framework. For this they worked together with tax experts from Deloitte, Haskins, and Sells.

This initial research generated two important findings. The first produced a new organizing principle centered on taxpayers. The design team identified a taxpayers filing status as the key entrance point for the new tax system. In a second discovery, the design team found that a third medium length tax form was missing that could mitigate life for millions of taxpayers. Within the IRS, the first finding was an appreciated and easily accepted insight, recalls the organization's design liaison at the time.

'I remember it [the filing status] was not clearly described upfront even though this is one of the most important things one needs to know from the beginning. This may have been brought by S&G.'[33]

However, opinions quickly split on the second conclusion, the call for a new intermediate tax form. Nonetheless, Siegel & Gale received encouragement to develop this new form that would represent a significant change in the tax form *system*. Phase I therefore ended with three concrete action items to be pursued in Project Phase II. These included:

1   Customize the tax forms and instructions according to taxpayers' filing status (i.e., head of household, single, married filing single and married filing jointly)
2   Redesign the forms and instructions
3   Develop a new income tax form for taxpayers who no longer qualify for the 1040A (the shortest and simplest tax form at the time) but whose tax situation is not nearly as complex as the long 1040 form they have to fill out.

Dueling design approaches and design competencies

Phase II, prototype development (spring 1980 to fall 1981)

In Phase II, the design team moved forward to develop and implement its vision for a three-tiered tax forms system. A question emerged around how to present these forms to the taxpayers. The design team proposed that the IRS offer nine distinct income tax form *packages* to tax payers. Each package itself would be customized to a particular filing status. A taxpayer filing single would receive a package tailored to her needs while an individual being married but filing single would receive a package with information and forms relevant to his situation.

The IRS team immediately questioned the feasibility of this plan and expressed a strong preference for a 'consolidated' version: a single tax form package that would contain the information and instructions *for all tax filing statuses*. In this case, every tax payer would receive the same package but only select the forms and materials appropriate for his tax situation. Simply put, the IRS staff was terrified by the thought of having to manage and maintain nine different packages with an ever-smaller workforce. This was an early indication that the design team's vision for the redesign of the forms had not translated in a rethinking of the larger organizational vision. It was also an early sign that a new tax form system could not be implemented without the participation of IRS employees.

The design team's vision for customized tax packages was further challenged when a new Tax Commissioner came to office. The previous Tax Commissioner, Jerome Kurtz, seemed supportive of the design team's attempt to design an overall system for income tax forms. Former project members feel that this support vanished when Roscoe L. Egger succeeded Jerome Kurtz as Tax Commissioner in 1980. The new Tax Commissioner had close links with the tax industry. It was rumored that he was more interested in maintaining a solid customer base for the tax preparer industry. Too much simplification might have possibly cut into their business. True or not, Egger did look for arguments against individually tailored tax information.

Egger instructed the *Long Range Tax Forms Simplification Study Commissioner's Control Group* (the name is worthwhile savoring) to investigate if taxpayers did *significantly* better when they received only those income tax forms and instructions that were newly customized to their tax filing status. Or, alternatively, if they did *significantly worse* when they received a newly designed consolidated package that included instructions for all tax filing statuses.

The answer to this question carried enormous weight for the organization. If the difference in performance by taxpayers would be significant, the IRS would see an increase in tax sheets it needed to produce and maintain. It would also need to sort the recipients of the tax packages according to filing status. A clearly preferred situation for the IRS would be to send every taxpayer the same tax package and leave the task of sorting through the information to the individual.

The issue of 'customized' versus 'consolidated' tax packages became such a big concern for the organization that it decided to put all further development of the 1040-Intermediate on hold until tests would prove which approach (customized or consolidated) was more successful.[34] The 1040-Intermediate was envisioned as a new form that would simplify life for taxpayers whose tax situation was slightly more complicated than what the short 1040A allowed but far less complicated than what the long 1040 assumed.

Research by the design team had shown that the addition of a third form that covered these in-between tax situations would allow millions of taxpayers to file their taxes in less time and with less effort. From the perspective of the organization, however, the introduction of a third form threatened an additional workload. The IRS was prepared to see through the re-design of the short tax form 1040A and the long tax form 1040. But it was not ready for another new tax form for which it would have to be responsible as well.

In the face of ever-smaller budgets and shrinking staff numbers, these two design developments were bound to alarm at least some people within the organization. It is not easy to establish today the exact resentments towards the 1040-Intermediate, but it seems that the question of consolidated versus customized packaging of tax information was a welcome opportunity for the IRS to pull the brakes on the looming third tax form.

The effect on the design team was immediate and devastating. In the eyes of the design team, the organization was dismissing and disregarding all the research results and findings the team had produced up to this point. Adding insult to injury, the Tax Commissioner 'one day mused about an old form' that could be turned into a third tax form.[35] The IRS junior staff member, to whom the Siegel & Gale team directly reported, remembers Tax Commissioner Egger asking: 'Could we not go back to the really simple postcard?' To the amazement of the junior staff, his immediate superior proudly responded: 'We are already working on that.'[36] Caught by surprise and utterly confused, the junior staff sought to get some clarity as he walked out the door with his boss. 'When', he inquired, 'had that form development begun?' He was in for another surprise (as well as for a lesson in organizational politics) when his superior responded: 'Just now.'

Ironically, this meant that the IRS had bought into the fairly radical idea proposed by the design team: to address the needs of '20-odd million taxpayers.'[37] Instead of following the design team's recommendation to develop a new intermediate form, the IRS returned to an earlier idea of a simple postcard to replace the short form and to expand the current short form (1040A) into an intermediate form.

According to a former official who was involved in the project, this was the point when 'the IRS turned the table.' IRS employees took back their design authority and insisted on applying its design competencies. Up till then, the Siegel & Gale team would present their findings and prototypes and 'run them by' the IRS Study Group, the Tax Forms Simplification Control Group and others. Now it was the IRS taking the initiative.[38]

Return to previous organizational design practices

Phase III, user testing

In March 1982, the IRS moved forward with its plan to subject the design prototypes to a large field test with 30,000 tax filers in America's Southeast. The agency halted all further forms development pending the outcome of this field test in Atlanta, Georgia, with 43,427 randomly selected taxpayers. Of the 43,427 questionnaires mailed out in Atlanta, 4,118 'usable' questionnaires were voluntarily submitted to the IRS. The test found that taxpayers had almost no preference as to a consolidated or customized tax package. Of the 4,118 returned questionnaires, 1,537 had chosen to file taxes using the consolidated 1040S and 1,469 had chosen to file their taxes using the customized 1040S. The remaining 1,112 filed the old 1040A. Despite the obvious numerical results, which the IRS interpreted to be preferences, the test revealed little about how long a filer spent on each form or how accurate the information was the person filled in.

This test was perceived as a blow by the design team and the solution it was still developing. The design team struggled with this decision because its prototypes were still incomplete works in progress and ill-suited for the kind of affirmative and ultimate evidence the IRS desired. Stunned with this obvious lack of understanding on the IRS side of how an iterative design process works, the team felt a need to respond with a detailed report on the project, revisiting the background, the development, and the status of the Tax Forms Simplification Project.[39]

In this report, the designers reiterate their initial assignment, defend their accomplishments so far, and articulate their goals for the future and their concerns. The design team gives voice to their concern that further testing 'risks losing momentum.'[40] In an attempt to remind the organization of the larger purpose of the project, the design team reiterates that the Request for Proposal (RFP) sent out by the IRS in 1978 'asked potential contractors to analyze, restructure, and simplify the tax reporting system used by the individuals.'[41] The design team acknowledges and commends the efforts already made by the IRS to simplify the forms.

'The RFP noted that forms simplification undertaken by the IRS in recent years had focused on isolated areas. For example, the readability of the most common tax forms and instructions had been reduced to an eighth grade level, and the explanation of specific tax items had been redrafted with a view towards simplification.'[42]

But it points out that these efforts have remained fragmented and not comprehensive enough. In the words of the design team, the IRS has not been able 'to mount a comprehensive evaluation and redesign of the entire system of individual tax forms and instructions.'[43] For these reasons, the designers appealed to the IRS to see the Tax Forms Simplification Project as an opportunity to redesign the *entire system* of tax forms, instructions and supplements as a whole.

An achievement or a disappointment?

On September 20, 1983, the IRS drafted a final report on the *Long-Range Tax Forms Simplification Study* of which the Tax Forms Simplification Project became the cornerstone. Tax Commissioner Roscoe L. Egger included the findings in his Report to Congress, celebrating among the many achievements of the Tax Forms Simplification Project 'a step-by step approach' and 'a new layout' of the tax forms.[44]

The *Final Report* of the *IRS Long Range Tax Forms Simplification Study Group* proudly included a copy of the *Certificate of Excellence* the *American Institute of Graphic Arts* awarded the new tax forms. The IRS had delivered what the GAO had asked for: new tax forms. A former project member from the IRS explains what the achievements looked like from an operational perspective. For him, the Tax Forms Simplification Project[45]

- Successfully brought down reading levels.
- Introduced user testing, 'which was not that easy because the tax forms people did not see a need for that but when I talked to the IRS customer service group, they immediately recognized its value.'
- Led to new instructions that were easier to fill out, caused people to make fewer errors, and reduced the time it took them to fill in the tax forms.
- Led to the discovery of error pattern with forms. 'This was new. For the first time, we could say there is a problem with line 11 or so.'
- Led to the identification of sticky spots in our new forms 'that we then improved with better language.'

About a month later, in October 1983, the design team drafted its own final report on ninety-six-pages. The *Final Report Tax Forms Simplification Project, Prepared by Siegel & Gale* is much less celebratory and expresses disappointment with the project and the organization. In it, the design team mourns a 'lost opportunity for major simplification' and considers the findings 'extremely disappointing.'[46] According to the design team, the IRS

> . . . chose to select bits and pieces of our simplification concepts and overlay them on existing forms. The resulting amalgam falls far short of the comprehensive simplification that the project sought to achieve and represents an irretrievably lost opportunity for fundamental simplification.[47]

In their view, the report by the IRS does not do justice to the scope of the project and the development and abandonment of the intermediate form. Specific complaints include:

- 'The report was far too limited in scope. The report fails to capture the three years of progressive simplification the project achieved and focuses almost exclusively on the mechanics of the Atlanta field test.'
- 'The report gives short shrift to the Intermediate Form, an extremely viable approach that contained some of the project team's most advanced concepts in forms simplification. No mention is made of why the approach was abandoned.'
- 'The report fails to clarify the important distinction between error rates – which are basically mathematical – and accuracy of completion, which measures whether

correct information is entered in the first place. In addition, the report fails to project the significance of reduced error rates and improved accuracy, which can both substantially reduce taxpayer burden and provide cost benefits to the IRS.'

- 'The report ignores the significance of reduced completion time and favorable taxpayer response, both of which have a direct impact on taxpayers' ability and willingness to prepare their own tax returns.'

The report by the design team reveals that the design project had failed in one crucial area: it never managed to transform the organization to think and act differently. The organizational design practice within the IRS did not change. The project did not succeed in providing a rationale for why or how it should change its design practice:

- 'The report concentrates on the 1040EZ, an offshoot of the project that the IRS undertook on its own initiative. The 1040EZ is no panacea to millions of taxpayers who itemize deductions, and claim common tax benefits, but who otherwise have uncomplicated tax situations.'
- 'The report notes that the IRS selected certain simplification techniques – principally involving [graphic] design, while rejecting others, but never provides a rationale for this seemingly arbitrary decision. This suggests the IRS will continue its piecemeal approach to simplification that the project, and the Congressional mandate, sought to overcome.'
- 'The report fails to deal with the fact that no action standards were established so that a clear determination could be made to adopt the new forms should they attain a certain level of superior performance. As a result, there was never any commitment made to implement fundamental simplification beyond the duration of the project.'
- 'The report's recommendations for continued simplification are fuzzy, and seem to call for more research, rather than for implementation of the simplified tax forms that proved so effective.'

All this reveals the Tax Forms Simplification Project as an ambitious project with the potential to re-orient public services and a public organization around people. Following in the footsteps of the *Document Design Project*, one can relate to the sense of disappointment expressed by the design team. It had worked hard to arrive at forms that were demonstrably easier for taxpayers. Yet, this seemed of little interest to the organization, which, in the eyes of the design team, had returned to its previous design practices:

> The [IRS final] report suggests that the IRS has continued to select language and design variables that 'appear' to work for taxpayers. Judging from the 1982 tax forms, the IRS focused on *design* modifications, including a new typeface, white space, and functional use of color but *not* on more substantial changes, such as simplified vocabulary and structural modifications.'[48]

Even decades later, the lead graphic designer lamented:

> 'It [the tax forms package] was well designed, all together. But they did not even buy the right typeface.[49]

The statement is revealing and warrants a closer look at the role and actions of the design team in this outcome.

Design practices and design methods matter

Despite all the talk and emphasis on a holistic system, there are indications that the design consortium itself had trouble talking about their own integrated design approach in a fashion that communicated coherence and unity. Established professional hierarchies and assigned ranking might have derailed some of the integration attempts within the team itself. Rather than describing organizing and wording as activities that are part of human-centered product development, the team talked about many of these activities as 'tasks' and techniques *distinct* and isolated from the activities that go into designing. By doing so, the team may have inadvertently undermined their comprehensive effort and effectively communicated to the organization that visual design in itself was a sufficient means for simplification.

> Regardless of which configuration of forms is eventually adopted, and whether or not customized packages are retained, the simplification techniques developed for prototypes, involving organization, language, and design, provide the framework for a simplified tax package.[50]

This segmentation fed right into the inherent tendency of the IRS to pick and choose those distinct techniques that were convenient to adopt. While the design team viewed these simplification techniques as inseparable parts of a systematic approach that could not be pieced up and divided, the organization took these words literally, accepting only those design changes that the design team had labeled 'design.' These 'design' changes also had the advantage of being highly visible, thus allowing the IRS leadership to show that it had heeded the GAO recommendations and that it had instituted change – all the while allowing it to stay the same.

Another factor that contributed to the dissatisfactory outcome was the design team's narrow focus on re-designing the product itself when the human system around it needed to be changed first – or at least brought along on the journey. In the Tax Forms Simplification Project, all the research that was undertaken focused exclusively on the tax forms. Already facing an immensely complex systems problem in the product itself, it is understandable that the design team was not eager to entangle itself in organizational issues. And yet, the design team had the tools and the means to effect internal organizational change. The design team, engaging in cutting-edge design research at a time when design was understood to be an art to create aesthetic visual expressions, gained insights into the general problems taxpayers had when interacting with the organization but did not pursue these organizational issues further with the IRS.

The combined effects of a failure to generate an overall vision for the organization, the lack of commitment and a broader lack of support from the organization's leadership eventually doomed any efforts to make lasting changes within the IRS. Under Egger, the status of the design team as design *consultant* over design *researcher* became quickly evident. The IRS had turned to the design consortium not to question the organization but to apply a remedy. A design *research* team, rather than a design team – similarly conceived, for example, as for the earlier *Document Design Project* – might have had more success in challenging the organizational perspective.

Design understanding and design awareness

How people think of and perceive of design and designing is consequential for the outcome of a design project. The question who can and who cannot design refers to skills and qualifications, talents and expertise that are required of a person actively to participate in the design project and influence the design outcome. Depending on the interpretation of this question, a design project can be more or less inclusive, allow for more or less participation of people with different design training. Since most employees in organizations are not trained in design methods like professional designers, this question immediately points to the possibility of collaborative practices and opportunities for organizational learning.

Our understanding of what can and what cannot be designed effectively sets the boundaries for the design activities and defines the areas to which design methods might successfully apply. Organizations are skilled in creating or maintaining 'No-Touch' zones – 'things' (including systems and organizational structures) employees feel cannot possibly change because of their complex nature or status.

This leads to the question of what does designing involve? The idea that designing means to introduce aesthetic principles is not wrong but also does not provide a complete picture of the activities that constitute design. The impact of product development on the four elements of the organization depends on the kind of design activities and methods a design team can employ. But it also depends on what the organization respects as design activities and design methods.

Finally, the vision for a design project and the purpose of the design activities matter. Unless those involved share the same overall purpose of the design outcome, there can be little agreement on the kind of design activities that might lead to the desired outcome. Also, if the purpose is not clear, success remains a moving target. We see evidence of this in the Tax Forms Simplification Project.

In the Tax Forms Simplification Project, professional designers have a strong opinion about who can design and who cannot. They are convinced they can and people working in the organization cannot. For the designers, the meaning of design is to help taxpayers file their tax returns. For the organization, design means improving the aesthetic look and changing words. These two meanings do not have to be in conflict but as we have seen, they can be the source of tension.

The involvement of the IRS as an organization was limited from the beginning. The key graphic designer recalls:

> We only worked with a handful of people at the IRS. These were open thinkers who got a special assignment in addition to their other responsibilities.[51]

According to this graphic designer, the design team did one 'walk-through' at the IRS where they met the in-house designers. These in-house designers, however, were not involved in the redesign and had little contact with the external designers. The lack of involvement of those people who issue and maintain the existing tax forms simultaneously presents a lack of learning opportunities for the organization and the design team. From the theoretical perspective developed here, the fact that the design team did not identify and consider this internal group as users counts as an oversight. Instead of bringing this group of people along with the journey, the design team preferred to dismiss their input since 'these in-house designers, they were not the very best designers and they did not have the freedom we had in generating new ideas and concepts.'[52] Says a former project member:

> The project was successful in that it was kept to a small group of people that shared ideas and pulled all of our good thoughts together. We had a big amount of freedom.[53]

Implicit in this statement is the fear that the more people who are involved in re-designing, the more restrictions will be imposed on the project. Another comment can be interpreted to support this concern: 'This group [the people that worked with Siegel & Gale] was successful in taking it all apart and restructuring it.'[54] It almost appears as if the system, from which parts were selectively taken in the re-design, had pushed back by selectively picking from the results, as the visual designer summarizes: 'The IRS accepted a number of fairly original ideas but was unable to accept the overall package.'

All this suggests that the design team did not provide sufficient opportunities for members of the organization to experience and engage in the design thinking and methods they applied. Education and information about the design process occurred mostly in the abstract and in written form, in overhead presentations and formal reports. IRS staff participated mainly in a controlling and correcting function in this project but not as partners in the discovery and invention of a solution. In the absence of workshops and work sessions that would have involved IRS members in user research and user testing, both sides began digging trenches early on.

At least some of the members of the design team were convinced that the majority of the organizational staff did not have 'it,' the ability to think and act 'designerly.' Moreover, these members of the design team did not think it possible that members of the IRS could acquire these abilities through learning by doing. Denying members of the organization these abilities aided the development of barriers that cut throughout the project.

Organizational understanding and organizational awareness

Why did the IRS retreat to reviving old forms rather than implementing new forms proven to be superior in many important aspects? The answer is multifold but becomes clear when viewed through the lens of organizational change: From the beginning the organization had little interest in internal change. The Tax Forms Simplification Project turned into a product development exercise to respond to external pressure from the GAO, politicians and citizens. Changing the look of the tax forms was a highly visible sign that the IRS responded to the demands from the GAO and to the new guidelines set by the Paperwork Reduction Act.

The design team was not prepared either to tackle organizational change issues. The design team was led to believe that once it generated a 'superior enough' solution, then the organization would proceed to implement the new forms. However, the precise criteria for 'superior enough' and 'justify change' were never established or articulated by the IRS. This turned out to be detrimental since the design team ever since faced a moving target. The design team should and could have taken a leading role in clarifying these criteria in collaboration with the organization.

The Tax Forms Simplification Project allowed the organization to maintain its basic assumptions about taxpayers. It never successfully challenged the organization to question its role or purpose in relation to the people it serves. But without addressing the vision of the organization, the design team was unable to develop an incremental approach. Instead, the design team had to rely on its own vision for the project and they had one shot to get it right. This, in turn, was too much for the organizational system to digest at once. As a result, outstanding design research and innovative, human-centered product development remained latched onto the pages of the tax form prototypes. The project never generated a larger vision for the organization of which the tax forms then would become a part as a first intermediary product, or an 'instance' of this plan. The tax forms were seen as an end in themselves, both by the design team and the organization.

The fundamental simplification the design team sought to instill with the tax form redesigns was not possible without significant changes within the organization. But while the designers had an understanding of the principles for clear communication and how they related to the tax forms, they did not understand how to apply these principles to the organization. One wonders if the outcome would have been more significant had the design team been able to turn the 'piecemeal process' that characterized forms development in the IRS to their advantage. Perhaps the problem of the design team was that it could not break down its own 'holistic' approach into workable strategy 'pieces' while the IRS was not able to aim its incremental changes towards a unified and coherent whole. Indeed, the opportunity for fundamental change was missed. It is not surprising that the project had a limited impact on the organization overall.

A demonstration of designing as organizational necessity

The Tax Forms Simplification Project remains fascinating and relevant for today's efforts at public sector innovation that increasingly recognize services as central to policy making and policy implementation. Though far from the changes envisioned by the design team, the IRS did expand the income tax form system by one additional form and did end up with a three-tiered tax forms system. Though this did not happen according to the design team's vision and intent, it nonetheless represents a shift within the organization's structure and can be described as a success of this project. According to the final report by the IRS, several techniques invented and adapted for researching general user experience with tax compliance and for measuring the usability of particular forms were adopted by the IRS for future tax form development. This includes learning about language simplification and basic usability concepts of the tax forms using newly developed and acquired techniques by the consortium.[55]

The IRS *Tax Forms Simplification Study Group* actually requested more staff to take on these new tasks.[56] But budget cuts and managerial philosophies smothered this attempt at a larger structural change. We have seen above that the key readability expert was replaced with a career bureaucrat who lacked the qualifications, skills and background to pursue forms design from a readability perspective. And while some of the former IRS members claim that new techniques in the development process of the forms were introduced the Tax Forms Simplification project did not effect a change in the values, norms and beliefs of the organization at the time.[57] The main changes resulting from the project therefore concern technical capabilities.[58] As the complexity of the tax laws continued to grow, fundamental issues remained unsolved. Tellingly, the main worry of the IRS Forms and Publication division – to this day – continues to be how to fit the annual changes in tax law onto as few lines as possible on a tax form.

Changing services involves organizational changes

The IRS Tax Forms Simplification Project remains an excellent example of an organization employing product development to avoid transformative organizational change and instead opting for accommodation. The accommodation consists of re-designing the tax forms while the organizational framework in which the tax forms are being developed remains the same. In this case, the product development remains organization-centered. The organization minimizes the organizational role of design methods and design thinking to produce forms that satisfy the congressional mandate by the General Accounting Office.

From the very beginning, the organization was astutely aware of the potential impact of the redesign on internal affairs. Among the criteria the final design results had to satisfy, the IRS listed these four as core: statutory complexity, administrative equity; taxpayer competence; and only much later the proof for cost effectiveness that justified change.[59]

Statutory complexity referred to the need for the new forms to reflect accurately the federal individual income tax laws, including annual legal and regulatory changes.[60] Statutory complexity addressed the operational concern of the IRS of updating and maintaining the income tax forms and ensured technical accuracy of the new forms. Also, the new system would have to accommodate the IRS' printing, distribution, and processing requirements, and the production constraints of the U.S. publishing industry.[61]

Administrative equity described the IRS' aim to ensure that every taxpayer was given enough information to take advantage of, or to comply with, all applicable provisions of the Internal Revenue Code. The new tax forms system would have to satisfy the obligations the IRS had to taxpayers of all filing statuses. Administrative equity called attention to the content of the income tax forms from a legal perspective. Although the improvements sought under 'taxpayer equity' are clearly beneficial to individual taxpayers, it appears in this context that the motivation for the IRS was to avoid legal troubles. This is important, because simply providing rules and laws can satisfy legal obligations. But doing so does not make it easier for people to make use of this information.

Of all four requirements then, 'taxpayer competence' was the only IRS requirement that looked at the difficulties taxpayers had with tax forms. And it was listed only as third criteria. Yet this was the priority and focus of the design team, which in turn were not as concerned with cost effectiveness. For the IRS cost effectiveness meant that any additional costs involved in changing over to the new system of forms should not significantly exceed the estimated collective benefits to taxpayers. The IRS specifically asked for the new system to be 'cost-effective to administer' and to be 'superior enough to the existing system to justify change.'[62] Again, the IRS stresses its concern over the operational implications for the organization. Not until the final report on the Tax Forms Simplification Project does the design team list cost effectiveness as a separate requirement.[63]

Despite the needs for measurement and evaluation, the organization never agreed to what the milestones in the project might be or might look like. As it turned out, the IRS had a reason to remain vague. From the moment the design team engaged in the redesign, the IRS was trying to solve the problem in-house. Thus success, from the beginning, remained a moving target. The design team, feeling the pinch of this situation, never managed to get the organization to commit to any of its achievements. Instead, the designers continued to work under constraints they felt increasingly uncomfortable with. In their words, 'the new system and the prototype forms themselves were to be judged by three independent (and sometimes conflicting) standards.'[64]

None of these tests focused on the experience of taxpayers. But the design team also did not make use of methods like story-telling to document and communicate these experiences. Testing and evaluation, like the notion of simplification remained focused on quantitative testing and evaluation. Can it be that the design team weakened its position rather than strengthened it? One might argue that because the research did not succeed in personalizing the struggle of an individual taxpayer to IRS officials 'from person to person', it was easier for IRS staff to remain detached and disinterested in an individual's difficulties. Moreover, it meant that the design team failed to produce its own evidence.

It would take almost two more decades before the IRS would realize that well-designed paper (and electronic) forms were *essential* but not *sufficient* to improve the citizen experience with taxation. To achieve this, the organization itself would need to re-orient itself around people. The effort by Vice President Al Gore to 're-invent services at the IRS' in 1998 focused on taxpayer experience and connected this with changes the IRS had to make internally.[65] It is around that time that the Australian Taxation Office, at the center of our next chapter, started the *Integrated Tax Design Project* explicitly with the intent to re-orient the organization around people. While in the US, the updated *Paperwork Reduction Act* continues to pummel government agencies to test and simplify federal forms,' the Australian Tax Office was less concerned about re-designing forms but about changing its design practices.[66]

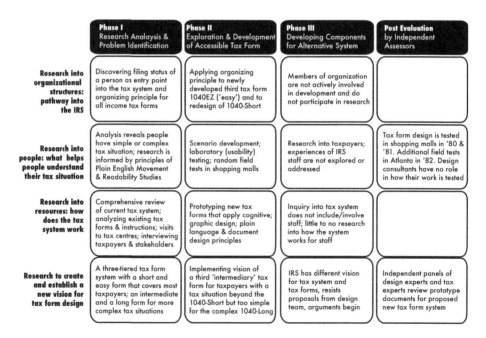

	Phase I Research Analaysis & Problem Identification	Phase II Exploration & Development of Accessible Tax Form	Phase III Developing Components for Alternative System	Post Evaluation by Independent Assessors
Research into organizational structures: pathway into the IRS	Discovering filing status of a person as entry point into the tax system and organizing principle for all income tax forms	Applying organizing principle to newly developed third tax form 1040EZ ('easy') and to redesign of 1040-Short	Members of organization are not actively involved in development and do not participate in research	
Research into people: what helps people understand their tax situation	Analysis reveals people have simple or complex tax situation; research is informed by principles of Plain English Movement & Readability Studies	Scenario development; laboratory (usability) testing; random field tests in shopping malls	Research into taxpayers; experiences of IRS staff are not explored or addressed	Tax form design is tested in shopping malls in '80 & '81. Additional field tests in Atlanta in '82. Design consultants have no role in how their work is tested
Research into resources: how does the tax system work	Comprehensive review of current tax system; analyzing existing tax forms & instructions; visits to tax centres; interviewing taxpayers & stakeholders	Prototyping new tax forms that apply cognitive; graphic design; plain language & document design principles	Inquiry into tax system does not include/involve staff; little to no research into how the system works for staff	
Research to create and establish a new vision for tax form design	A three-tiered tax form system with a short and easy form that covers most taxpayers; an intermediate and a long form for more complex tax situations	Implementing vision of a third 'intermediary' tax form for taxpayers with a tax situation beyond the 1040-Short but too simple for the complex 1040-Long	IRS has different vision for tax system and tax forms, resists proposals from design team, arguments begin	Independent panels of design experts and tax experts review prototype documents for proposed new tax form system

Research into People, Structure, Resources and Vision: The IRS Tax Form Simplification Project

Figure 10.4 Research into people, organization, resources and vision for the IRS tax forms transformation project

Notes

1 The project is sometimes also referred to as the *Long-Range Tax Forms Simplification Study*.
2 Olsen, Nina E. 'Tax Payer Advocate', http://www.taxpayeradvocate.irs.gov/reports/2015-annual-report-to-congress [accessed January 2016].
3 See https://www.irs.gov/uac/The-Agency-its-Mission-and-Statutory-Authority [accessed January 2016].
4 See: Last Week with John Oliver, IRS (HBO): https://www.youtube.com/watch?v=Nn_Zln_4pA8 [accessed January 2016].
5 See http://www.taxpayeradvocate.irs.gov/2013-Annual-Report/budget-cuts.html.
6 See http://trac.syr.edu/tracirs/trends/v10/irsStaffG.html [accessed January 2016].
7 See: http://www.c-span.org/video/?324602–1/treasury-secretary-lew-irs-commissioner-koskinen-testimony-fiscal-year-2016-budget [accessed January 2016].
8 http://www.nytimes.com/2013/05/16/opinion/the-real-irs-scandal.html?_r=0 [accessed January 2016].
9 Ibid. The Siegel & Gale report quotes the 1975 study by the *U.S. Office of Education* from the original *Request for Proposal* by the IRS.
10 *Further Simplification of Income Tax Forms and Instructions Is Needed and Possible*, GAO Report No. GGS-78–74, July 5, 1978.
11 Ibid.
12 See: *Technical Assistance and Training from the Document Design Project*. Final Report. Prepared for the National Institute of Education, Washington, D.C. under contract No. NIE-400–78–0043, November 1981 by the American Institutes for Research with Siegel & Gale and Carnegie Mellon University.
13 Ibid.
14 The original *Guidelines for Document Designers* were published as *Writing Contracts in Plain English* by Carl Felsenfeld and Alan Siegel (St. Paul, Minnesota: West, 1981). Joanne Locke's overview is available at Locke, J. (2004). 'History of Plain Language in the United States Government', published on http://www.plainlanguage.gov/whatisPL/history/locke.cfm.
15 *Paperwork Reduction Act–Implementation at IRS*, November 1998. United States General Accounting Office, Report to the Chairman, Subcommittee on Oversight of Government Management, Restructuring, and the District of Columbia, Committee on Governmental Affairs, U.S. Senate. GAO/GGD-99–4.
16 See Beth Mazur's article "Revisiting Plain Language", May 2000, Vol. 47 (2), issue of *Technical Communication, the Journal of the Society for Technical Communication*.
17 Shriver, Karen (1997) discusses Plain English and its role in document design in *Dynamics in Document Design*, John Wiley & Sons, New York. For an example of Plain English in technical writing, see Carliner, Saul (2000). 'Physical, Cognitive, and Affective: A Three-Part Framework for Information Design', *Technical Communication*, Fourth Quarter 2000/2: 561–576.
18 Source: Joanne Locke's (2004). 'History of Plain Language in the United States Government', published on http://www.plainlanguage.gov/whatisPL/history/locke.cfm.
19 *Tax Forms Simplifications Project: Background, Development, and Status, March 8, 1982*, prepared by Siegel & Gale, p. 1.
20 This date is established in the report *Tax Forms Simplifications Project: Background, Development, and Status*, prepared by Siegel & Gale on March 8, 1982.
21 This is a quote from retired IRS official who was at the time in a key position at the Tax Forms and Publication Division. According to this official, taxpayers' statements about tax forms are not reliable since the majority of the taxpayers never even look at the tax forms themselves but have them prepared by somebody else.
22 Comments made by a member of the Senior Executive Association. Most members of this organization are former senior IRS officials. Author notes, July 12.
23 In its final report, the IRS describes the Tax Forms Simplification Project as a "two-phase project." It appears that the IRS uses "phase" synonymously with "year" as the Siegel & Gale contract ran over two years. This may explain the differences in the respectively issued documents about length and achievements in each phase. I am following the Siegel & Gale concept of phase as it allows for a more detailed narration of the events.

24 See Figure 10.3 for the expert design panel that was called on at the end of the project.

25 See Project Objectives, *Final Report*, Siegel & Gale.

26 In its *Final Report*, the IRS claims that the project virtually involved all levels of the agency, making it even more promising for the project to effect changes within the organization.

27 In 2003, Barnett criticizes the IRS for using the 1975 numbers to feed their assumption that it's the user's fault if they cannot read and understand a form. Instead, Barnett argues that it is the forms that confound people and make them look stupid. Barnett, Robert. 2003. 'How Do You Know Your Forms Fail?' updated 2005 and 2007: http://c.ymcdn.com/sites/www.bfma.org/resource/resmgr/Articles/07_46.pdf.

28 See Siegel & Gale's report *Tax Forms Simplification Project, Background, Development, and Status,* March 8, 1982.

29 Author phone interview with former senior IRS member, August 4, 2005.

30 *Final Report Long Range Tax Forms Simplification Study*, September 20, 1983, Tax Forms and Publications Division, Research Division, Internal Revenue Service, p. 3.

31 Adam Smith's Division of Labor continues to have implications for organizational design. Smith, A. (1904 [2010]). *An Inquiry into the Nature and Causes of the Wealth of Nations*, originally Methuen & Co. Ltd., London, reprinted by Capstone Publishing, Chichester, UK, 2010.

32 *Final Report Long Range Tax Forms Simplification Study*, September 20, 1983, Tax Forms and Publications Division, Research Division, Internal Revenue Service, p. 1.

33 Author phone interview with former design liaison at the IRS, August 5, 2005.

34 *Final Report, Long Range Tax Forms Simplification Project*, IRS. 1983.

35 Author phone interview with former senior IRS project member, August 4, 2005.

36 Phone interview with former IRS member, August 4, 2005.

37 The "20-odd million taxpayers" are quoted from the *Final Report* of the IRS, September 1983.

38 Not long after the completion of the Tax Forms Simplification Project, in 1985, the IRS suffered one of its worst crises in history under Tax Commissioner Egger when a newly installed computer system failed to process thousands of tax returns properly.

39 *Tax Forms Simplification Project–Background, Development, and Status, March 8, 1982* by Siegel & Gale.

40 Source: *Long-Range Tax Forms Simplification Study, Final Report*, September 20, 1983, p. 10. Testing methods and results for Denver and San Francisco were not available.

41 *Tax Forms Simplifications Project: Background, Development, and Status,* March 8, 1982.

42 This was the result of a six-month internship by a graduate student in readability and reading from Rutgers University. The IRS particularly liked his ability to device readability formulas. The student later assumed a leading role in the Tax Forms Simplification Project as the IRS internal readability specialist and, somewhat ironically, works today for the United States Postal Service (the organization of focus in my second case study).

43 This is an excerpt from a status report prepared by Siegel & Gale: *Tax Forms Simplifications Project: Background, Development, and Status, March 8, 1982*. Since I do not have a copy of the *Request For Proposal* itself, it is not entirely clear how much of the wording is an interpretation by the design team. It could indeed be that, at least initially, the design team and the IRS had very different ideas about what the entire system of individual tax forms and instructions constituted.

44 *1983 Report to Congress*, Tax Commissioner Roscoe L. Egger (The IRS project was completed in 1982).

45 Information based on author phone interview, August 4, 2005.

46 "Response to the IRS Report", *Final Report Tax Forms Simplification Project* prepared by Siegel & Gale, p. 66.

47 Ibid.

48 Quoted from the *Final Report* by Siegel & Gale, March 1983 (emphasis in original).

49 Author phone interview, April 30, 2005.

50 *Background, Development and Status Report*, 1982, p. 11.

51 Author phone interview, April 30, 2005.

52 Author phone interview with former member of design team, April 30, 2005.

53 Ibid.

54 Ibid.

55 At least one of the IRS members did not want to or could not follow the language simplification guidelines. I quote from page 21 of the *Final Report* issued by the IRS: 'IRS should therefore be directly benefited by lower math error rates to be expected to result from applying to our current tax forms

the techniques embodied in the prototypes.' One can only imagine the terror of the plain language experts at Siegel and Gale reading this useless assembly of words. One is also left to wonder about the IRS intent to apply 'the techniques embodied in the prototypes to its 'current tax forms' when it seemingly did not care to apply these principles to their own final report.

56 I have been unable to confirm that this request had been made or granted. My information is based on the request made by the *IRS Long Range Tax Forms Simplification* Study Group in the *Final Report on the Long Range Tax Forms Simplification Project*.

57 The publication *Reinventing Service at the IRS* compiled by Vice President Al Gore, Treasury Secretary Robert E. Rubin with the Frontline Employees if the IRS in 1998 demonstrates a shift in awareness and attitude under President Clinton. Department of The Treasury Internal Revenue Service Publication 2197 (3–98). Catalog Number 25006E.

58 This is in line with the findings of Bowen et al I discuss in the final chapter of this book.

59 In its report to the Commissioner of Internal Revenue in 1981, the design team lists only three 'sometimes conflicting' requirements of the newly designed forms. 'Cost-effectiveness' appears as a fourth requirement in the 1982 report on background, development and status of the project.

60 *Report to the Commissioner of Internal Revenue–Status of the Tax Forms Simplification Project*, November 30, 1981, p. 5.

61 While the design team does not always explicitly list the technical demands on the new system it respects this important constraint throughout the project.

62 Ibid.

63 *Final Report Tax Forms Simplification Project*, prepare by Siegel & Gale, p. 1.

64 *Report to Tax Commissioner Internal Revenue – Status of the Tax Forms Simplification Project*, November 30, 1981, p. 4. Note that the design team does not yet list cost-effectiveness and the need to justify change as their requirements.

65 See *Reinventing Service at the IRS* by Vice President Al Gore and Treasury Secretary Robert E. Rubin with Front-line Employees of the IRS. Published by the Department of Treasury Internal Revenue Service: Publication 2197 (3–98) Catalog Number 25006E, Government Printing Office 1998.

66 Memorandum by Cass R. Sunstein, dated August 9, 2012. Available online at http://www.whitehouse.gov/sites/default/files/omb/inforeg/memos/testing-and-simplifying-federal-forms.pdf.

11 Developing design capability at the Australian taxation office

To sustain an end-to-end process we must articulate a tax design methodology and ensure our staff are fully trained and supported to become truly professional designers. Design is about making products; a professional tax design practice will require the support of highly developed product strategies.[1]

In this third and final case illustration, we focus again on taxpayers and the challenge of public organizations to develop services that fulfill desired policy intents. The chapter centers on the ongoing *Integrated Tax Design Project* by the Australian Taxation Office. Though its precise starting point can no longer be pinpointed (Terrey 2012, p. 6), there is agreement that things began to happen for real in 1999.[2] A precursor to the design work now underway in many public innovation labs, it predates the 'lab wave' by nearly 20 years. The project attests to the centrality of people and services to successful policy implementation and demonstrates how greater design awareness; a more nuanced design understanding and the use of human-centered design methods contribute to better integration of policy making with policy implementation.

This chapter traces the key events and developments that led the Australian Taxation Office to turn to human-centered product development and shows how the agency introduced design thinking and design methods into the organization. In contrast to its American counterpart, the Australian Taxation Office chose to work with external design mentors to change organizational design practices and to introduce new design principles and methods. As part of this project, members of this government agency learned about their own roles as designers. They were designing tax products before but did so without applying human-centered design principles and human-centered design methods.

At the start, this project's ambitions aimed to develop 'an integrated design capability for tax policy, legislation and administrative processes.'[3] It was nothing less than a radical attempt to align the design of policies with the design of people-centered services for policy implementation. Much of what is happening today in government public innovation labs echoes the principles and methods employed in this project. However, there was no dedicated lab. There were different areas of the Taxation Office that committed to developing design capabilities that would lead to better quality products for taxpayers and better results for the organization.

I will focus on the early years to show how the organization went about developing internal design capabilities. During my visits in 2003, I spoke with staff from different business areas in the Australian Taxation Office (ATO) and met with people at the Treasury. I revisited Australia again in 2011 to conduct follow up interviews with staff at the ATO, the Treasury and Think Place in Canberra as well as with Second Road in Sydney. Since then, Nina Terrey, herself a former member of the ATO and project manager on the *Integrated Tax Design Project*, has provided additional insights into this fascinating project in her doctoral dissertation (Terrey 2012).[4]

Australian taxation and the Australian Taxation Office

Attitudes towards taxation in Australia differ from those in the US. Many Australians still view taxes 'as the price to live in a great society.'[5] To this day, the country benefits from a 'predominantly cooperative and willing taxpayer community' (Terrey 2012, p. 97).[6] As in other countries, the complexity of the Australian tax law had made it increasingly difficult for individuals to pay their annual tax bills. For a long time, the agency thought it best to leave it to the industry and third-party providers to figure things out. Registered private tax agents that offer advice in return for compensation now match the number of ATO staff. In addition, numerous third party providers make a business out of books and software targeting and aiding confused taxpayers.

Any time a new tax law comes into effect, the ATO has to have all relevant tax products ready and available. If the Treasury decides that a baby bonus is available to parents, say, on July 12 in a given year, the ATO has to develop all tax products that allow taxpayers with children to file for their bonus as of that date. The ability to deliver tax products in and on time was a recognized strength of the ATO. This ability remains crucial in an environment where policies put forth by Treasury need to get implemented according to timelines and deadlines the ATO has little control over. In Australia, the Treasury makes the policy decisions about collecting revenues and raising funds. The Office of Parliamentary Council translates these policies into legislation, or laws, and the Australian Taxation Office is in charge of administering these laws.

In the late 1990s, the ability to deliver promptly suffered from an understanding of how to design tax products people could actually use, reminisced a senior tax official who was involved in the Integrated Tax Design project:

> 'The Tax Office is really good at bringing stuff in on time. We do that well. But we let some other things suffer, like the customer and the quality of [the tax product].'[7]

The 'customer', the taxpayer, indeed, was an afterthought, admitted another senior tax official involved in the project.

> We just developed products till we turned them on and then taxpayers told us and it was too late to fix them.[8]

The way the Treasury, the Office of Parliamentary Council and the Australian Taxation Office went about designing and implementing policies can best be described as a relay-style design process: handing over the baton from one person to the other, from one department to the other.[9] The characteristics of a relay design approach include linear and fragmented design activities that allow people involved to withdraw without further responsibilities for a design outcome after they have 'done their part'. In a relay design approach, there is no incentive for anyone to maintain or guard a vision, let alone a policy's intent.

We have seen in chapter 3 how common policy cycle representations insinuate linear and fragmented design approaches to policy makers and public managers. I am often reminded of a popular children's game when I come across such design approaches: One child starts whispering a secret sentence into the ear of another child. The second child now whispers whatever it understood to the next child, and so on. By the time the game is over, the message is usually thoroughly distorted and produces some kind of funny nonsense. What is a laughing matter for children is no joke for lawmakers and governments. Second Tax Commissioner Alan Preston was among the first to articulate the need for an integrated approach to tax systems design.

> Many hands are involved in both formulating and executing policy intent. The interactive non-linearity between intent and execution further muddles the waters of tax systems design. Since most design measures also involve delivery of numerous products across all our product families, in essence our search for quality must again focus on the unity of a balanced and functioning whole.[10]

Like most organizations, the Australian Tax Office, too, has lived through several significant waves of organizational change. The first one, 'modernization,' took place in the mid-1980s and signified the transition from paper forms and processes to computer technologies. The second one, 'Total Quality Management,' followed on its heels in the 90s. Total Quality Management introduced cross agency teams and emphasized continuous improvement of internal processes. But the exclusive focus of TQM on internal processes failed to include and consider needs of people external to the organization. One ATO staff member remarked: 'The limitation [with TQM] is you can fix the process, still deliver quality products but still not satisfy your customer.'[11] With the *Integrated Tax Design* project, the organization made a conscious effort to re-orient itself around people.

At the time of the project's start, the ATO serviced a nation of twenty million people and employed a staff of 20,000 to collect outstanding taxes and to reinforce the tax laws.[12] During 2003, ATO staff members conducted more than eleven million phone calls and handled more than one million written inquiries per year.[13] The agency was responsible for generating up to 92% of the Australian government's revenue. Naturally, these numbers have changed since, but they express the situation and circumstances that frame this project and became the core focus of the *Integrated Tax Design*.

Identifying the need for design capability

Staff members unanimously pointed to three key developments in the late 1990s that prepared the ground for design thinking and design methods to enter the Australian Taxation Office. There was, at first, a growing recognition that the taxation of businesses no longer provided the incentives needed to encourage growth and innovation. Australia, in 1998 found itself in the midst of a global economy and subject to international competitive pressures and technological developments. Seeking to understand the implications of the new circumstances, the Commissioner of Taxation ordered a study of the prevailing practices and policies of business taxation. He assigned a renowned and respected Australian businessman, John Ralph, to chair this review.

Ralph soon discovered that many weaknesses in business taxation were rooted in a systemic problem that plagued the Australian tax system. About every eight or ten years or so, the Australian tax system required a major overhaul or reform because 'its wheels came flying off.'[14] In his final report *A Review of Business Taxation*, Ralph documented that the

instability and unsustainability of the tax system was due to a highly fragmented and disconnected design approach by the Australian Government. Although tax design involved policy
design, law design, and the design of tax products, he found that there was no comprehensive
method that aligned the needs of the Treasury with those of the Office of Parliamentary
Council or that of the Australian Taxation Office. Thus, the legislative, executive and administrative arms of the government each interpreted a new tax law according to their own
needs and operations. This effectively muddled the original intent of any law and over time
caused so many inconsistencies and incompatibilities that the system broke down.

The Ralph Report, as it became known, presented this problem as a problem of design.
Its first three chapters were dedicated to a discussion of taxation design and designing
taxes.[15] In its conclusion, *The Review of Business Taxation* called for the immediate redesign
of the Australian tax system that would take an integrated approach to tax design, break
the pattern and result in a sustainable tax system. This new system would provide a sense
of fairness, ensure the integrity of the taxation process and facilitate compliance for individual taxpayers and businesses.[16] It would achieve this by viewing tax design as an 'end-
to-end process' that focused on the needs of taxpayers.[17]

The introduction of a new *Goods and Services Tax* in 2000 finally demonstrated how
the disintegrated and fragmented approach to tax design fell short of delivering desired
outcomes. The *Goods and Services Tax* was an attempt by the Australian Government to
introduce a Simplified Tax System for businesses. In this effort, however, the government had 'moved the burden of tax collection and compliance to the private sector
while significantly increasing tax revenue.'[18] In addition, this initial round of 'simplification' concentrated on cutting the number of pages of legislative paperwork. This echoes
the early simplification efforts undertaken by the USPS and the IRS presented in the
previous chapters. *Guidelines for Document Design* and *Plain English* remain relevant for
government today and have also played, if a minor role, in the Integrated Tax Design
Project.

Especially small businesses were hit hard by the new requirements. In more than one
way, the rocky introduction of the new *Goods and Services Tax* exemplified the unintended
outcomes of a disintegrated tax design approach. It came to mark the second government
development that pointed to the need for a different approach to product development
within the ATO. There was another significant change in the tax system, as the ATO
shifted from a 'pay-as-you-went' to a 'pay-as-you-go' method. Technically, the introduction of the 'Pay-as-you-go' method did not constitute a change *of* the tax system. However, ATO members who had to change a number of rules and laws to implement the
new payment method referred to these changes as 'a change of the tax system'.[19]

The third development leading up to the Integrated Design Tax project was an internal
recognition within the Australian Taxation Office that somehow moving from vision to
implementation was a problem for the organization.[20] A disconnect existed between the
'thinkers' and the 'makers.' This disconnect was rooted in the prevailing ATO conception of
the tax design role, writes former Second Commissioner of Taxation, Dr. Alan Preston.

> The accent was far less on design expertise per se, and much more on the writing of
> tax law as an expression of the technical skill of the drafter. The complementary tasks
> of administrative design – encompassing the myriad of products that support the tax
> law and make it operational – had always been, and were widely recognized as, the
> poor cousin of law design.[21]

A vision and a strategy for integrated tax design that delivers for people

For many senior government officials, the Ralph Report was a revelation. But perhaps nobody was as convinced about the need *for Integrated Tax Design* as Dr. Alan Preston, who at the time oversaw the *Review of Business Taxation* in his position as Secretary for the Department of Treasury. Shortly after the conclusion of the Ralph Report, in November 1999, the Governor-General appointed Preston to the position of Second Tax Commissioner in the Australian Taxation Office. He thus became one of three Second Tax Commissioners who directly reported to the Commissioner of Taxation.

Preston championed the *Integrated Tax Design* (ITD) initiative and immediately assembled an *Integrated Tax Design Sponsor Group* at the ATO to explore what human-centered design meant in the context of taxation. This group included a representative of the Board of Taxation, the chair of the Ralph Report who also functioned as representative for the business community, as well as senior representatives from the Treasury, the Office of Parliamentary Counsel, and the Australian Taxation Office. Simultaneously, Preston invited three international design experts to mentor the ATO in the development of its own internal design capability. Their initial inquiry affirmed the need and opportunities to reorient the organization around people.

> Many of the senior leaders understood the idea – as well as the driving forces for organizational change. But the organization seemed to focus most of its energy and talent on the enforcement of rules rather than helping people comply.[22]

The organization needed to learn how to design products for people. So far, it had paid little attention to user pathways or user experience.

> To focus that consciousness, the ITD Project has defined the role of pathway custodian for major tax regimes that affect key groups of users. The pathway custodian is charged with capturing and holding the evolving vision for the defined group of users and ensuring that implementation takes place in accordance with the design blueprint and faithfully delivers on policy intent. Above all the pathway custodian role deliberately emphasizes design leadership from a user's perspective.[23]

But the organization also needed a strategy for how to develop and apply design thinking and design methods. With the help of the three design mentors experienced in designing in the context of organizations, a two-tiered strategy emerged. The first tier concerned the development of the individual design skills; the second tier concerned the distribution and integration of these skills within the organization. Committing itself to a ten year project, the ATO set out to accomplish an unusual feat: to set up and integrate design education within a government agency.

Design explorations: Connecting systems, processes and people

The organization already had a vision – to design interactions for people – but it needed to understand how systems, processes and people needed to work together to realize this vision. With the strategy in place and a rough outline of what was needed to develop design capabilities on an individual and organizational level, the *ITD Sponsor Group* began a concerted effort to educate 'key internal opinion makers' about human-centered design and to familiarize them with design thinking and design methods. These staff members would form the *Integrated Tax Design Team*. Their design education happened in a series of design conferences. For this purpose, the ATO chose three design mentors to work with its staff. Each design mentor explored one of three relevant topics with the organization: systems, processes and people. Three in-house design conferences became part of a systematic effort to introduce design thinking and design methods into the ATO. With each conference, the circle of participants and design proponents grew bigger. The conferences included hands-on exercises and activities to teach participants about design methods in action. The conference also provided opportunities for staff to engage with design issues and to discover their relevance to taxation and their own work.

In a first for the organization but most likely in a first for any government agency, *Design Conference 1* took place in February 2000. Several interviewees recollect the purpose of the event as 'sensitizing' about eighty key staff members 'to the integrating role of design.'[24] The Head of the School of Design at Carnegie Mellon led through this first event. As design mentor, he introduced staff members to 'the art of shaping arguments about the artificial or human-made world, arguments which may be carried forward in the concrete activities of production in each of these areas, with objective results ultimately judged by individuals, groups, and society.'

The second event, *Design Conference 2,* was held eight months later, in December 2000. Its theme centered on 'Design Strategy in Action.' Jim Faris, a renowned interaction design practitioner, worked with an audience of about two hundred staff members on the strategic role of design in an organization. The second conference effectively pointed to organizational design processes.

By the time Darrel Rhea, an expert in strategic design, mentored roughly two hundred ATO staff members on 'Designing for People' for the last of the conference series (*Design Conference 3),* there were encouraging signs of growing organizational design capability: The ITD team had begun to apply the lessons from the previous two conferences. They had managed to visually represent how processes, systems, and people related to each other in the ATO. In addition, they had begun work on mapping the design process within the ATO. The ITD team had also began to compile a design handbook for staff members, *The Guide.*

Articulating organizational design practices

The Guide contained two key visualizations: *The Wheel* and *The Stacker* articulated and explained how design applied to individual taxation projects and how each of these projects fit in with other projects by the ATO. In 2002, the Prototype Version of *The Guide 2.0* describes the two models as follows.

The Wheel

The Wheel is the descriptive name given to the ITD Process Cycle, one of the two foundational models of the ITD process. The Wheel represents the ITD process at the level of an individual project. It consists of six sequential but overlapping stages with clearly defined gateways and quality assurance processes throughout.[25] Although the development of distributed design capability happened on a voluntary basis, the design teams themselves were instructed by the Tax Design Group to make use of the wheel.[26]

> Although there is a long way to go on the quality front, we have instituted the mechanisms of independent reviews of design implementation at appropriate stages of The Wheel, particularly to assess the quality of implementation of policy intent.[27]

The Stacker

The Stacker is the descriptive name given to the ITD Process Framework, the second visualization that models the ITD process. The framework comprises three elements: The constitutional foundation for tax design; the context for tax design; and the infrastructure (in the areas of people, process and product) that is necessary to support and sustain an integrated tax design capability.[28]

The Blueprint

Another important achievement was the introduction of the *Blueprint* as part of every development project. In the *Blueprint*, a project team articulated the intent of a particular project, the goal it was trying to accomplish and the means it felt would be necessary and successful to arrive at the desired outcome. Starting out with a concept and a plan that took the overall development into consideration was a change in action for ATO members, says this senior tax official.

> So we used the analogy of 'you would not build a house, you would not do the drawings, the wirings diagrams for the house until you had drawn an outline for the design for the house.' And that was a new step we introduced.[29]

The first *Blueprint* was developed in 2000. In 'Reforming the Tax Design Process – A blueprint for building an integrated tax design capability,'[30] the team demonstrated the power and utility of the blueprint method while simultaneously sharing its ideas and approaches for a major policy change. The *Blueprint* explained the vision and values future tax design practice should adhere to. The Blueprint constitutes an early commitment to human-centered design aligned with a strategy and a vision. The ITD team sought to develop

> . . . an integrated tax capability in which tax design professionals operate creatively and collaboratively within an articulated and disciplined design process to implement tax system products that coherently connect policy intent with user needs.[31]

These first outcomes can be understood and viewed as products on their own, highlighting the productive nature of design. Yet, these were not merely products. These were tools for further exploration of design in the ATO as well as tools for articulating and clarifying design processes and design principles that put people and their experiences in the center. They were evidence of growing design awareness, greater design understanding and shifting design practices within the ATO. They were indications for new design capabilities tailored to the needs of the organization but driven by a concern for the experience of taxpayers.

How do we know it works?

But was the investment worthwhile? ATO's leadership was asking to see evidence that the ideas and core concepts that had been developed so far were workable. Was it worth the eight million dollars that funded the project with 30 staff members over ten years? For many in the ITD design team, the request for evidence came as a surprise. Testing was not a common practice in the Taxation Office at that time, as one staff member explains:

> So we developed these ideas but the organization by this time was saying 'well you need to go and get your hands dirty and test it.' So. . . one of the ideas was before you

start making individual products, try and sketch out an outline of design. We never did that in the past. So we did not know how that worked.[32]

There was also a lingering concern among some of the organization's leaders that despite the promises of the new design approach, it would ultimately fail to deliver when confronted with organizational reality.

The ATO is full of accountants and lawyers, investigators, systems builders. They are very pragmatic people. So the tolerance of the organization for new ideas, it drives them on but if they cannot see how to convert that into better outcomes in what they would call the real world, it drops them.[33]

As it turned out, there was no reason to worry. The ITD team applied the new principles and methods successfully to several policy projects. By the end of 2001, the ATO leadership called for all projects concerning tax policy changes to follow the ITD process. Moreover, the *Integrated Tax Design Team* assisted in setting up the *ATO Tax Design Group*. This new *Tax Design Group* was 'working with select policy change projects.' In addition, a *Policy Implementation Forum* (PIF) was set up to provide a channel to see these changes implemented.

Embedding new design practices within the ATO

By June 2003, the organizational structure of the ATO accommodated a whole new set of practices that centered on designing and on developing an integrated approach to tax design. The approach demonstrated the organization's commitment to develop and distribute new design capabilities within the organization systematically and over time. 'Design Thinking' – understanding the development of products and services that fulfilled policy intent by meeting the needs of people as a design problem – had begun to change the way the organization operated.

Already, the ATO had committed to six design principles. These design principles were consistent. With growing experience and insights they were expanded on or adjusted. By the end of 2003, staff and leadership had agreed to seven design principles. These were printed on large and highly visible posters that hung across different ATO areas, including PTAX. These principles were:

1   taking a user centered approach, creating products and services that are easier, cheaper and more personalized
2   making the emerging design visible early through documentation and prototypes that focus dialog, sustain energy and facilitate co–design
3   working collaboratively in interdisciplinary teams, helping ensure that changes to the tax system are fully integrated
4   building a shared understanding of intent and ensuring that, when change is implemented, the user experience reflects that intent
5   following a disciplined yet flexible process that stays true to our design principles and achieves a higher quality in less time
6   mapping the user pathway and other layers of design upfront to create a coherent blueprint for change
7   looking for innovative solutions that align with corporate directions and achieve a balance between tax systems integrity and user expectations.

In addition to the principles, three *Service Delivery Teams* had been set up.[34] Service Delivery Teams provided expertise and support by leading Intent Workshops; providing Blueprinting Process and Documentation; organizing Creative Workshops; guiding through Walkthroughs; conducting Usability Testing, and User Research but also through Prototyping and User Based Design. In addition, Service Delivery Teams paid attention to Quality Assurance Processes, Design Facilitation and Information Design. In short, the Service Delivery Teams functioned as a design resource for all ATO areas. Each team included a team leader, a design facilitator, an information designer and a user testing and user research expert.

Members of one Service Delivery Team began to meet regularly with colleagues of the other two teams to form 'Communities of Practice' (Wenger 1998). Every gathering was an opportunity for design facilitators, information designers, user researchers and user testers to discuss their role specific challenges, issues and methods. Through these communities, they assumed a key role in the further development of ATO's design capability, spending up to 20% of their time on capability building activity.[35] By learning with and from each other, individual members received continuous encouragement while developing new approaches they fed back to their Service Design Teams and applied in their own projects.

Leaders of the three Service Delivery Teams worked closely with the organization's *Practice Management*. *Practice Management* formed the primary point of contact for all ATO clients, which freed the *Service Delivery Teams* from 'management' and allowed their focus to remain on actual design activities. ATO clients who might request design services at the time included Change Program Sub-Program Leaders or project managers but also Distributed Design Areas, Policy Change Project or individual, 'ad-hoc corporate requests.' *Practice Management* allocated job requests to the Service Delivery Teams and assisted their team leaders in the assembly of Core Design Teams that met a specific design support request.[36]

In the effort to continuously develop, build, and distribute design capability, the *Knowledge Capture and Sharing Team* was formed. This team captured the methodologies and learnings that emerged within the *Service Delivery Teams*. The task of the *Knowledge Capture and Sharing Group* was to make new approaches, tools and techniques accessible to the 'wider ATO design community.' While the *Knowledge Capture and Sharing* team documented particular design methods and techniques, the *Design Capability Build Team* assumed a more fundamental role in building the design capability across the ATO. Their work resulted in the *Integrated Administrative Design Guide* and handbooks for the four different Community of Practice areas. They also sought to establish a distributed design strategy in other ATO business areas, for example in the Business Service Lines. Figure 11.1 shows how the ATO sought to integrate administrative design in 2003 while developing organizational design capabilities. The figure shows how the design specific Service Delivery Teams work and engage with the Practice Management Team and ATO clients. The latter could request design support for specific design projects but also turn to the Service Delivery Teams for an introduction to the new design approaches and methods.

The presence of these different teams, all linked to the efforts of the ATO to develop internal design capabilities, attests to the growing recognition that people and services matter to policy making and policy implementation. In addition, they exemplify the implications of a design approach for public organizations. To this day, few organizations in the public and the private sector have shown such a commitment to re-orienting their internal workings around people.

A chart with the organizational structure of the Australian Taxation Office from June 2003 depicts seven business service lines engaged in developing internal design capabilities.[37] Two of them, the Personal Tax (PTax) group and the APP/SOLS/CDC group already had developed

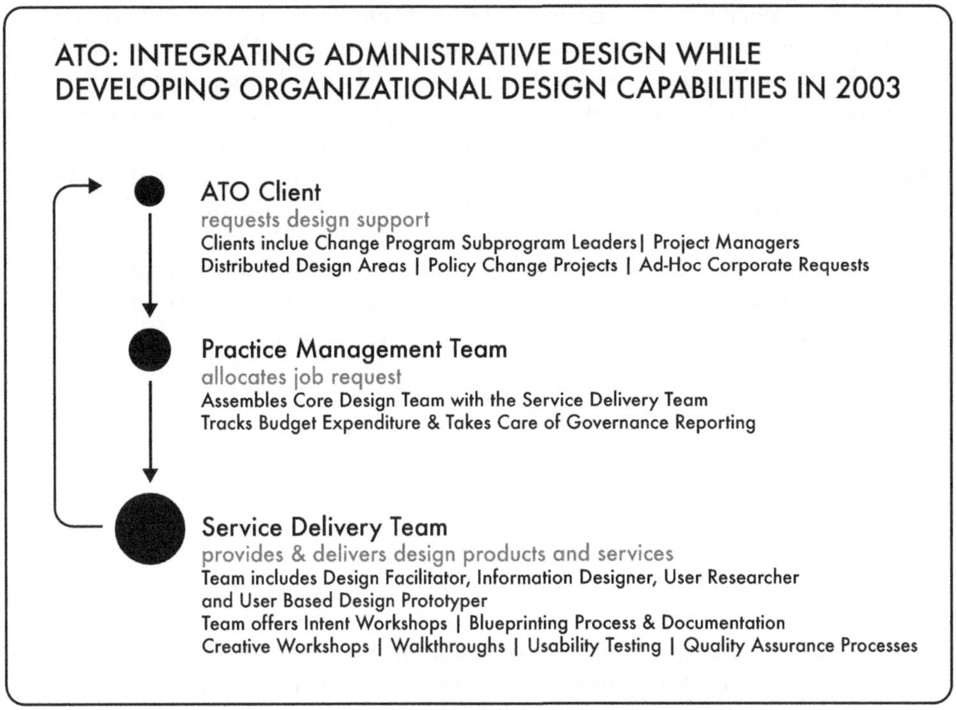

ATO: INTEGRATING ADMINISTRATIVE DESIGN WHILE DEVELOPING ORGANIZATIONAL DESIGN CAPABILITIES IN 2003

ATO Client
requests design support
Clients inclue Change Program Subprogram Leaders| Project Managers
Distributed Design Areas | Policy Change Projects | Ad-Hoc Corporate Requests

Practice Management Team
allocates job request
Assembles Core Design Team with the Service Delivery Team
Tracks Budget Expenditure & Takes Care of Governance Reporting

Service Delivery Team
provides & delivers design products and services
Team includes Design Facilitator, Information Designer, User Researcher
and User Based Design Prototyper
Team offers Intent Workshops | Blueprinting Process & Documentation
Creative Workshops | Walkthroughs | Usability Testing | Quality Assurance Processes

---

Figure 11.1 ATO's original approach to develop and distribute internal design capability

internal skills for design leadership, design facilitation, user testing and user research. However, information design was not well developed yet in 2003. Only two out of the seven positions had been filled. The role of the information designer itself seemed still poorly understood. In the team meeting I observed in 2003, for example, the information designer acted as note taker documenting the meeting. In 2004, four new relevant design specialties had been recognized and added to the list of emerging design capabilities. These were Business Process Design; Knowledge and Infrastructure Design; Applications Design, and Design Management.

The distribution of design capability happened incrementally and was carefully guarded. None of the ATO business areas were forced to develop design skills. Instead, they were encouraged to request design services from the *Service Delivery Teams* to explore what, how and why design thinking and design methods were relevant for them. In addition, the seven principles provided ample space to experiment, adopt or refine existing design activities. Rather than imposing a particular or singular approach to design on the different ATO areas, individual ATO areas were encouraged 'to own design and understand design in their own terms.'[38] Figure 11.2 shows how the design action loop initially worked.

The design facilitators and the design capability distribution teams played a crucial role in this effort, devising strategies that accommodate their particular group's needs. Guided by the principles and a vision but not controlled or contained by rules, distributed design teams were free to explore within their groups what the seven principles meant in the context of their own work. This exploration was supported by several initiatives that continuously built confidence and skills in the design teams.

In September 2004, the ATO had five major agency wide initiatives in place to support and develop continuous design capabilities. These initiatives included the *Capability*

Framework which identified the core and specialist capabilities central to the Tax Office achieving its corporate business goals; the *Design Curriculum* which offered continuous opportunities in training and skilling for design practitioners; *The Design Guide* (later becomes known as *The Guide*) which described the end to end process for developing a new tax product using human-centered design principles and techniques and contributed to a shared understanding of the process; regular *Communities of Practice* meetings for each of the (now) seven design disciplines for support and exchange; and a quarterly *Design Council* which offered senior managers a forum to discuss 'the health of design' in the Tax Office. All these initiatives were supported by additional '*buddying, coaching and mentoring initiatives*' that offered specific support to new staff members and to transfer design skills. Together, these initiatives signaled to current and new members of the ATO that human-centered design thinking and design methods were taken seriously by the leadership and played a key role in the way the organization approached the design of taxation products.

Developing and distributing design capability within PTAX

The Personal Taxation Group (PTax) emerged as an early adopter of human-centered product development. It was one of the first ATO business areas to maintain its own design group, PTax Design. At the time, Personal Tax was responsible for a client base of roughly 8.9 million taxpayers; 25,500 tax agents and a range of other 'intermediaries'. Intermediaries include tax practitioners who mediate between the Taxation Office and individual taxpayers. They provide services, ensure compliance, interpret laws, engage in benefits distribution and apply the private health insurance rebate. It was the task of the Personal Tax group to manage the ATO's relationship with these professional intermediaries. In addition, Personal Tax provided services to the Department of Family and Community Services for the Family Assistance Office and the Child Support Agency.[39] PTAX remains the most visible face of the Australian Taxation Office because the majority of taxpayers will pay their taxes through products and services offered by this organizational business area. PTAX has to ensure that everyday taxpayers 'understand and report their tax obligations and claim their entitlements.'[40]

By late 2003, the PTax Group had emerged as one of the internal advocates for improving their own design capability. Members of PTax Design, like design team members from other business areas, had been trained following a design curriculum that was specifically developed for the ATO. Like them staff had participated in design seminars and creativity workshops. For two design facilitators at PTax, this was not enough. They still had questions. As one of them recalls:'At one point, we just sat down and said: "Let's try to figure out this design thing."'

She recalls that they 'grabbed a whiteboard and started to sketch out' what they understood about design and its relevance to their work. As morning went into afternoon and afternoon into evening, the whiteboard filled with all sorts of questions: 'What is it?' 'Why should we care?' 'How do we use it?' 'What do we need?' By the end of the session, the two design facilitators had developed answers for themselves that led to the creation of a new model of how design worked and how design could be useful, usable and desirable in the specific context of PTax. Moreover, they had produced a visual illustration that explained the value of design in their work context. Figure 11.3 shows the final model, which has come known as the 'Three Cogs' diagram and one of the earlier hand drawn working sketches. Design is shown as the central cog that connects project management with governance, effectively linking theory and practice.[41] It is this drawing that inspired the cover for this book and affirms once more how public services by design are the key to re-orienting services, organizations and policies around people.

Encouraged and informed by this work, other PTax design team members began to conduct their own design inquiries into PTax. They mapped current user pathways and reviewed them for opportunities of improving the taxpayer's experience. They produced discussion papers, such as the one on 'Individual Client Segment Pathways', which further clarified how and why the concept of user pathways related to the tasks of PTax.[42] Within a year, the PTax Design team, on its own, had produced a blueprint for distributing design capability within PTax, a design skilling document and a draft for distributing design strategy. It had also organized and conducted its own design coaching workshop.[43]

Some of the design work that emerged in the PTax group has facilitated the design work in other Business Line Services. Especially their exploration of the interaction between design, project management and governance has had an impact outside of PTax.

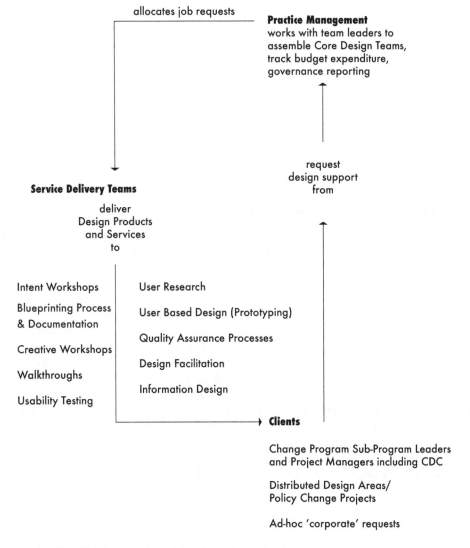

Figure 11.2 The ATO integrated administrative design action loop

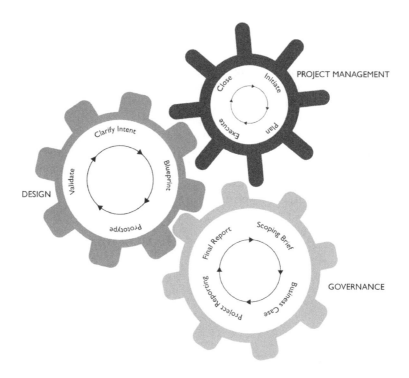

Figure 11.3 Diagram generated by IRS staff to situate design within the ATO

Will transformation by design last?

For all the efforts the ATO made to transform public services by design, to re-orient its own organization around people, the question remains how sustainable these changes turn out to be and how these changes positively contribute to the ATO over time. The answer to this question is of great import to current design-informed public sector innovation efforts. On the individual level, there is ample evidence that the efforts to skill people in design thinking and design methods were successful. So successful in fact, that some staff members felt equipped to leave the government and set up their own consulting firm. Others accepted innovation leadership positions in the private sector. Yet others advanced their public career based on their newly acquired design capabilities. On the agency level, design thinking had been understood and promoted in many different areas and on all management levels from the Tax Commissioner down. But not every manager or every staff member of the ATO subscribed to a human-centered design approach. One of the design mentors, invited to review and evaluate the development of design capability in late 2003 assessed the situation then as follows:

> I cannot judge whether the new ideas have penetrated deeply into the entire organization, but there is now a critical mass of individuals in the central office who are working in a new way.[44]

At times, these newly minted design roles struggled to reach out and failed to draw in colleagues. This was noted, for example, in the 2004 Audit, which called for more participatory design *within* the organization in its recommendations.

Promote awareness of design disciplines by encouraging Business Solutions staff to participate in design related work (not just as part of the formal core design team), to participate in a number of Communities of Practice meetings and by recording this information on the Business Solutions website.[45]

The 2004 Audit points out that staff involved in design activities generated unique insights concerning their organization and their business area while staff members not involved in these activities 'lack[ed]' behind. In order for the organization to move on and to progress, that knowledge needed to be accessible to all staff. This clearly indicates a growing recognition of design capability as a core organizational capability.[46]

But how do things look a decade later? From 2006 through 2011, the ATO lost some of its key design staff. Some were moving on to other government agencies, or others left the public sector for good. This had a negative impact on the organization's design capability. During my follow up visit in 2011, those in charge of design at the ATO were not as engaged with the design approach in 2003. Neither of them had recognized how the organization relapsed into old practices. By early 2011, design had become synonymous with *IT and Rapid Solution Design* and design solutions now had 'to fit' the organization. This presented a shift back to the organizational perspective, though user pathways and customer experience were still terms employed and considered.

Significant changes were also evident in the actual *Design Guide*. This document was originally considered to be an important tool to communicate the role and practice of design at the ATO. By 2011, staff no longer treated it as a living document. It had undergone its last update three years earlier, in 2008 and had since withered into a container for ever more and ever more complicated and detailed principles. This was in marked contrast with earlier versions, which received updates about every 18 months.

In August 2011, staff at the Australian Taxation Office no longer seemed to believe in or no longer saw the need for articulating and reflecting on their design principles. Almost nobody seemed to notice the gradual vanishing of visualization. The principle to visualize early, while still verbalized, had become more difficult to adhere to since the team had been moved into a new building. The new building's regulations did not permit the team to hang posters or attach anything else on the wall. While staff pointed to this situation, they seemed resigned to the situation and were either not aware or not concerned about losing this aspect of their recently acquired design practice. Remarkably, the innovation principle was dropped as well. Again, this did not seem to trouble staff members talked to. They argued that creativity was implicit in the system and that it was not necessary to state innovation as an explicit principle.

> Dropping the innovation principle was taken as we are not allowed to be creative. But that is not what is the case. If you take poetry, there is the structure of the sonnet it is remarkably rigid and can generate innovation nonetheless.[47]

In an indication that the ATO continues to value design and remains vested to developing its own design capabilities, the agency re-invigorated and strengthened its design teams with several new design related hires in the end of 2011. The vision for an Integrated Tax Design is still alive today. In his 2014 address to participants of the ATAX 11th International Tax Administration Conference in Sydney, Australia's Commissioner of Taxation, Chris Jordan reiterated the continuous relevance and need for *Integrated Tax Design*. He underlined that the work undertaken by the ATO and its direct involvement with people and services ('solutions') generated important and actionable insights for lawmakers at the Treasury.

> It is important to me that the ATO is able to influence law design. We have the advantage of seeing what works and doesn't in practice and can use those insights to advise Treasury. Our new Integrated Tax Design Unit will ensure requests to Treasury are prioritised and presented from a whole-of-system perspective – there is limited capacity to change law and we are looking at other ways to resolve issues. Seeking the community's perspective through consultation – knowing what problems exist and their ideas for possible solutions is vital for us to provide the right advice to Treasury.[48]

Two years later, in January 2016, a new Deputy for Design and Change Management assumed her position at the ATO. In her words, her task is

> To bring together functions in the ATO that focus on an enterprise-wide view of experience design, program and project activity and change management. It includes our corporate research and intelligence function, consultation hub and the software developers' partnership office as well as our design, change and portfolio management capabilities.[49]

A different approach

The approach chosen by the Australian Taxation Office to re-orient itself around people is strikingly different from that of the two case studies we looked at in Section Two of this book. From the start, the ATO expected to be in for the long haul. These efforts have not stopped and continue to evolve. There have been disruptions and slow-downs. There have been moments where the efforts seem to be in danger of being derailed. For anyone interested in studying human-centered design in government, the *Integrated Tax Design* project remains a unique case for its longevity and commitment.

Overall, the ATO continues to be successful in developing internal design capability. It succeeded in establishing design teams and new design roles. It managed to change its organizational design practices by developing a common set of design principles, a framework for design processes and blue prints staff could apply. The original seven principles applied design thinking and design methods systematically to the problems of specific business areas. And while the integration of the design teams into their business area was not always successful or easy, design specialties have been nurtured in a protective environment that allowed the individual to understand their role as information designer or user researcher while acquiring relevant techniques.

The ATO *Integrated Tax Design* project demonstrates that transformation by design takes resources and time. Moreover, it shows how easy it is for people within institutions to default to previous behavior and thinking when the support for design vanishes. In the ATO, this was evident in the period from 2008 through 2011 when new staff without design knowledge replaced the one with design training and design exposure. In a sign of remarkable resilience, the design principles still lived on and methods were still used. But their application and their interpretation had changed significantly, weakening the focus of user experience.

Contributing factors

There are several factors that have sustained and advanced the development of design capability in the Australian Taxation Office. Among these count a voluntary approach that encouraged and promoted design thinking and design methods, providing the tools and the training but also the space for individual exploration. Staff was provided with opportunities, resources, and support to inquire into how this new design approach works for them rather than being told to make use of a method degreed from above. A set of design principles that were communicated and lived guided these explorations. However, the departure of a key person also played a role.

In February 2002, Second Tax Commissioner Dr. Preston abruptly departed the organization. He was a key promoter of the *Integrated Tax Design initiative* recommended by John Ralph and had supported Ralph's efforts at improving the taxation system.[50] What could have been a turning point for the ITD project remained with little impact since by then '[His successor] was on board with the design approach, even though he did not promote it initially.'[51] By the time Preston left the organization in February 2002, his leadership in tax reform had instilled the principles and techniques of user-based design and generated enough internal support to continue the further development of distributed design capability.

In retrospect, Preston's departure counts as one of the reasons for why design thinking could begin to grow roots within the ATO. When he left, the ATO had to make a conscious decision about where to take the idea of design. By deciding to develop the capability, the organization made an important commitment that strengthened the ongoing initiatives and led to new ones. In addition, Preston's departure presented a much-needed opportunity for re-scoping the project. Rather than trying to change everything at once, rather than trying to get the Treasury, the Office of Parliamentary Counsel and the Australian Taxation Office to integrate their design processes simultaneously, the project scaled down. The ATO served as a pilot study to learn and deliver. This system within a system could then become a model for other government areas.

From the onset, leadership played a key role in the efforts by the ATO to change from being a rules-enforcer to being a support for people paying taxes. It was no coincidence that the Governor-General appointed one of the key team members of the Ralph Report to a top executive position in the ATO. And it was no accident that the Commissioner of Taxation immediately charged the new Second Tax Commissioner with overseeing the change efforts. In his annual report 2001–2002, the Tax Commissioner highlighted the design efforts that were underway in the ATO by including a case study on user-based design.[52] Michael D'Ascenzo, previously Second Commissioner of Law at the Australian Taxation Office, assumed the position of Tax Commissioner in January 2006. He has embraced design thinking and discusses the activities of designing in his public presentations.[53] His successor, Chris Jordan, appointed as the 12th Commissioner of Taxation on 1 January 2013, continues to support the advance of ATO design capabilities. The question is, will the design principles continued to be adhered to, and if so, will the organization continue to re-orient itself around people.

Moments of derailment and drifts

So far, there have been three moments were the project was drifting and in danger of derailing. These instances show the continuous temptation of a living organization to drift away from a stated vision and goal and highlight the role of an alert leadership to prevent that drift. These three instances are the *ATO Change Program* in 2003; the merging of the *Integrated Administrative Design Group* with a technology-driven group central to ATO, *Business Solutions* in 2004 and the slow depletion of design expertise from roughly 2008 to 2011.

Drifting 1: The ATO change program

In 2003, the Commissioner of Taxation introduced the ATO Change Program. The program focused on changes within the Taxation Office and aimed at making the process of paying taxes more transparent to taxpayers. The goals of the effort include making the dealings of the agency with taxpayers transparent and repeatable, 'with everyone understanding the rules.'[54] The ATO Change Program promised taxpayers easier, cheaper and a more personalized program to pay taxes. Originally planned to run for three years, the program was a direct result of the *2002 Listening to the Community* program that the Commissioner had initiated after the flawed introduction of the Goods and Services Tax.

Prepared with heavy involvement of the *Integrated Tax Design Group,* the *Listening to the Community* program began in March 2002. It successfully employed user-based design principles and included discussion groups, product development workshops and observation of taxpayers of all walks of life (individuals, small business operators and tax agents) 'to get an idea what the tax system is for them.'[55] Among the results of the *Listening to the Community* program were new insights into four main ATO customer segments: individuals, small businesses, tax agents and internal ATO staff.

The findings from the *Listening to the Community* program led to a new and public change initiative by Tax Commissioner Carmody. He announced the *ATO Change Program* to taxpayers in a small brochure. Titled *Making it Easier and Cheaper to Comply,* the brochure directly addressed taxpayers and explained why taxes exist and how the ATO was working on improving people's experience in fulfilling their tax obligations.[56] Carmody referred to the brochure as 'my contract with the community.'[57] The introduction of the *ATO Change Program* signaled a shift to a new business model that emphasized a high level of ease and a low level of cost for taxpayers in fulfilling their obligations, all the while providing a sense of closure, a sense of certainty of the outcome. As a result of the Change Program, the ATO expected three of its main business areas, client services, work management and integrated processing to undergo significant changes.[58]

Former Second Assistant Tax Commissioner Preston once said that for the Integrated Tax Design to take hold, it needed to overcome two challenges. First, the organization needed to be persuaded that indeed a systematic and integrative discipline of design existed.[59] Second, the organization needed to engage in the activities of designing to discover or invent a solution appropriate for its *particular* situation. 'There are simply no off-the-shelf-solutions – each organization must fashion its own solution.'[60] However, to fulfill his 'contract,' Carmody increasingly turned towards information technology solutions, raising concerns 'that the technical vision of an IT system will lose connection with the high quality of user experience that is now the foundation of human-centered design thinking in the ATO.'[61] This concern was shared internally, especially after an international management consulting firm was hired.[62] Their stated 'one-solution-fits-all' approach to the needs of the ATO represented a significant departure from the newly developed design capabilities and a possible organizational drift towards old behaviors, values and norms.

Drifting 2: Merging integrated administrative design with business solutions

By 2004, the steady ATO efforts at developing and distributing design capability within its various business areas were so successful and productive that the focus needed to shift to another level – to capturing and integrating the new knowledge into the overall organization. There existed by now a number of productive individual 'design cells' that generated new knowledge and developed new skills around their particular business area's needs. The next step would mean to organize the evolving design capability organization-wide to 'respond quickly and appropriately to corporate priorities.'[63]

The ATO decided to merge the *Integrated Administration Design* team (up to that time responsible for the design process within the ATO) with the Corporate Design Center (which has been responsible for new policy design content). The new group was called *Business Solutions*.[64] The design mentors watched this development closely for a number of reasons. First, it represented yet another step towards aligning the design capabilities 'even more closely with improvement of the quality of user experience in interacting with the tax system.'[65] The move thus represented a positive development. However, there was concern that the heavily technology-driven existing Business Solutions group might, perhaps inadvertently, pull the focus away from user-based design and lose the vision that interaction design of the client experience had provided. A valid concern as it turned out.

The ATO leadership took this concern seriously as the subsequently emerging *2004 Blueprint for Business Solutions* shows. Distributed Design Capability was attributed a key role in designing a sustainable tax system. These distributed design teams already established have proved their value many times over by pushing the boundaries of the Tax Office's existing level of knowledge around administrative design, and by successfully capturing and sharing their experiential learning with other practitioners. They have also contributed to the emerging knowledge economy around implementation of practical design solutions by providing input into new versions of corporate documents and by participating in regular communication forums like the Design Council and various communities of practice.[66]

Drifting 3: When initial success becomes the detriment

As I have already explained, another period of drifting set in sometime around 2008 and lasted through the end of 2011. During these three years, it could have been expected for design capabilities to disappear completely. During this time, the design capacity and capability were significantly weakened but they never disappeared completely. One of the explanations is that by that time, human-centered and user-centered design had become a topic across national government. It was no longer the ATO alone that had an interest in design and developed capabilities, other public organizations, too, had begun to turn to co-designing and user-experience. Incidentally, this also meant that ATO staff with the best design understanding had an easy time moving up and moving out of the ATO and into other government agencies. The Australia Service Delivery Reform, which was enacted in 2010, gave another push to human-centered design, co-designing and user research in the public sector. I have speculated elsewhere that in a small government like Australia, it is difficult to keep people tied to one government organization throughout their career. Instead, people move from one ministry to another, from one government institution to the next. While this development weakened the ATO's ability to foster its own design capabilities further, it also meant the ideas, principles and methods spread across the national government.[67] The loss of knowledge and expertise produced a vacuum in design leadership. Inside the ATO, lack of leadership in turn allowed for loose application of the original design principles. At the same time, new principles sprung up in practice without being referred to as 'principle'. This includes the 2011 efforts to 'design to fit the organization,' which framed product development around digital IT solutions. By 2011, the original vision was also no longer clearly articulated. Members of the Treasury interviewed in 2011 also noted a lack of ownership 'of the design philosophy' espoused at the top level of the ATO. They referred to Tony Golsby-Smith's 'Voice of Intent of Design', which calls for someone very senior to be prepared to act as design champion in the organization.[68] 'We have not abandoned hope but we delayed it,' they stated at the time.[69] They found the fundamental vision still intact but a change in the strategies.

The importance of a shared vision and a long-term view

The project's original vision for designing interactions rather than products and services grew out of *The Review of Business Taxation* and pointed the organization to human-centered design. This vision was anchored in seven principles that were generated in the early stages of the project. The seven principles were made visible in word and image, for example, in form of posters. They were clearly articulated and communicated to all staff members working on projects. Staff members were encouraged to apply these principles and to adhere to them. The vision and the principles were part of an incremental implementation strategy.

An incremental implementation strategy

The strategy for implementing change in the ATO project is described by some as one of 'organic growth.'[70] Indeed, the project evolves: At first, there is an idea. Then a group of five people immerses itself in user-based design theories, methods and techniques to understand how they might be applied to the Australian Tax System. They identify and develop the basics, test them and refine them by applying them to initial projects. The success of these projects provides the group with the confidence to replicate its structure and approach, thus making it possible to work on ever more projects and creating ever more opportunities for exploration, refinement and testing. Now the activities are no longer limited to one group within the agency. Instead, copies of the original group begin to emerge in all seven Business Service Lines. The knowledge and insights these new groups generate individually leads to the formation of a new group that consolidates this information and makes it accessible to the collective. This effectively contributes to the evolution of the organization.

But this 'organic growth' was all part of a human-centered product development strategy that focused on people from the beginning. The strategy began with a search for understanding and resulted in initial design capability. In the second step, the newly acquired design capability was 'put to the test' in an effort to discover and work out potential problems at an early stage. So refined, the capability was being applied to ever more challenging tasks and projects, thus allowing for further refinement and sophistication. Once the elements and the architecture of the basic prototype design team were established, the strategy was to distribute the capability throughout the ATO.

Creation of new positions and changes in
the organizational structure

The effort to distribute the design capability is supported with the internal creation of four new job profiles that are all related to particular design tasks: Design Leader, Design Facilitator, Information Designer and User Researcher. Not one of these positions existed before and not one of these positions is directly linked to the day-to-day operations in the organization. Instead, the task of these new staff members is to continue to develop the design thinking and design methods within a particular ATO business area.

1) User researcher and user tester

By June 2003, five out of seven Business Service Lines engaged in the development of capability for user research and listed at least one user researcher, if not two, as members of their design team. Early user researchers appear to have strong backgrounds in usability testing. For some, the methods applied within the ATO are 'nothing novel or innovative, just the usual basics.'[71]

2) Design team leader

This role is also referred to as the Treasury leader and thus is the ATO contact in the Treasury (which is responsible for policy formulation). The Treasury leader or design team leader ensures that policy formulation and policy realization are integrated processes. The Treasury leader is accountable to the Budget Group Executive Director.

3) Design facilitator

By November 2003, between 15 and 20 design facilitators were part of this Community of Practice.[72] The role of design facilitator is rather unique and novel. Therefore, the organization screens applicants for their potential capability for design thinking and formally trains them in-house. Because design facilitators end up having a highly visible role in the Integrated Tax Design effort and in the various sub-Change Programs, it is particularly interesting to explore how they join the organization and how they are being prepared for their role. Many design facilitators have a background in facilitation and organizational change. Most of them found their way to the ATO through a newspaper advertisement seeking design facilitators. The following description of the application process by a current design facilitator seems to be shared by most of his colleagues.

> You apply for the position, go to assessment center, and do an activity on an open-ended problem with 60 people watching. This is followed by a formal interview. I did self-initiated research and formal training.[73]

In this case, the formal training involved a three-day course led by one of the design mentors, four days of induction training, and two to three days of design methodologies 'where *The Wheel* was being explained to me.' Current ATO design facilitators have a role in shaping this position as this draft text, e-mailed between two design facilitators shows.

The Design Facilitator works with project teams to apply and implement good design principles and methods to administrative design issues. In partnership with the client and project teams, Design Facilitators establish how the ATO's design methodology should be applied to a particular case, mapping out a program of design activities to achieve the outcomes the client is seeking. Their work involves conversation with project teams and other clients to bring design principles to life in the products and services that help make the revenue system easier and cheaper for the community.[74]

'Design facilitators see themselves as here for the user,' shared a design facilitator attending the Community of Practice meeting for design facilitators in late 2003.[75] This weekly meeting is intended to provide an internal support group and forum to discuss what individual facilitators have learned, are working on and how their efforts at instilling design thinking and design methodologies in their particular area succeed.

In their own words, design facilitators consider themselves 'intelligent non-experts.'[76] They claim to have a good understanding of the policy process but are not necessarily familiar with detailed tax issues. The weekly meetings served as reminder that they were always 'in danger' of becoming too familiar with their special business areas' way of going about tax design. They raised the question as to what point in the process will they become less effective as 'outsider' and no longer able to see the big picture. This vulnerability is heightened by the fact that many of them find themselves the lone representative and promoter of design within their business area. It is for these reasons that the Community of Practice meetings are so meaningful and important. Design facilitators were enjoying particular attention and respect from senior management in the ATO. Other design team members who tended to be overshadowed by design facilitators, sometimes mockingly referred to design facilitators as 'whiteboard specialists' or even 'whiteboard slaves'.[77]

4) Information designer

Of the three original roles in the design teams, the information designer had been the least visible. By June 2003 only two out of seven distributed design capability teams had developed capability in information design. The few information designers that were part of design teams were mostly asked to capture discussions, notes and sketches, i.e., to document ongoing work. At least during the early stages, information design was almost synonymous with recording and not well understood as a creative capability in its own right. Other design specialists were referring to information designers as 'upgraded secretaries.'[78] There are indicators that the ATO has developed and clarified the role of the information designers since 2003.[79]

Newly emerging design capabilities

In 2004, the design stream was expanded to include four more capabilities: business process design, knowledge and infrastructure design, applications design, and design management.

Visualization of core concepts

Being able to capture core concepts of the vision in three early diagrams facilitated the discussion, communication and development within the ATO core design team. By visualizing these concepts, the ATO arrived at a common ground that then served to familiarize people joining the project with the issues. For example, *The Wheel* was used in training and preparing newly hired design facilitators about the design process but it also used internally to introduce the idea of designing. Says one of the Assistant Tax Commissioners: '*The Wheel* seemed to gain acceptance in the organization as a sensible way to think about applying design.'[80]

Prototyping

The ATO stayed committed to evaluate core ideas quickly in one or two projects. The results from these evaluations provided insights that were then used to refine principles. Prototyping was not previously part of the ATO tax design process. Now it is established in the Blueprinting Process.

Direct dialogue with taxpayers

The first product directly aimed at the general public was the *Listening to the Community* Program. This was followed by the brochure *Making it Easier to Comply*. The brochure represents a commitment by the organization to continued user-based product development and continued integration efforts. Both the program and the brochure were well perceived by the public. In many ways, this was a risky move, recalls one of the Assistant Tax Commissioners.[81] Until that time, the Australian Taxation Office had never made promises to the public. Now it was putting itself on the spot, making its actions accountable. The ATO had therefore began to engage in a direct dialogue with taxpayers.

Cultural and demographic factors

There are two other distinguishing factors that figure into the ATO project. Age is one of them. Staff members of the ATO are on average significantly younger than those working for the USPS or the IRS at the time. Age can play a role in people's attitude toward change. Cultural differences in values and norms are another one. Australia is indeed a nation that is more community centric than the United States, which tend to be individual centric. This means that Australians generally may have a more positive attitude about paying taxes than do Americans.

Organizational impact

As we have already seen above, the development of design capability within the Australian Taxation Office was touching on every aspect of the organization.

Changes along organizational structures

1) Several new organizational areas and functions are now dedicated to the development of design skills. Already in 2002, Tax Commissioner Carmody reported on the expansion of the Office of the Commissioners line to include the Tax Design Group, Integrated Tax Design and Strategic Directions and Programs.[82]
2) The structural flow of information has changed from a linear flow to one that is non-linear and allows information to flow directly back into the organization.
3) Basic tasks have changed from 'meeting deadlines' to 'designing user experiences.'

Impact on Staff

1) There are now 'centres of expertise,' i.e., people with expert knowledge about design, in each business line who use the corporate methodology to solve line specific design issues.
2) The new skills include the art of engaging and maintaining a dialogue with other people and an emphasis on interdisciplinary teamwork.
3) There is a general shift in awareness among staff members that they are in the business of design.[83]

Changes related to organizational resources

1) Prototyping was not previously part of the ATO tax design process. Now it is established in the Blueprinting Process. Most of the artifacts took the shape of prototypes, indicating their incompleteness and openness to further input.
2) The Blueprinting Process itself represents a new resource for the organization that aids the planning and design of new tax products.
3) The Tax Design Group and the Integrated Tax Design Team have turned into valuable internal resources. The Tax Design Group is the resource for building and deploying an integrated tax design capability whereas the Integrated Tax Design Team is the internal resource for developing corporate strategy and design, including the ATO Change Program and ensures an integrated and coordinated approach to planning and governance activities.
4) The blueprinting process also introduced a new language that is helpful in the product development efforts, as this statement by a senior tax official documents.

   People familiar with the methodology and that's lots of people now . . . we have got a language that allows us to do that more easily. So I can tell you 'hey we are diving into details now and we have not even got a blueprint for this.' So it has given us a tool to help manage discussion like that. Or 'I don't think we have a shared understanding of intent here may be we should spend ten minutes and sort out the differences so it is useful in this sense. Or what's the user's experience. That is another question that is often asked. So it is part of the language.[84]

Changes related to organizational vision

1) The organization has shifted its understanding and efforts from enforcing rules to designing interactions for its customers.
2) Evidence that the new vision is taking hold comes from statements by the highest tax officials. The official website of the Australian Taxation Office talks deliberately about human-centered design and ATO's commitment to design interactions for people.

Integrating Tax design: An ongoing effort involving struggles and successes

The Integrated Tax Design project has linked designing for interactions with organizational development and it continues to do so today, almost 20 years later. From its inception, the ATO project had a strong organizational champion. But whenever the leadership wavered, the project and its vision became vulnerable. Stewarding the project, guarding the overall vision and creating new user pathways became explicit tasks for the design teams and their design facilitators. Many of these had a previous career in organizational facilitation who combined their expertise and work on organizational change with the principles and methods of human-centered design. It is noteworthy that during the last major drifting period (2008 and 2011) none of the external design mentors were called on. During this time, the vision did shift and one important principle was dropped. It is almost astounding then – and a credit to the ATO – that the design efforts have been revived and reinvigorated by the end of 2011 when a new head of design was installed.

Above all, the ATO corporate plan 2011–12 committed once again to integrating services, organizations and policies. It states as one of the goals of ATO's corporate planning:

> We work with Treasury and continue to consult, collaborate and co-design with taxpayers and our consultative forums to address those issues of uncertainty and contention in the law.[85]

The ATO made this commitment against challenges and opportunities it is aware of and discusses openly. These concern, as in so many public organizations:

- the problem of involving users early, often and iteratively through a design process
- providing adequately for co-design in their project management and delivery methods
- ensuring the voice of the user is carried to the ears of decision makers
- balancing the goals of their organization and the needs of users
- working with new enterprise solutions whilst delivering individual experiences
- maintaining a responsive and experience co-design capability across a large change agenda.

In 2011, the ATO formulated the following answers:[86]

- 'We continue to work with project managers who feel unsure about taking out low fidelity and rough drafts to the community. To successfully involve users in the design process they need to be included as early as possible. The opportunity for changing and influencing design is significantly reduced if scheduled after other corporate sign off processes (eg: technical sign offs) have taken place.'
- 'Co-design costs in time and resources. We continue to work closely with our design and project leads and new policy team to capture both the time and financial costs of co-design.'
- 'We continue to work on our co-design and usability documents (which can be detailed and wordy) and governance processes to look how we synthesis [sic] findings and ensure they are presented to the right person for embedding into design.'
- 'This [balancing] will forever be an ongoing challenge, ensuring we have run the right processes, with the right people to ensure we have the right information when we have to design solutions that provide the right balance between our organization and community.'

- 'Our enterprise solution is still maturing and with that our understanding for how we adapt the overarching design framework, whilst adapting for different types of clients and use contexts, ultimately leading to better experiences.'
- 'We continue to develop and grow the co-design capability, many who now have long term experience within this discipline to ensure we can be responsive to our large organizational change agenda. We are also more mindful of our capacity and come to programs of work more strategically when looking for areas to target co-design.'

One can argue that the focus on co-design has provided the ATO project with another opening to continue its work on integrating tax design around people. It will be interesting to see what shape and form design thinking and design practice will take in the future. What is already evident is that at least in some parts of the Australian government, civil servants have become aware and have taken on responsibility for their own design work. Many private businesses would to reflect in similar fashion on their own product development approaches to improve the services they offer and to re-orient their organizations around people.

The current version of the Blueprint (from March 2015) uses eleven client stories for every kind of client in the ATO, this is making taxation personal in the tax office. It also tells six staff experience stories. Human experience in the ATO includes people inside and outside the organization. It is an acknowledgment that services do not stop at the desk of an organization but run through the organizational system and effect staff as much as they affect citizens. The stories are introduced as 'bringing design to life'.[87]

We find the same two-tiered strategy today employed other innovators in the public sector, for example by Laboratorio Gobierno in Chile and Inovagov in Brazil, by Mindlab in Denmark and by The Lab at the US Office of Personnel Management. However, few government agencies and innovation initiatives enjoy the benefits of a long-term commitment the Australian government has bestowed on the Australian Taxation Office.

The ongoing efforts by ATO to develop internal design capabilities deserve to be looked at by researchers and practitioners across different fields. It is a rare live case with many lessons for professionals concerned with public management, policy making and design. But it also points to new models of design education in a time when design emerges as central not only to developing consumer goods but to envisioning and developing desirable social outcomes.

Notes

1 Preston, A. (2004). 'Designing the Australian Tax System', in R. Boland and F. Collopy (eds.), *Managing as Designing*, Stanford University Press, Stanford, CA, pp. 208–213.
2 Terrey, N. (2012). *Managing by Design – A Case Study of the Australian Taxation Office*, Doctoral Thesis, University of Canberra, Faculty of Business, Government & Law, Canberra, Australia.
3 See Body, John, Farris, Jim, Golsby-Smith, Tony and Rhea, Darrel (2003). 'Tax Design in Australia', *AIGA Annual National Conference*, The Power of Design, Vancouver, BC.
4 Terrey, *Managing by Design*.
5 This statement is attributed to ATO Tax Commissioner Michael Carmody. See D'Ascenzo, M. (2010b). 'Working for All Australians: The ATO and the Community', *Public Lecture to Charles Sturt University*, Albury-Wodonga Campus, New South Wales, Australia, 6 October 2010 and D'Ascenzo, M. (2011). 'Keynote Address by the Commissioner of Taxation: Protecting the Community and Its Tax System', *Institute of Chartered Accountants of Australia, National Tax Conference*, 7 April 2011, Canberra, Australia.
6 Terrey, *Managing by Design*.

7   Author interview with senior tax official, November 24, 2003.

8   Author interview with senior tax official, November 24, 2003.

9   For more on relay style design see Archer, Bruce (1961). *A Systematic Method for Designers*, Design Council, London.

10 Preston, 'Designing the Australian Tax System,' p. 212.

11 Author interview, November 21, 2003.

12 In 2014, 16.5 Million tax returns were lodged. Source: https://annualreport.ato.gov.au/sites/g/files/net376/f/Annual-Report-2013–14/01-overview/reinventing-ato.html [accessed May 2016].

13 Richard Tait, 'Information Management and Analytics, Australian Taxation Office,' The Australian Taxation Office, PowerPoint presentation. November 18, 2003.

14 Comment by senior tax official, October 2003.

15 Ralph, John, *A Tax System Redesigned–More certain, equitable and durable*, July 30, 1999. Also known as The Ralph Report or Ralph Review. Australian Taxation Office.

16 Ibid.

17 Second Commissioner Dr. Alan Preston in a Foreword to *The Guide. Applying an Integrated Approach to Tax Design*, February 2002, Australian Taxation Office.

18 "TVM yet to be tested," online article by the Australian Institute of Company Directors, November 2000. http://www.companydirectors.com.au/Director-Resource-Centre/Publications/Company-Director-magazine/2000-to-2009-back-editions/2000/November/TVM-yet-to-be-tested [accessed June 2016].

19 Author notes, October 31, 2003.

20 Author notes from conversation with ATO staff, October 31, 2003.

21 See 'Designing the Australian Tax System,' by Dr. Alan Preston, formerly Second Commissioner of Taxation, Australian Taxation Office, in *Managing as Designing*, Richard Boland and Fred Collopy (eds.) (Stanford: Stanford University Press, 2004), pp. 208–213.

22 Also see Michael D'Ascenzio, then Second Commissioner of Taxation: 'Designing the delivery of legislative measures' presented at the International Quality and Productivity Conference: Strengthening the links between Policy Development and Implementation – Strategies to ensure the successful delivery of government policy decisions in Canberra, May 17, 2004.

23 Author notes, November 2003.

24 Preston, 'Designing the Australian Tax System,' p. 212.

25 This account of the first design conference is in line with the description by Dr. Preston, 'Designing the Australian Tax System.'

26 Definition taken from the Glossary of Terms, *The Guide–Applying an Integrated Approach to Tax Design*. Integrated Tax Design Group, (ATO, Version April 2002).

27 Author interview with senior tax official, November 24, 2003.

28 Preston, 'Designing the Australian Tax System,' p. 212.

29 Definition taken from the Glossary of Terms, *The Guide–Applying an Integrated Approach to Tax Design*. Integrated Tax Design Group, (ATO, Version April 2002).

30 Author interview with senior tax official, November 24, 2003.

31 'Reforming the Tax Design Process – A Blueprint for Building an Integrated Tax Design Capability', ATO, December 2000.

32 The Guide, Version April 2002. Prototype only, ATO.

33 Author interview with member of ITD design team, November 24, 2003.

34 Author interview with senior tax official, November 24, 2003.

35 Status as of November 25, 2003.

36 Source: IAD (SD&P) Organisational Structure, ATO undated.

37 Ibid.

38 Printed undated chart provided by ATO staff.

39 *Distributing Design in Personal Tax*, June 13, 2003, ATO.

40 ATO Annual Report 2002.

41 Ibid.

42 Author reconstructed diagram based on the PTax original provided by a PTax design facilitator.

43 'Individual Client Segment Pathways,' a discussion paper prepared by Helen Barnes, PTax Design (undated).

44 See PTax Design Environment. PowerPoint slide July 31, 2003; PTax Design Skilling Document. PTax. November 21, 2003; PTax Blueprint Distributing Design in Personal Tax. October 13, 2003;

PTax Key Messages. V1.6. July 28, 2003; PTax Design Coaching Workshop. Tuesday November 25, 2003; PTax Distributing Design Strategy. Draft.

45 2003 report on the development of design capability.

46 ATO Business Solutions User Research Report Knowledge Audit 2004. Published by ATO Business Solutions Knowledge and Design Infrastructure August 25, 2004, page 4.

47 Personal conversation with senior ATO staff August 2011.

48 ATAX 11th International Tax Administration Conference, Sydney, 14 April 2014, https://www.ato.gov.au/Media-centre/Speeches/Commissioner/Reinventing-the-ATO-building-trust-in-Australia-s-tax-administration/ [accessed June 2016].

49 See: https://au.linkedin.com/in/jane-king-a7724521 [accessed May 2016].

50 The Second Tax Commissioner is mentioned in the Ralph Report as an "apt leader."

51 Author Interview with senior ATO official, November 24, 2003.

52 'Case Study: User-Based Design Reaches New Heights,' ATO Annual Report 2002, 3.3. *Innovations in Tax Administration*. Michael Carmody, Commissioner of Taxation 1993–2005.

53 See for example D'Ascenzo, Michael, Second Commissioner of Taxation. "Designing the delivery of legislative measures" presented at the International Quality and Productivity Conference: Strengthening the links between Policy Development and Implementation–Strategies to ensure the successful delivery of government policy decisions in Canberra, May 17, 2004.

54 See *Making it Easier and Cheaper to Comply*, ATO, July 2003. NAT9497-7.2003.

55 Ibid., p. 5.

56 Ibid.

57 Former Tax Commissioner Michael Carmody as quoted by a First Tax Commissioner during a presentation of the ATO Change program to a group of international tax officials.

58 This information is based on a presentation of the ATO Change Program during the OASIS TaxXML Technical Committee Conference, hosted by the Australian Taxation Office, January 31st–February 4th, 2005 Sydney Australia *Technology Conference*, PowerPoint Slides.

59 Preston, 'Designing the Australian Tax System.'

60 Ibid.

61 Concern was expressed in a confidential 2003 report by one of the original design mentors.

62 The ATO hired Accenture for this.

63 2004 *Business Solution Blueprint*, ATO internal document.

64 2003 report on the development of design capability by a design mentor.

65 Ibid

66 See *Business Solutions Blueprint for Building Design Capability*, Draft 1.0, September 8, 2004, p. 2 (dated September 2, 2004).

67 Junginger, S. (2012). 'Public Foundations of Service Design', in S. Miettinen and A. Valtonen (eds.), *Theory of Service Design*, Lapland University Press, Rovaniemi, Finland, pp. 21–26.

68 Reference to Tony Golsby-Smith from Second Road in Sydney who also had a key role in the early stages of developing design capability at the ATO.

69 Interviews with members of the Treasury, August 2011.

70 Author interview with Assistant Tax Commissioner, November 24, 2003.

71 Author interview with user researchers, November 24, 2003.

72 Author interview with design facilitators during Community of Practice Meeting, November 21, 2003.

73 Author interview with design facilitator after design facilitator meeting, November 24, 2003.

74 Excerpt from an e-mail between design facilitators to draft a design job advertisement to recruit new design facilitators dated October Friday 13, 2003.

75 Comments by design facilitator during design facilitator meeting November 24, 2003.

76 Author interview with design facilitator, November 24, 2003.

77 Author interview, November 21, 2003.

78 Author interview November 25, 2003.

79 ATO Strategic Paper 2004 details more formal education and training for information designers.

80 Author interview with Senior Tax Official, November 24, 2003.

81 Author interview with Assistant Tax Commissioner, November 24, 2003.

82 ATO Annual Report 2002. ATO.

83 Course: ATO official website: http://www.ato.gov.au.
84 Author interview with senior tax official, November 24, 2003.
85 Co-design in the ATO, Australian Taxation office, 2011, p. 4.
86 Ibid., p. 11.
87 Reinventing the ATO, March 2015, Australian Taxation Office.

12 Expanding design discourse and design practice across government

When managers begin to think, speak and act as designers, a profound change can take place. When they accept that what they are about is changing existing circumstances to preferred ones (as Herbert Simon says), and when they begin to adopt the distinctions of design conversation, and some of the methods of traditional design practice, new possibilities for collaborative work become available.

—Jim Faris, Designer[1]

Presenting theories and practices of design in one book is a challenge and not without its problems. The temptation to segment the content into two volumes, one with a focus on theory and the other with a focus on practice accompanied this work from start to finish. Succumbing to the temptation, however, would have undercut one of the very characteristics of designing, and worse, lost sight of what distinguishes design from many other fields: the ability to bridge critical thinking, research and analysis with actual making. Keeping the two sections together illustrates the broader implications of specific design practices and design principles for organizations, especially those we put in charge of translating policies into public services. It is our understanding of design, designers, designing and our notion of what can be changed – that is perceived newly and re-designed – for the better that leads to novel consumer products and great fashion design. But the same principles and practices inform how we go about designing policies and the services that bring them to life.

The arguments put forth in this book position policy work as a creative and productive art. People concerned with policy intent, policy making and policy implementation all participate in the making of policies that shape the lives of many, often millions of people. The design perspective put forth here does not deny the presence of many stakeholders with conflicting interests. Instead, it suggests a different approach to arrive at a common ground that enables us to act. Design is an art that helps us overcome situations that appear to be stuck. Design thrives on the challenge of creating new possibilities. A design perspective does not seek to brush over the intricate legal and political context in which policy designs are being developed. Instead, a design perspective encourages us to assess our development processes, our design capabilities and our use (i.e., non-use) of specific design methods.

The examples suggest that when design puts people and services in the center of policy making and policy implementation, those in charge benefit from a range of new design methods and new design practices that open new avenues for useful, usable and desirable citizen-centric public services. This indicates that human-centered design aids policy makers and public managers to re-orient policies, organizations and services around people while equipping civil servants with new tools to achieve better outcomes.

Designing policies and services

One of the points this book has made is that design is integral to the public sector. Policies, organizations and services are, and always have been, products of human thinking and doing. The historic examples in Section II showed that specific design principles, certain kinds of design thinking and particular design methods are put to work by every government organization. The same is true for private businesses and non-profit organizations. They all are built around specific design principles that may or may not serve them well in today's rapidly changing technical, social and economic contexts. Interestingly, we can still find the same design approaches with the same predictable design outcomes, both in public and private organizations. It seems clear then that our opportunities for public sector innovation therefore rest in our ability to engage critically with our design tasks and practices.

This is, of course, easier said than done. We can look to the rise of design thinking in business and most recently, in the public sector.[2] Design thinking can be a vehicle for transformative organizational changes. Yet, for this, design thinking has to be understood not only as a new technique or a novel method. Techniques and methods merely inject new spirits into the organizational skeleton. Only when design thinking guides a comprehensive approach to integrate and re-align an organization, its structures, resources and people with its purpose, does it reach the strategic depths of the organization, where it can have a lasting impact.[3]

From Pilot Study to Project Commitment: Embedding Design

The examples in Section II as well as the pilot studies mentioned throughout Section I convey that it is fairly easy for organizations and designers to set up an initial pilot study. The demands on resources in the early stages are negligible: A six week-pilot project sufficed for the USPS project and a small curious in-house team got things initially underway at the ATO. The UK Library design research project ran for less than ten weeks while students looking into the German employment agency spent a total of six hours with that organization, applying the research methods they acquired in class to produce significant and actionable insights. And yet, every pilot study spawned a new vision and generated valuable insights for a new strategy and new services.

Any sustained and purposeful inquiry that involves organizational change, in contrast, requires long-term organizational commitment, a dedicated team and a budget. A serious design project involves the development of design skills and design knowledge in house and on the job. This will be the case for as long as public administration and public policy schools fail to address design education and design training in their curricula and programs. Only a handful of public managers and policy makers currently have opportunities to advance their design skills and to learn about relevant design capabilities. Tentative interest has been expressed by national academies in France (ENA) and Brazil (ENAP), the latter making room on its own campus for a public innovation lab. Even German academies like the Bundesakademie or the Verwaltunghochschule Speyer have or are opening their doors to design thinking workshops, for example.

Efforts to embed human-centered design approaches within broader government and across different levels (i.e., the national, international, local and regional levels) are not easily compatible with existing organizational structures and processes. Actual development projects are important because they provide opportunities for staff to engage, learn about and experiment with new approaches relevant to their own work and problems. After attending a workshop session by a local initiative that embraces design for public sector innovation, a senior member of a German government funded political foundation affirmed that proximity, engagement and participation are key to shifting organizational design practices: 'they have to experience it themselves. Experience sticks, you cannot take away someone's experience.'[4] Employees need opportunities to engage with designerly ways of thinking and doing and they need support from the organization's top levels. This is also one of the conclusions from the projects throughout this book.

It is a reminder that 'innovation bubbles' and 'public innovation labs' must pay particularly attention to connect their work from the start with the work of staff across the organization. Even the most formidable design-driven public sector innovation project will be difficult to sustain. The inability to anchor its work in the local and national context emerged as one of the reasons for why the Helsinki Design Lab has been defunded. This team, along with design director Marco Steinberg, conducted cutting-edge work on public sector innovation and continues to inspire many public innovation lab initiatives around the globe. Through projects, the Helsinki Design Lab demonstrated and validated the relevance of design approaches to public sector problems. It connected people, services organizations with policies. Yet, its international impact and success did not resonate locally or nationally. Its funder, SITRA, the Finnish government's innovation unit, never grasped its value and effectively shut down the lab when it did not extend its funding.[5]

Leaders of other public innovation labs, for example, at Mindlab in Denmark, have taken notice and are actively developing their national and local relationships. Mindlab's engagement portfolio is based on civil servant *Secondments*, a diverse advisory board made up of national and international experts, local projects and, last but not least, international validation.

Mindlab celebrated its tenth anniversary in 2016. These were not ten easy years and have been accompanied by substantial changes in how Mindlab operates and works, both in terms of methods and strategies. Even after a decade of success, the lab does not take the support from its ministerial sponsors for granted. Mindlab continuously seeks to engage people from its ministries. It offers secondments to individual public servants who then spend several months working on a project in the lab. Secondments present an opportunity for public servants to immerse themselves in new ways of working, thinking and making. Secondments also serve as a reality check for Mindlab staff. Are they addressing issues of relevance to their ministries? What are the challenges and obstacles to develop a broader culture of learning and applying new design approaches? Secondments therefore offer insights into what adds value to the operations and objectives of these organizations.

Mindlab has also emphasized project engagements with smaller cities and communities, like the city of Odense, and taken an active role in the 'testing of principles for modernization through Governance labs' in Fall 2014. Mindlab's team offered support during the development of the seven principles that were meant to guide the six targeted 'governance labs.' In addition, it sought to engage participants in discussions about 'how forms of administration based on the seven principles might contribute to increased efficiency, productivity and the levels of service or democracy'.[6]

The advisory board played a particular role in strategically positioning and anchoring Mindlab. Its members include experts from academia, business, civil society and government who are annually invited to reflect on the lab's strengths and weaknesses. The majority of the advisors in 2015 came from Denmark. They included CEOs from start-ups, senior academics, professional designers and senior administrators of non-profit

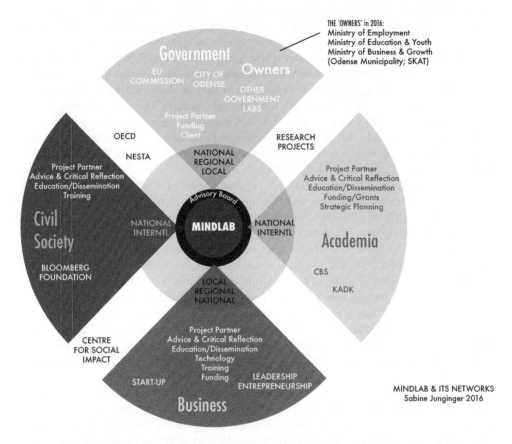

THE 'OWNERS' in 2016:
Ministry of Employment
Ministry of Education & Youth
Ministry of Business & Growth
(Odense Municipality; SKAT)

MINDLAB & ITS NETWORKS
Sabine Junginger 2016

Figure 12.1 How Mindlab developed its network across governments, business, academia and civil society

organizations. International professionals and scholars familiar with politics and policies as well as design and research complemented the group.

Beyond its advisory board, Mindlab developed an international network of actors and researchers that has allowed it to bring together knowledge and insights beneficial to its own work. In this process, Mindlab has also emerged as a leader for new public innovation lab initiatives. Figure 12.1 shows what Mindlab's network looked like in Spring 2016. The diagram positions Mindlab in the center, tightly surrounded by its advisory board. We can see how the advisory board cushions and connects the team with the government, business, academic and civil society sectors. In between we find relationships with organizations that do not neatly fit in any of these sectors but contribute additional valuable insights, knowledge and strategic connections.

Inviting, Engaging and Enabling People

The Internal Revenue Service (IRS) was publicly chided for not being creative enough and judged incapable of producing citizen-centric solutions when the Tax Forms Simplification Project started. The organization was forced to hand over its innovation project to external experts. Staff was effectively excluded from the research and the development of the new solution. They were not able to 'have an experience' of their own. They were neither invited, nor engaged to participate actively in the design project. Instead, the external design team denied this government agency and its staff, which included their own in-house design team, the ability to contribute to a creative user-friendly solution. Worse, the external design experts did not want to have to deal with staff they judged to be lacking imagination and inclination for a radical solution. The external design team did not understand staff as users with needs and concerns. This resulted in a predictable confrontational situation where each side remained suspicious of the other. No matter what the design team was to produce, it was doomed to be inacceptable for the organization, which trusted more in its own solution.

This shows that identifying, inviting and engaging people for whom a design outcome will matter remains one of the key tasks for any design project. Projects like this remind us of the importance of understanding staff as users, as people who need to be invited and engaged in a participatory development process. To do so challenges the design team and the organization to engage in a broader design discourse, to entertain new ideas about who designs, what can be designed and how something can be designed in ways that instill lasting and meaningful changes. A participatory design process enables people to come to terms with new structures, new processes, new procedures and new attitudes about their work and the people they serve. This is a lesson for designers of all backgrounds who are entering public organizations or working on public services. When designers are prepared to recognize and articulate an organization's current design practices and design approaches, they can better connect with people in the organization and enable staff to embrace design as an organizational problem (Junginger 2015).[7]

The inclusion of ATO staff as co-designers remains a model for other organizations. Design was not removed from the ATO. Design was also not simply added on top of existing practices. Instead, design was identified as central to the organization and articulated within its context, tasks and purpose. From the start, staff was encouraged to experiment with design methods on their own. Individual employees explored and experimented with design concepts within their own work environments.[8] The organization deliberately supported the development of new design practices by setting up design 'communities of practice' (Wenger 1998). These provided opportunities for individuals pursuing new design approaches to advance the design discourse for the ATO and to adjust it to its needs.[9]

In contrast to the IRS project, staff at the ATO was encouraged and supported to experience design hands-on and within the contexts of their own everyday tasks and responsibilities. The design mentors did not do the design work for the organization. They only shared design principles and familiarized staff with design methods. They also facilitated design conversations. Not least important, they conveyed to staff that they were capable of applying human-centered design principles and methods themselves. Though it did not completely eliminate the perception of design as somewhat foreign to professionals trained in law and accounting, it succeeded in connecting design to the organization's objectives. Moreover, it connected the design activities of the ATO with those at the Treasury by articulating organizational design practices and presenting alternative approaches. I always find it amazing that it took more than a decade before the Integrated Tax Design project received the attention it deserved. To this day, the design developments at the ATO remain unique and distinct from most public innovation efforts. Inviting, engaging and enabling people, be they taxpayers, ATO staff, or tax lawyers, have been central to this approach.

Developing Arguments for Change

Introducing new organizational design practices poses a challenge. The USPS example shows how those leading a redesign effort can create an environment where change is possible by making strategic use of human-centered design. The designers involved staff at the headquarters throughout the project. They set-up and maintained a project website; they conducted workshops to inform staff about the aims of the project; they explained how staff expertise contributed to the project; they facilitated design conversations. In addition, they familiarized public managers with user pathways and user research methods. In parallel, the design team conducted user research with USPS staff across the US, across many departments and facilities.

The visualization of user research revealed itself as a powerful tool to persuade USPS senior experts about the need to change its services around people. Interviews with USPS staff, current mailers and potential mailers clarified areas for action and allowed the design team to develop its own understanding of the situation. All work was meticulously documented on film, captured in handwritten notes and photographs. User research, participation and visualization, part of a human-centered design approach, became the means to reflect on and articulate current organizational design practices. User research provided the insights necessary to create a momentum for action by establishing new facts based on human experiences and human interactions.

Changing Times: Kitchen Analogies for Policy Making

In government, much designing still takes place within silos and in isolation from the real world. This is an increasingly anachronistic way of developing products and services. Yet it is the one deeply ingrained in many government structures whose origins can be traced to ideas that ruled the early industrial age.

Kitchens are great for illustrating organizations and organizational design principles. Kitchens are organizations whose purpose is to produce products and services for people. If we look at a kitchen from 1926, we find very different design principles at work than in a kitchen, say designed in 2009. The Frankfurt kitchen, for example, was designed by Margaret Schütte-Lihotzky in 1926. Everything in this kitchen has its place. Even the person running this kitchen is assigned her place: a chair in front of a work desk. All cupboards are closed, keeping pots, spices, and tools out of sight. It is the task of the person in charge to know where things are and where things go. Likewise, the processes of how meals come together remain a guarded secret. The room is enclosed and kept apart from the rest of the home. Whoever works here works in isolation. Nobody interferes, nor is anyone expected to. This kitchen is perfectly designed to tackle the production of meals and the preservation of foods following rational economic principles, which include short ways and few moves to work as efficiently and effectively as possible.[10] One of the aims of this kitchen is to keep the mess of peeling, frying and cooking hidden from family and visitors. All we are meant to see from this kitchen is the perfect meal, ideally presented by a flawless woman who herself has freshened herself up and changed clothes to make her work look effortless.[11]

This 1926 kitchen design and its implications for working resonates with many civil servants today. The design thinking and the design principles that informed the design of the Frankfurt kitchen are the same we can still find shaping many offices and cubicles in the public sector.

I contrast this 1926 kitchen with a design from 2009 by German kitchen manufacturer Bulthaup, the B2.[12] There are no walls or doors in this kitchen. Rather it is set up centrally in an otherwise open space. A workbench in the center of the room invites everybody in the room to join in, to engage in the process of 'developing' a meal. Nearby chairs around a large dining table invite people to sit down, talk and socialize. The few cupboards are open and reveal their contents. It is a design built on the notion of participation. Anyone in the room, regardless of status (family, friend, visitor, etc.), can observe, grab a knife or stir a pot.

The design principles that inform the 2009 kitchen reflect a radically different understanding of the role of the cook ('the expert') and the task of cooking ('product development'). In the 1926 kitchen, the meal is the product. The kitchen is conceived around optimizing and economizing kitchen work to get to the meal fast and under economic considerations. In the 2009 kitchen, the meal is no longer the product. Rather, the meal turns into a byproduct of the actual product: establishing and strengthening human relationships. The B2 is built around the design principles of human experiences and human interactions.

It is a fair guess that a housewife teleported from the Frankfurt kitchen into the 2009 kitchen would feel a loss of control and struggle to find her place and role. We can understand when she feels uncomfortable in the open environment where she is no longer the absolute expert and more like a relative expert: someone with expertise in context. Many policy makers and public managers find themselves teleported in precisely this way today. They are not trained for co-designing with citizens and still work in offices that physically and mentally manifest the design thinking and design principles of a bygone era. Few are prepared to work across ministerial units or across organizational boundaries. Just as we can understand that the modern kitchen requires a different attitude, different skills and different methods, we can easily see why the demands for more collaborative and co-designing practices can be difficult for civil servants to apply.

The observations made by the former project manager for the USPS Domestic Mail Manual Transformation Project resonate with efforts that re-orient the public sector around people: When I asked her why the design team did not immediately redesign the whole Domestic Mail Manual but chose to tackle the task in increments, she responded:

> The human system needed to be persuaded of the need for change; required a demonstration of what the change could look like; required a demonstration that the change could be done.[13]

When the task is to move from one kitchen into another, from one era into the next, we need to become aware of our own design thinking that is giving shape to our own design practices and favors particular methods of making. In 1926, the Frankfurt kitchen was revolutionary and at the top of the Zeitgeist. In 2009, the B2 was a better match for how we think about families, women and kitchen work. We have yet to make a similar adjustment to the public sector.

User Experience Remains Central to Human Experience

Research into user experience has emerged as valuable and viable approach to generate insights into problematic situations. Human experiences and human interactions matter from the earliest steps in any development that ultimately concerns people. Who is included, considered and invited to participate in the different stages of design? What kinds of interactions and experiences are envisioned and pursued? What specific outcomes are we trying to achieve? These questions drive many of today's public sector innovation efforts mentioned throughout the book. The examples presented serve as demonstrations for how different answers to these questions lead to different outcomes. And therein lies the value of the cases: they illustrate that how we go about designing in the public service matters and has direct consequences for the kinds of innovations we can achieve. They also show how developing better public services for people inevitably calls for changes on the organizational level.

Aside from the challenges of securing resources for an innovation lab, the question of participation remains one of the key issues for those seeking to open new ways of going about business in the public sector. In Brazil, members of the Hackerlab, an innovation group created by civil servants in the basement of the House of Deputies wing of the Brazilian congress wonder how they might draw in more citizens. Only those in the know might suspect to find a pro-citizen Hackerlab in the basement of a chamber known mostly for its corrupt politicians.

Despite their surprisingly casual looks (jeans and polo shirts), the congressional environment they are surrounded by remains intimidating for many people. One reaches the Hackerlab only by crossing the intimidating halls of congress where one is likely to encounter famous senators, deputies, press and lobbyists dressed up in dark formal suits and ties imbued with a body language full of gravitas. To get to the Hackerlab, which is located in the basement of the building, one first has to cross this official environment. And one has to know that there is a lab down there.

To reach a diverse group of Brasilia's population, the team would need to leave its basement hub and venture out into their neighborhood. The nearby central bus station and several shopping malls in the neighborhood provide ample opportunities for such 'outings'. There, the team could observe, engage and converse with real people. They could test and evaluate their own assumptions and developments. Rather than speculate about how many people on limited budgets have access to smart phones, methods of observation and conversation would generate reliable data in a short amount of time. Conducting user research even just for one day at the bus station across the street from the congress halls, for example, would allow the team to observe the phone habits and phone usage of hundreds of people they were concerned about. Instead of pondering the worthiness of 'developing a smart phone app for this user group' the answer would present itself.

User research here presents an opportunity to engage in conversations and to learn about what matters to these very citizens the hackers hope will use their product – in this case an online platform for learning about new laws and lawmaking that are being proposed in congress. It would guide their own development to arrive at meaningful, usable and accessible outcomes. Theories and methods from human-centered design as well as from service design would support and complement this project. This, however, requires training and education not readily available in most government agencies.

The Hackerlab team has made its goal to increase citizen participation and create a new level political transparency through online tools that publish the laws under consideration.

In addition, the online tools strive to give citizens a voice by allowing them to change paragraphs and wording of a given law proposal. The success of the Hackerlab depends very much on its ability to engage people. 'What can we do to engage more people?' I was asked. 'We are bringing people into our lab,' was the answer. 'In this case', I responded, 'the answer is easy': you have to go out and engage with people where they are.[14] The team had yet to work with real people in real situations.

Public Sector Innovation in the Digital Age: Making technology work for people

Innovation in the public sector can easily be confused with the task of implementing digital technologies in government offices. But social innovation and public sector innovation cannot and should not be reduced to the invention and implementation of technical solutions. Without a doubt, the digital possibilities for the public sector are immense. But digital achievements, as the Hackerlab shows, have to be informed by real life insights in order to arrive at useful, usable and desirable public services.

In this regard, the findings of a study conducted by the Manufacturing Vision Group conducted in the early nineties (Bowen et al 1994) foreshadowed the problems technological innovations pose for much-needed transformations in the public sector.[15] The purpose of this study was to identify the keys to 'perpetual' innovation in manufacturing through product development. It did not include public sector organizations. Nonetheless, it revealed why technological solutions fail to transform an organization: because the needs of the technologies in development and the needs of the organization for which they are being developed diverge.

Several participants reported that they were aware of their opportunity to develop new organizational core capabilities along with their technological innovation. In other words, they could have renewed and thereby transformed the organization as they went on developing their technology-based product. Yet, all of those who recognized this opportunity stated that they consciously chose not to pursue this potential. Rather, they perceived their own role as one of delivering and implementing only those changes necessary to ensure the functioning of the new technology.

One of the participating corporate members explained this with the existence of an 'expectation boundary that limits any kind of change except technical change' among product developers (Bowen et al, p. 278). Study participants also admitted to making conscious decisions about ignoring any organizational change opportunities: 'There is a tendency to specifically not use product development as change agent' for fear that it will 'put the technological development at risk' (Bowen et al, p. 279). Both statements highlight that many people concerned with technology development prefer to stay away from the organizational system. They justify this stance either with the situation, i.e., the organization that does not call for any change beyond the product in development, or with the objective to protect the product, i.e. technology, in development. In either case, transformations beyond the product in development are not foreseen or desired. Instead, all efforts on innovation concentrate on fine-tuning specific technologies originating from within the current organizational thinking, i.e., the very innovation box we want to free ourselves from. Moreover, these boundaries are being acknowledged, accepted and validated with each new technological device so created.

While the study by the Manufacturing Vision Group did not pursue where these expectations originate and if they indeed presented barriers to innovation in the organization, a more recent study has found that in many cases, barriers to innovation are a myth and not a reality (Cels, de Jong and Nauta 2012).[16] Cels et al. identify four possible sources for the myths. In the first instance, employees are prevented from taking action because of 'phantom regulations'. These are regulations employees imagine, but do not actually exist. In the second instance, staff and employees are acting in accordance with unwritten and unspoken rules. Here, daily 'work practice feels like there are official procedures in place' (de Jong, 2014 OECD). Everyday practices thus remain unchallenged. The study identified as another source the perception staff and employees have about their ability to move within their space. They often feel that the space they can move within 'is narrower than it actually is'. Finally, the study identified that some people hide behind rules and procedures to avoid change. The source for innovation barriers here are the very people who are against innovation. This latter group is actively creating innovation barriers to explain and excuse their inaction.

It is a speculative exercise to try to get to the bottom of the motivations of the participants in the Manufacturing Vision Group study. Can we argue that these innovators were actually against innovation when they drew their innovation boundaries around a technological product – without addressing the innovation framework under which they work and of which that very product would be part? Were they led by a myth when they perceived of an 'expectation boundary that limits any kind of change except technical change'? Again, we do not know. But what we do know is that the attitudes expressed by these innovators are now echoed in public sector innovation projects.

It is necessary to emphasize that the study participants were all engaged in traditional new product development, like, for example, the design of a better and cheaper printer. None of the projects concerned a service. But it is easy to extend the implications of this technological stance to a service organization where digital solutions drive innovation. For public sector innovation, the consequences of the technology innovation approach are that minor technological changes are heralded as 'break-through innovation in government'. The successful implementation of a new digital parking meter system in a municipality presented by Sahni et al. (2013), for example, reflects a similar understanding of innovation discovered by the Manufacturing Vision Group: The digital parking system becomes the object of innovation and transformation in isolation and in ignorance of internal organizational change opportunities.[17]

Sure, the introduction of new technologies into the complexities of a city-system is not without its challenges, and to see such a project through to completion is an achievement. Doubtless, the municipality has improved its service touch-points and perhaps its service encounters for its citizens and visitors. It is likely that the digital system reduces the city's overall cost as the new parking system is easier to control and requires less manpower to check on parking offenders. All this is beneficial and confirms that there is a role for technology in innovation. And yet, there is something amiss when it comes to public sector innovation that seeks to transform government. Just ask a civil servant who is trying to get out of her 1926 'kitchen' office.

The integration of policy making, policy implementation and services can be viewed as a matter of human systems integration (HIS), a term proposed by William B. Rousse. Rousse, too, has studied human-centered design (Rousse 2007) for its role in integrating systems and people (Rousse 2011).[18] In one of his studies, he takes a look at the economics of human systems integration to weigh their costs and benefits. What he observes in regards to investments in the public sector is that they suffer from all the uncertainties private businesses suffer, too. These include the spatial and temporal separation from investment and gain or return on investment. What is certain for public organizations, however, is that there may be no one who 'owns the future'. In the absence of any one being able to claim a return on investment in the future, any 'investment is treated as cost' (Rousse 2011). It is a cost to the people today who will not know if they get to see or benefit from the return:

> Although these expenditures may yield assets that can provide future returns, government agencies – and congress – have no balance sheet on which to tally the value of these assets. Thus, no value is explicitly attached to the future (Rousse 2011).

From this vantage point, we can see why it is tempting for public managers to decide for a technological project over fundamental organizational change. The benefits of any future outcome might be a product one can point to, no matter where one gets transferred. Sadly, the biggest management consultancies are eager and willing to provide public managers with technological band-aids. The 2015 Government Summit in Dubai, themed on the topic 'The Future of Government Services', exemplifies how global management consultancy giants present their own digital visions of government services as inevitable. I attended this session and was not the only one thinking it odd that the discussion of the future of government services was left to the CEOs of major management consultancies. Not a single civil servant was invited on stage; no public manager was invited to share their perspective. The discussion was left to three people whose business interests are closely intertwined with a public sector that buys their technologies and fulfills their business vision.[19] I did not need to point this out to the senior civil servant from Dubai sitting next to me who freely expressed his disappointment. The 2016 *Zukunftskongress* in Berlin, Germany indicates that the German government is not heeding the lessons from the Manufacturing Vision Group either. Not services or people, but digital technologies are to drive public sector innovation and the future of government. And like in Dubai, the promoters are the businesses that have the most to gain.[20]

Transforming Public Service by Design: Re-orienting services, organizations and policies around people

Not everyone involved in public sector innovation is 'thinking, acting or speaking like a designer'. But more and more civil servants with all levels of responsibility are beginning to engage with design in new ways. They are broadening their design understanding, fostering design awareness among their staff and consciously experimenting with new design methods that make people the central focus of their actions.

Many put their hopes in the creation of a 'public sector innovation lab' – a space where experimentation is encouraged, where staff is experiencing new methods and applying new thinking to cope with both new and lingering challenges. They provide new opportunities to learn how to develop more citizen-centric services and policies. Judging by the commitment of resources, manpower and time, it appears that the most ambitious developments in human-centered design in the public sector are being set up in Latin America.

Here, many democracies are still young and in search for the right balance of government power, individual freedom and responsibility. At the same time, cruel government experiences are still in the minds of those seeking to establish new ways of governing. In

Chile, for example, the idea of a 'future state' (*Estado Futuro*) that focus on innovation to serve people resonates with many senior government officials who fled under the Pinochet dictatorship and now return to lead the country into a new future. One of the key members involved in establishing Chile's public innovation lab (*Laboratorio Gobierno*) is an architect by training in his late thirties. He explains: 'Our ideas and our methods find open ears and actual support from senior government officials. Some view us as continuing the work they had started before they had to flee'.[21]

In Brazil, a country shaken by high-level political corruption and a major economic crisis in 2016, the Ministry of Planning, Development and Budget pursues its own innovation lab and actively supports innovation initiatives across government. The ministry established its own public innovation lab on the grounds of ENAP, Brazil's official School for Public Administration, and has engaged in networking activities through Inovagov in an effort to overcome intra-governmental roadblocks to innovation.[22] 'No matter who comes into power next', so their assessment, 'we have to change the ways we are working. The problems and challenges we face now will not go away and we will need to experiment with new approaches to generate new solutions.'[23]

Colombia, too, has begun to experiment on a government level with design approaches to social innovation. Based on the 2012 CONPES Document, the Council for Economic and Social Policy degreed a guideline for social innovation. It has created an opening for a small group to explore the possibilities of setting up an innovation lab. These developments are taking place in the equivalent of the Ministry of Planning in Brazil, though they are much less structured at the time of writing.[24]

Are these all good developments? For some, the turn to design endangers the classical foundations of the civil society (cf: Havel 2000).[25] When everyone participates, when everything is transparent, they worry: are we inadvertently shifting powers, blurring the very boundaries on which democracy is built? There are reasons to be vigilant and attentive. The best design intents can lead to the worst unintended consequences. Bad designs, too, express design thinking and involve design principles. The task ahead is to articulate and challenge the ways we go about conceiving, planning, developing and delivering public policies and services to arrive at better outcomes. The honorable Jocelyne Bourgon provides a final rational for expanding the discourse on design in the public sector, especially in regards to policy making and policy implementation:

> A broader perspective is needed to focus on what matters most and to productively engage Ministers, elected officials as well as senior public sector leaders in a much needed discussion about the challenges of preparing government fit for the time.[26]

This broader perspective examines the relationship between policy intent and social change. Although social changes can and do take place independent of policies, most policies seek to affect some kind of desirable social change. In this sense, social change can be described as a policy outcome. Looked at it this way, social change begins to take form at the earliest stages of policy making and depends on sensible and meaningful policy changes. Furthermore, social change requires relevant public organizations to develop and deliver the kinds of services necessary to fulfill a policy's intent. As I stated earlier, people do not experience policies: they experience services. Therefore services that are built to enhance human experiences and human interactions are they key to policy success. Figure 12.2 captures and summarizes this relationship.

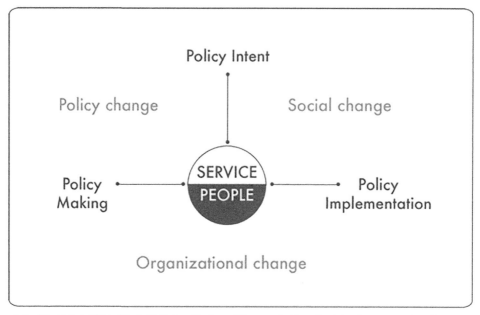

Any change in public policy is likely to affect a public organization. Applying human-centered design principles and methods to these design challenges from the start can ensure that the resulting policies and services fulfill the policy's intent, can be sustained by the respective organizations and contribute to positive outcomes and desirable social changes.

Figure 12.2 From policy intent to actual social change

Re-orienting policies, organizations and services around people may come with a price tag, but the return on investment is guaranteed. Besides, systemic fragmentations and system breakdowns are costly for governments because they lead to mandatory follow-ups and repeat appointments. Our trust in our governments remains priceless.

Notes

1 Quote taken from Jim Faris, "Remarks to the American Society for Cybernetics Conference," presented at the American Society for Cybernetics ASC 2002 Conference, June 13-16, Santa Cruz.
2 See for example, Jon Kolko (2015). Design Thinking Comes of Age, *Harvard Business Review*, September 2015: 66–71.
3 See Junginger, S. (2016). Thoughts on Design as a Strategic Art in the Organization, in Junginger, S. and Faust, J. *Designing Business*, Bloomsbury, Oxford, UK: 37–49.
4 Statement by senior member of Stiftung Politik und Wissenschaft in Berlin, Germany, Spring 2016, at the end of an introductory meet-up workshop by Politics for Tomorrow. Also see politicsfortomorrow.de
5 See www.helsinkidesignlab.org
6 Internal Mindlab document: 'Testing of principles for modernization through Governance labs', dated September 4, 2014, Mindlab Copenhagen.
7 See Junginger, S. (2015). 'Design Legacies and Service Design', *The Design Journal, Vol. 18 (2), Special Issue on Emerging Issues in Service Design*: 209–226.

8 See Junginger, S. (2006). Human-Centered Interaction Design: A Study In Collective Creativity. Discussion Paper presented at the Critical Management Study Stream Collective Creativity at the 2006 Academy of Management pre-conference sessions in Atlanta, Georgia.

9 Wenger, E. (1998). *Communities of Practice: Learning, Meaning, and Identity*, Cambridge University Press, Cambridge, UK.

10 https://en.wikipedia.org/wiki/Frankfurt_kitchen [accessed May 2016].

11 In 1926, the kitchen still was the domain of women.

12 See www.bulthaup.de: the B2 kitchen.

13 Statement made by Angela Meyer, the former project manager for Carnegie Mellon University's design team in a reflection on the course and strategy of the Domestic Mail Manual Project in 2004.

14 Personal meeting April 27, 2016 in Brasilia.

15 Bowen, K.H., Clark, K.B., Holloway, C.A. and Wheelwright, S.C. (1994). *The Perpetual Enterprise Machine–Seven Keys to Corporate Renewal Through Successful Product and Process Development*, Oxford University Press, Oxford, UK.

16 See Cels, S., de Jong, J. and Nauta, F. (2012). *Agents of Change: Strategy and Tactics for Social Innovation*, Brooking Institution Press, Washington, D.C.

17 Sahni, N.R., Wessel, M. and Christensen, C.M. (2013). 'Unleashing Breakthrough Innovations in Government', published on *Stanford Social Innovation Blog* (Summer 2013), http://ssir.org/articles/entry/unleashing_breakthrough_innovation_in_government

18 See Rousse, W.B. (2007). *People and Organizations: Explorations of Human-Centered Design*, John Wiley and Sons, Hoboken, NJ, and Rousse, W.B. (2011). *Economics of Human Systems Integration: Valuation of Investments in People's Training and Education, Safety and Health and Work Productivity*. John Wiley & Sons, Hoboken, New Jersey.

19 Dubai Government Summit Report 2015. See https://worldgovernmentsummit.org

20 *Zukunftskongress*, Berlin 2016. Also see *Jahrbuch Innovativer Staat 2016, 17th edition, www.wegweiser.de.*

21 Observation shared by one of the members of the Laboratorio Gobierno during the 2016 state sponsored two-day conference "Estado Futuro–Future State" which centered on people. President Bachelet opened the conference via video. 70 percent of the attendees were civil servants. See https://lab.gob.cl/#intro

22 See http://inovagov.blogspot.de and http://www.enap.gov.br

23 Response by a senior official in the Ministry of Planning, Development and Management to my question of the sustainability of innovation in Brazil.

24 Based on presentation by Javier Guillot at the Hertie School of Governance, April 2016, Berlin and personal conversations.

25 Havel, V. (2000). "Civil Society and its New Enemies," http://www.project-syndicate.org/commentary/civil-society-and-its-new-enemies [accessed May 2016].

26 Excerpt from Bourgon, J. (2015). *Public Innovation and Public Purpose: A Follow-Up to the OECD Conference Innovating the Public Sector: From Ideas to Action,* Public Governance International (PGI), Ottawa, Canada, p. 9.

Bibliography

Adebowale, O. and Starkey, K. (2009). *Engagement and Aspiration–Reconnecting Policy making with Frontline Professionals*, Sunningdale Institute Report for the UK Cabinet, March 2009.

Aldersey-Williams, H., Bound, J. and Coleman, R., eds. (1999). 'The Methods Lab–User Research for Design', *Published by the Design for Ageing Network (DAN for the Presence Conference Held at the Geographical Society)*, June 25, 1999.

Alvin, R. Tilley and Henry Dreyfuss Associates (1993). *The Measure of Man and Woman: Human Factors in Design*, Whitney Library of Design, New York. Originally published: New York: Whitney Library of Design, under title: The measure of man, 1960.

Amatullo, M. (ed.) (2016). LEAP *Dialogues, Career Paths in Design for Social Innovation*, DesignMatters, Art Center College of Design, Pasadena, CA.

Andrews, M. (2013). *The Limits of Institutional Reform in Development*, Cambridge University Press, Cambridge, UK.

Andrews, M., Pritchett, L. and Woolcock, M. (2012). 'Escaping Capability Traps through Problem-Driven Iterative Adaptation (PDIA)', *Center for Global Development, Working Paper 299*, June 2012.

Arnstein, S.R. (1969). 'A Ladder of Citizen Participation', *Journal of the American Institute of Planners*, Vol. 35 (4): 216–234; Peters, G. (2015). *Advanced Introduction to Public Policy*, Edward Elgar, Massachusetts, USA.

Atfield, J. (1999). *Utility reassessed–The role of ethics in the practice of design*, Manchester University Press, Manchester, UK.

Barnett, R. (2003). 'How Do You Know Your Forms Fail?' updated 2005 and 2007 http://c.ymcdn.com/sites/www.bfma.org/resource/resmgr/Articles/07_46.pdf

Bason, C. (2010). *Leading Public Sector Innovation*, The Policy Press University of Bristol, Great Britain.

Bason, C. (2014a). 'Design Attitude as an Innovation Catalyst', in Chris Ansell and Jacob Torfing (eds.), *Public Innovation through Collaboration and Design*, Oxford, UK: Routledge.

Bason, C. (2014b). *Design for Policy*, Gower, Farnham, UK.

Battarbee, K. and Koskinen, I., (2005). 'Co-Experience: User Experience as Interaction', *CoDesign*, Vol. 1 (1): 5–18.

Baxstrom, R. (2011). 'Even Governmentality Begins as an Image: Institutional Planning in Kuala Lumpur', *Focaal, Journal of Global and Historical Anthropology*, Vol. 61: 61–72.

Binder, T., de Michelis, G., Jacucci, G., Linder, P. and Wagner, I. (2011). *Design Things*, MIT Press, Cambridge, MA.

Body, J. (2007). 'Design in the Australian Taxation Office', *Design Issues*, Vol. 24 (1): 55–67.

Bonsiepe, G. (2010). *Civic City Cahier 2: Design & Democracy*, edited by Jesko Fezer and Matthias Görlich, Bedford Press, London, UK.

Borins, S. (2014). *The Persistence of Innovation in Government*, Brookings Institution Press, Washington, DC.

Bourgon, J. (2015). *Public Innovation and Public Purpose: A Follow-Up to the OECD Conference Innovating the Public Sector: From Ideas to Action*, Public Governance International (PGI), Ottawa, Canada. Accessible online: http://www.pgionline.com/publications/.

Boyer, B., Cook, J.W. and Steinberg, M. (2013). *Legible Practices: Six Stories about the Craft of Stewardship*, Helsinki, Finland: Helsinki DesignLab.

Brafman, O. and Beckstrom, R.A. (2008). *The Starfish and the Spider: The Unstoppable Power of the Leaderless Organization*, Portfolio Trade/Penguin Books, New York, NY.

Brown, T. (2008). *Change by Design: How Design Thinking Transforms Organizations and Inspires Innovation*, Harper Collins, New York, NY.

Buchanan, R. (1992). 'Wicked Problems in Design Thinking', *Design Issues*, Vol. 8 (2) (Spring): 5–21.

Buchanan, R. (1995). 'Rhetoric, Humanism and Design', in R. Buchanan and V. Margolin (eds.), *Discovering Design: Explorations in Design Studies*, University of Chicago Press, Chicago, 23–66.

Buchanan, R. (2001). 'Human Dignity and Human Rights: Thoughts on the Principles of Human-Centered Design', *Design Issues*, Vol. 17 (3) (Summer): 35–39.

Buchanan, R. (2006). 'Human Dignity and Human Rights: Thoughts on the Principles of Human-Centered Design', in M. Bierut, W. Drenttel and S. Heller (eds.), *Looking Closer Five: Critical Writings in Graphic Design*, Allsworth Press, New York, 140–144.

Buchanan, R. (2016). 'Design on New Ground: The Turn to Action, Services, and Management', in S. Junginger and J. Faust (eds.), *Designing Business*, Gower, Farnham, UK.

Buchanan, R. and Margolin, V. (eds.) (1995). *Discovering Design*, University of Chicago Press, Chicago, IL.

Carliner, S. (2000). 'Physical, Cognitive, and Affective: A Three-Part Framework for Information Design', in *Technical Communication* 47 (4), 561–576.

Carmody, M. (2002). 'Listening to the Community: Easier, Cheaper, More Personalized', *Presentation to the American Chamber of Commerce*, Sydney.

Cels, S., de Jong, J. and Nauta, F. (2012). *Agents of Change: Strategy and Tactics for Social Innovation*, Brooking Institution Press, Washington, DC.

Christiansen, J., Væring, A. and Utzon, A. (2015). *The Journey of Mindlab*, Mindlab, Copenhagen, Denmark. See www.mind-lab.dk.

Churchman, C.W. (1968). *The Systems Approach*, Dell Publishing, New York.

City Hall Innovation Team Playbook, The Innovation delivery approach to develop and deliver bold innovation (2015). Bloomberg Philanthropies, New York, NY. Available from www.bloomberg.org.

Clancey, W.J. (1984). 'Classified Problem Solving', *Proceedings Fourth National Conference on Artificial Intelligence*, Austin, TX, August 1984, 49–55.

Clancey, W.J. (1985). 'Heuristic Classification', *Artificial Intelligence*, Vol. 27 (3): 289–350.

Colomina, B. (2001). 'Enclosed by Images: The Eames Multimedia Architecture', *Grey Room*, Vol. 2: 6–29, Grey Room and Massachusetts Institute of Technology.

D'Ascenzo, M. (2010b). 'Working for All Australians: The ATO and the Community'. *Public Lecture to Charles Sturt University*, Albury Campus, New South Wales, Australia, 6 October 2010 and D'Ascenzo, M. 2011, 'Keynote Address by the Commissioner of Taxation: Protecting the Community and Its Tax System'. *Institute of Chartered Accountants of Australia, National Tax Conference*, 7 April 2011.

Dewey, J. (1927 [1954]). *The Public and Its Problems*, Swallow Press, Ohio University Press.

Dewey, J. (1934). *Art as Experience*, Minton, Balch and Company, New York, NY.

Dewey, J. (1938). *Logic: The Theory of Inquiry*, Henry Holt and Company, New York, Chapter VI, 'The Pattern of Inquiry'.

Diller, S., Shedroff, N. and Rhea, D. (2005). *Making Meaning—How Successful Business Deliver Meaningful Customer Experiences*, New Rider Press, Berkeley, CA.

DiSalvo, C., Clement, A. and Pipek, V. (2012). 'Communities: Participatory Design for, with, and by Communities', in J. Simonsen and T. Robertson (eds.), *The International Handbook of Participatory Design*, Routledge, Oxford, UK, pp, 182–209.

Doordan, D. (2000). *Design History, An Anthology*, MIT Press, Cambridge, MA, second print.

Downie, M. Eshkar, S. and Kaiser, P. (2009). *Creative Collaborations*, Helsinki Design Lab/SITRA, Helsinki, Finland. Available under a Creative Commons Attribution Non-Commercial-ShareAlike 2.0 license.

Ehn, P. (1993). 'Scandinavian Design: On Participation and Skill', in *Participatory Design: Principles and Practices*, CRC Press, Hillsdale, NJ, pp. 41–77.

Ehn, P. (2008). 'Participating in Design Things', *Proceedings of the Tenth Anniversary Conference on Participatory Design 2008*, Indiana University, Indianapolis, IN, 92–101.

Engeström, Y. and Escalante, V. (2001). 'Mundane Tool or Object of Affection? The Rise and Fall of the Postal Buddy', in Nardi, B. (ed.), *Context and Consciousness*, MIT Press, Cambridge, MA, pp. 325–373.

Eppel, E., Turner, D. and Wolf, A. (2011). 'Future State 2–Working Paper 11/04'. *Institute of Policy Studies, School of Government Victoria University of Wellington*, New Zealand, June 2011.

Felsenfeld, C. and Siegel, A. (1981). *Writing Contracts in Plain English*, West, St. Paul, Minnesota.

Fischer, F. and Forrester, J., eds. (1993). *The Argumentative Turn in Policy Analysis and Planning*, Duke University Press, Durham, NC, 167–185.

Freeman, B. (2013). 'Revisiting the Policy Cycle', *ATEM Developing Policy in Tertiary Institutions*, 21 June 2013, Northern Metropolitan Institute of TAFE, Melbourne.

Garud, R., Sanjay, J. and Tuertscher, P. (2008). 'Incomplete by Design and Designing for Incompleteness', *Organization Studies*, Vol. 29 (3): 351–371.

Gorb, P. and Dumas, A. (1987). 'Silent Design', *Design Studies, Vol. 8 (3), pp. 150–156.*

Gore, A. and Rubin, R.E. with frontline employees of the IRS (1998). *Reinventing Service at the IRS*, Department of Treasury Internal Revenue Service: Publication 2197 (3–98) Catalog Number 25006E, Government Printing Office, Washington, DC.

Gupta, A.K., Smith, K.G. and Shalley, C.E. (2006). 'The Interplay between Exploration and Exploitation', *Academy of Management Journal*, Vol. 49 (4): 693–706.

Halpern, D. (2015). *Inside the Nudge Unit, How Small Changes Can Make a Big Difference*, WH Allen, London, UK.

Hanington, B. (2003). 'Methods in the Making: A Perspective on the State of Human Research in Design', *Design Issues*, Vol. 19 (4), pp. 9–18.

Haring, K., Silvera-Tawil, D., Takahashi, T., Watanabe, K. and Velonaki, M. (2016). 'How People Perceive Different Robot Types: A Direct Comparison of an Android, Humanoid, and Non-Biomimetic Robot', *Proceedings of the 2016 8th International Conference on Knowledge and Smart Technology (KST)*, Burapha University, Chonnburi, Thailand.

Head, B.W. (2008). 'Wicked Problems in Public Policy', *Public Policy* [online], Vol. 3 (2): 101–118.

Head, B.W. and Alford, J. (2013). 'Wicked Problems – Implications for Public Policy and Management', *Administration and Society*, Vol. 47 (6): 711–739.

Heskett, J. (2002). *Toothpicks and Logos, Design in Everyday Life*, Oxford University Press, Oxford, UK.

Holmes, B. (2011). *Research Paper No. 1 2011–12: Citizens Engagement in Policymaking and the Design of Public services*, Politics and Public Administration Section, Parliamentary Library, Parliament of Australia, Canberra, Australia.

Howlett, M. and Ramesh, M. (2003). *Studying Public Policy*, 2nd Edition, Oxford University Press, Oxford.

Junginger, S. (2012a). 'A Human-Centered Design Perspective on Participatory Government – And Its Implications for the Practice and Education of Design Management', *Conference Proceedings of the 19th DMI Academic Conference*, London 2012.

Junginger, S. (2012b). 'Matters of Design in Policy making and in Policy Implementation', *Annual Review of Policy Design*, Vol. 1 [online] http://ojs.unbc.ca/index.php/design/article/view/542

Junginger, S. (2012c). 'Public Foundations of Service Design', in Miettinnen, S. and Valtonen, A. (2012). *Service Design with Theory*, Lapland University Press, Rovaniemi, Finland, pp. 21–26.

Junginger, S. (2012d). 'Public Innovation Labs: A Byway to Public Sector Innovation?' in P. Christensen and S. Junginger (eds.), *Highways and Byways of Radical Innovation*, University of Southern Denmark and Kolding School of Design, Kolding, Denmark, pp. 137–156.

Junginger, S. (2014). 'Policy making as Designing: Policy making Beyond Problem-Solving and Decision-Making', in Bason, C. (ed.), *Design for Policy*, Gower, Farnham, UK, pp. 57–69.

Junginger, S. (2015). 'Design Legacies and Service Design', *The Design Journal*, Vol. 18 (2): 209–226, Special Issue on Emerging Issues in Service Design.

Junginger, S. and Sangiorgi, D. (2009). 'Service Design as a Vehicle for Organizational Change', *IASDR Conference*, Seoul, Korea 2009.

Kaplan, T.J. (1993). 'Reading Policy Narratives: Beginnings, Middles, and Ends', in F. Fischer and J. Forrester (eds.), *The Argumentative Turn in Policy Analysis and Planning*, Duke University Press, Durham, NC, pp. 167–185.

Kettl, D. and Fessler, J. (2009). *The Politics of the Administrative Process*. CQ Press, Washington, DC.

Kimbell, L. (2010). 'Design Practices in Design Thinking', *Proceedings of the European Academy of Design 2009*, presented at the European Academy of Management, Liverpool, UK. http://www.lucykimbell.com/stuff/EURAM09_designthinking_kimbell.pdf

Kimbell, L. (2015). *Applying Design Approaches to Policy making: Discovering Policy Lab*, University of Brighton, Brighton, UK.

Kleinman, K. (1973). 'Design and the Federal Government', *Print*, July/August, Vol. 27 (4): 54–59, 83.

Krippendorff, K. (2006). 'The Semantic Turn – A New Foundation for Design', *Policy Sciences*, Vol. 4: 155–169.

Leadbetter, C. (2009). 'An Original Essay for Cornerhouse, Manchester Draft March 2009', published under a Creative Commons License and available online at http://www.charlesleadbetter.net [accessed August 2012].

Leadbetter, C. (2010). 'To, For, With and By' published online at http://charlesleadbeater.net/2010/05/for-with-by-and-to/

Leonard-Barton, D. (1992). 'Core Capabilities and Core Rigidities: A Paradox in Managing New Product Development', *Strategic Management Journal*, Vol. 13 (S1) (Summer): 111–125.

Linder, S.H. and Peters, B.G. (1995). 'The Two Traditions of Institutional Designing: Dialogue Versus Decision', in D. Weimer (ed.), *Institutional Design*, Kluwer Academic Publishers, Dordrecht, 133–160.

Locke, J. (2004). 'History of Plain Language in the United States Government' published on http://www.plainlanguage.gov/whatisPL/history/locke.cfm

Lynch, K. (1965). 'The City Sense and City Design', *Design Issues*, reprint 2000, originally published in *Scientific American*, Vol. 213 (3): 209–214.

Manzini, E. (2015). *Design, When Everybody Design – An Introduction to Design and Social Innovation*, MIT Press, Cambridge, MA.

March, J.G. (1991). 'Exploration and Exploitation in Organizational Learning,' *Organization Science*, Vol. 2 (1): 71–87, Special Issue: Organizational Learning: Papers in Honor of (and by) James G. March (1991).

Margolin, V. (1989). *Design Discourse, History, Theory, Criticism*, University of Chicago Press, Chicago, IL.

Margolin, V. (1995). The Product Milieu and Social Action, in Buchanan R. and V. Margolin (eds.), *Discovering Design: Explorations in Design Studies,* The University of Chicago Press, Chicago, IL, pp. 121–145.

Margolin, V. and Buchanan, R. (eds.) (1998). *The Idea of Design*, MIT Press, Cambridge, MA, Third Printing.

Mazur, B. (2000). 'Revisiting Plain Language', May 2000, Vol. 47 (2), *Technical Communication, the Journal of the Society for Technical Communication*. Accessed online: http://www.plainlanguage.gov/whatisPL/history/mazur.cfm.

Michlewski, K. (2015). *Design Attitude*, Gower, Farnham, UK.

Micklethwait, J. and Woolridge, A. (2015). *The Fourth Revolution–The Global Race to Reinvent the State*, Penguin Books, UK.

Miller, D. and Rudnick, L. (2011). 'Trying It on for Size: Design and International Public Policy', *Design Issues*, Vol. 27 (2) (Spring), pp. 6–16.

Moor, L. (2009). 'The State and Design, in Design and Creativity', in J. Gulier and L. Moor (eds.), *Design and Creativity: Policy, Management and Practice*, Berg, Oxford, UK, pp. 23–39.

Mulgan, G. (2014). *The Radicals Dilemma: An Overview of the Practice and Prospects of Social and Public Labs – Version 1*, Nesta, London, UK.

Nelson, G. (1974). *Problems of Design*, Whitney Library of Design, New York, NY, Third edition.

Norman, D. (1988). *The Design of Everyday Things*, Doubleday, New York, NY.

Papanek, V. (1984). *Design for the Real World: Human Ecology and Social Change*, Thames and Hudson, London, UK.

Peters, G. (2015). *Advanced Introduction to Public Policy*, Edward Elgar, Northampton, MA, USA.

Puttick, R., Baeck, P. and Colligan, P. (2014). *i-teams: The Teams and Funds Making Innovation Happen in Governments Around the World*, Nesta, London, UK.

Ralph, J. (1999). *A Tax System Redesigned–More Certain, Equitable and Durable*, July 30, 1999, Australian Taxation Office. Also known as The Ralph Report or Ralph Review.

Rein, M. (1983). *From Policy to Practice*, M.E. Sharpe, Inc., Armonk, NY.

Rein, M. (1970). *Social Policy: Issues of Choice and Change*, Random House Trade, New York, NY.

Rein, M. and Schön, D. (1977). 'Problem Setting in Policy Research', in C.H. Weiss (ed.), *Using Social Research in Public Policy Making*, Lexington Books: Lexington, MA, 235–251.

Rein, M. and Schön, D. (1993). 'Reframing Policy Discourse', in F. Fischer and J. Forrester (eds.), *The Argumentative Turn in Policy Analysis and Planning*, Duke University Press, Durham, NC, 145–166.

Rein, M. and Schön, D. (1994). *Reframing: Controversy and Design in Policy Practice*, Basic Books, New York.

Rittel, H. and Webber, M. (1973). 'Dilemmas in a General Theory of Planning', *Policy Sciences*, Vol. 4: 155–169.

Rosenbaum, R. (1999). *Explaining Hitler–The Search for the Origins of His Evil*, Harper.

Rousse, W.B. (2007). *People and Organizations: Explorations of Human-Centered Design*, John Wiley and Sons, Hoboken, NJ.

Rousse, W.B. (2011). *Economics of Human Systems Integration: Valuation of Investments in People's Training and Education, Safety and Health and Work Productivity*, John Wiley & Sons, Hoboken, NJ.

Sahni, N.R., Wessel, M. and Christensen, C.M. (2013). 'Unleashing Breakthrough Innovations in Government', *Stanford Social Innovation Blog*, (Summer), http://ssir.org/articles/entry/unleashing_breakthrough_innovation_in_government.

Sanders, B.N. (1992). 'Product Development Research for the 1990s', *Design Management Journal*, Vol. 3 (4): 49–54.

Sanders, E.B.N. and Stappers, P.J. (2008). 'Co-Creation and the New Landscapes of Design', *Co-Design*, March, Vol. 4 (1): 5–18.

Sanderson, I. (2002). 'Evaluation, Policy Learning and Evidence-Based Policy Making', *Public Administration*, Vol. 80: 1–22.

Sangiorgi, D. and Meroni, A. (2011). *Designing for Services*, Gower, Farnham, UK.

Schön, D. (1983). *The Reflective Practitioner: How Professionals Think in Action*, Temple Smith, London.

Schön, D.A. (1988). *The Reflective Practitioner*, Ashgate, London, UK.

Shields, P.M. (1998). 'Pragmatism as Philosophy of Science: A Tool for Public Administration', *Research in Public Administration*, Vol. 4: 195–225.

Shirky, C. (2008). *Here Comes Everybody: Organizing without Organizations*, Penguin Press, New York, NY.

Shriver, K. (1997). *Dynamics in Document Design*, John Wiley & Sons, New York.

Simon, H. A. (1957). *Administrative Behavior: A Study of Decision-Making Processes in Administrative Organization*, The Macmillan Co., New York, NY, 2nd Edition.

Simon, H.A. (1996 [1969]). *The Sciences of the Artificial*, MIT Press, Cambridge, MA, p. 111.

Smith, A. (1904 [2010]). *An Inquiry into the Nature and Causes of the Wealth of Nations*, Originally Methuen & Co Ltd, London, reprinted by Capstone Publishing, Chichester, UK, 2010.

Soetzu, Y. (1989), *The Unknown Craftsman*, Kodansha International, Tokyo, JP/New York, NY.

Sørensen, E. and Boch Waldorff, S. (2014). 'Collaborative Policy Innovation: Problems and Potential', *Innovation Journal*, Vol. 19 (3): 1–17.

Sunstein, C.R. (2013). *Simpler: The Future of Government*, Simon & Schuster, New York, NY.

Suri, F.J. (2007). 'Involving People in the Process', *Keynote Delivered at the 2007 Inclusive Conference*, in Toronto.

Sydow, J. and Schreyögg, G. (2009). 'Organizational Path Dependence–Opening the Black Box', *Academy of Management Review*, Vol. 34 (4): 689–709.

Terrey, N. (2012). *Managing by Design – A Case Study of the Australian Taxation Office*, Doctoral Thesis, University of Canberra, Faculty of Business, Government & Law, Canberra, Australia.

Torfing, J. and Ansell, C., eds. (2014). *Public Innovation through Collaboration and Design*, Routledge, Oxon, UK.

Verganti, R. (2009). *Design Driven Innovation: Changing the Rules of Competition by Radically Innovating What Things Mean*, Harvard Business School Publishing, Boston, MA.

Walker, D. (1980). 'Two Tribes at War', in M. Oakley (ed.), *The Handbook of Design Management*, Blackwell Reference, Oxford, UK, pp. 145–154.

Weick, Karl, E. (2004). Rethinking Organizational Design, in Boland R. and F. Collopy (eds.), *Managing as Designing*, Stanford University Press, Stanford, CA, pp. 36–53.

Wenger, E. (1998). *Communities of Practice: Learning, Meaning, and Identity*, Cambridge University Press, Cambridge, UK.

Whyte, W. H. Jr. (1956). *The Organization Man*, Double Day, Garden City, NY.

Williams, R. (1977). 'Residual, Emergent and Dominant Culture', in I. Szeman (ed.), *Cultural Theory*, Oxford University Press, New York, NY, 121.

Winner, L. (1995). Political Ergonomics, in Margolin, V. and Buchanan R. (eds.) *Discovering Design*, University of Chicago Press, Chicago, IL, pp. 146–170.

Winograd, T. and Wood, D.D. (1997). *The Challenge of Human-Centered Design*, Report from Working Group 3, Version of April 9, 1997. Unpublished Working Paper, http://www.ifp.illinois.edu/nsfhcs/bog_reports/bog3.html

Woodham, J. (1997). *Twentieth Century Design*, Oxford History of Art, Oxford University Press, Oxford, UK.

Woodham, J. (2010). Formulating National Design Policies in the United States: Recycling the "Emperor's New Clothes"? *Design Issues*, Vol. 26 (2), pp. 27–46.

Online sources

Agentes de Innovacion, Mexico: http://www.presidencia.gob.mx/agentesdeinnovacion/#proyectos

Design for America: www.designforamerica.com

DesignGov, Australia: http://innovation.govspace.gov.au/2012/01/27/a-pilot-centre-for-excellence-in-public-sector-design/

d-school design thinking: http://dschool.stanford.edu/dgift

Escola Nacional de Administração Pública: http://www.enap.gov.br

Geminoid-FbyMariaVelonaki:http://www.techradar.com/news/world-of-tech/meet-the-geminoid-f-the-first-humanoid-robot-to-star-in-a-movie-1310108

http://www.irs.gov

Inovagov Brazil: http://inovagov.blogspot.de

IRS Taxpayer Advocate: http://www.taxpayeradvocate.irs.gov

Kent, UK: http://socialinnovation.typepad.com/silk/meet-the-silk-team.html

La27iemeregion, France: See http://www.la27eregion.fr/en/ and

The Lab at the United States Office Of Personal Management: http://www.federalnewsradio.com/520/3004758/OPMs-innovation-lab-spurs-new-way-of-problem-solving

Laboratorio Gobierno, Chile: https://lab.gob.cl/#intro and http://www.bnamericas.com/news/technology/public-innovation-lab-among-key-digital-initiatives-for-chile-govt

Mindlab, Denmark: http://mind-lab.dk/en

Nesta, UK: http://www.nesta.org.uk/event/labworks-2015 and http://theiteams.org/case-studies/policy-lab-uk

SITRA, Finland: http://www.sitra.fi

Superpublic, France: http://superpublic.fr

TACSI, Australia: http://www.tacsi.org.au/who-we-are

University of Syracuse http://trac.syr.edu/tracirs/trends/v10/irsStaffG.html

Reports

1983 Report to Congress, Tax Commissioner Roscoe L. Egger.

DMM Transformation Project Report Internal Stakeholder Interviews, July 3, 2003.

Domestic Mail Manual 100: A Customer's Guide to Mailing: http://pe.usps.gov/cpim/ftp/manuals/dmm100/dmm100.pdf

Dubai Government Summit Report 2015. See https://worldgovernmentsummit.org

The Economist, "Test-Tube Government–Governments Are Borrowing Ideas about Innovation from the Private sector" Schumpeter, December 6th Print Edition.

Final Report Long Range Tax Forms Simplification Study, September 20, 1983, Tax Forms and Publications Division, Research Division, Internal Revenue Service.

Further Simplification of Income Tax Forms and Instructions Is Needed and Possible, GAO Report No. GGS-78-74, July 5, 1978.

The Guide, Version April, 2002, Australian Tax Office (ATO).

Jahrbuch Innovativer Staat 2016, 17th edition, www.wegweiser.de

Last Week with John Oliver: https://www.youtube.com/watch?v=Nn_Zln_4pA8

The New York Times: http://www.nytimes.com/2013/05/16/opinion/the-real-irs-scandal.html?_r=0

Outline for Discussion: Concepts for Postal Transformation. Submitted by the *United States Postal Service* to the Chairman of the *Committee on Governmental Affairs*, October 1, 2001.

Paperwork Reduction Act–Implementation at IRS, November 1998. United States General Accounting Office, Report to the Chairman, Subcommittee on Oversight of Government Management, Restructuring, and the District of Columbia, Committee on Governmental Affairs, U.S. Senate. GAO/GGD-99-4.

Prepared for the National Institute of Education, Washington, D.C. under Contract No. NIE-400-78-0043, November 1981 by the American Institutes for Research with Siegel & Gale and Carnegie Mellon University.

Public Governance and Territorial Development Directorate Public Governance Committee, OECD Report, February 2013.

Report to the Commissioner of Internal Revenue–Status of the Tax Forms Simplification Project, November 30, 1981, page 5.

Tax Forms Simplifications Project: Background, Development, and Status, prepared by Siegel & Gale on March 8, 1982.

Technical Assistance and Training from the Document Design Project, Final Report.

United States General Accounting Office, GAO-01-598T, April 4, 2001.

United States Postal Service Transformation Plan, K-14-16 Appendix, APPENDIX K–Growth- and Value-Based Strategies: Promote Greater Ease of Use, April 2002.

Index

For Product Safety Concerns and Information please contact our EU
representative GPSR@taylorandfrancis.com Taylor & Francis Verlag GmbH,
Kaufingerstraße 24, 80331 München, Germany

Printed and bound by CPI Group (UK) Ltd, Croydon, CR0 4YY
01/05/2025
01858379-0001